THE LANDS IN BETWEEN

THE LANDS IN BETWEEN

*Russia vs. the West and
the New Politics of Hybrid War*

MITCHELL A. ORENSTEIN

OXFORD
UNIVERSITY PRESS

Oxford University Press is a department of the University of Oxford. It furthers
the University's objective of excellence in research, scholarship, and education
by publishing worldwide. Oxford is a registered trade mark of Oxford University
Press in the UK and certain other countries.

Published in the United States of America by Oxford University Press
198 Madison Avenue, New York, NY 10016, United States of America.

Library of Congress Cataloging-in-Publication Data
Names: Orenstein, Mitchell A. (Mitchell Alexander), author.
Title: The lands in between : Russia vs. the West and the new politics of
hybrid war / Mitchell A. Orenstein.
Description: New York, NY : Oxford University Press, [2019]
Identifiers: LCCN 2018032433 | ISBN 9780190936143 (hc ; alk. paper)
Subjects: LCSH: Hybrid warfare—Russia (Federation) | Russia
(Federation)—Foreign relations—Western countries. | Western
countries—Foreign relations—Russia (Federation)
Classification: LCC DK510.764 . O74 2019 | DDC 327.470182/1—dc23
LC record available at https://lccn.loc.gov/2018032433

9 8 7 6 5 4 3 2 1

Printed by Sheridan Books, Inc., United States of America

In the 1990s and in the 2000s, influence flowed from west to east ... in the 2010s, influence flowed from east to west.

—TIMOTHY SNYDER, *The Road to Unfreedom*

CONTENTS

LIST OF FIGURES

ACKNOWLEDGMENTS

I have incurred many debts in writing this book. First, I would like to acknowledge my students at Johns Hopkins University School of Advanced International Studies (SAIS), Northeastern University, and the University of Pennsylvania, who helped me to form and refine ideas through many conversations, questions, and interactions inside and outside the classroom. Thanks to Jacob Cohen, whose research assistance and senior thesis on Russia's oil trade with Europe provided valuable insights, and to Nicholas Emery at Penn. I owe a special thanks to the SAIS students who accompanied me on several wintry trips to Russia and Eastern Europe to study international relations in the region and helped to set up and conduct interviews; it is always a pleasure to hear from you on Twitter and follow the progress of your careers. I would like to extend thanks to our local partners, colleagues, and hosts on these trips as well. In particular, thanks to Ramūnas Vilpišauskas of Vilnius University, who helped facilitate the organization of one trip to Lithuania and Belarus and to the students and faculty from Vilnius University. I learned a lot from you all. Thanks to Oleg Kravchenko, Chargé d'Affaires of the Belarusian embassy in Washington, DC, and Victor

Shadurski, Dean of International Relations at the Belarusian State University, for organizing a fascinating and unforgettable trip to Belarus and also to the European Humanities University in Vilnius for providing an alternative perspective. Thanks to the Washington, DC, European Union Center, particularly Director Dan Hamilton and Gretchen Losee, who helped to sponsor, administer, and advise us on these trips. I am grateful to all my interlocutors on the faculty at Johns Hopkins SAIS who helped in numerous ways to enhance my understanding of the diplomacy of the region.

Special thanks to my many colleagues and interviewees in Belarus, Bulgaria, Hungary, Latvia, Lithuania, Romania, Russia, Ukraine, and Brussels in the course of my research trips to the region over ten years. It has always been my pleasure to speak with you, whether or not the interview went well. I have a great deal of respect for the government officials, academics, think tank analysts, business people, political fixers, drivers, and translators with whom I have met, often together with student groups, and thank you for your gracious willingness to spend time discussing your perspective and the perspective of your organization. Even the small number of difficult encounters taught me a lot. A particular shout out to Ilian Cashu, my former student at the Maxwell School of Syracuse University and now member of the city council of Chisinau, Moldova, for his incredible assistance in helping to arrange my trip to Chisinau and explain the ins and outs of Moldovan politics, as well as to Valery Yakubovich, who accompanied me on a fascinating trip to Kiev, Berdichev, Pavoloch, and Odessa, Ukraine, and served as a sometime translator, and to Viktoria and Ostap Sereda in Lviv.

I owe a special thanks to US Ambassador Adrian Basora, with whom I organized a conference on democratic backsliding in Central and Eastern Europe in Washington, DC, in 2007, in cooperation with the Foreign Policy Research Institute (FPRI) and the German Marshall Fund, the first of many undertakings together. I have been proud to serve with you in the Project on Democratic Transitions and the Eurasia Program at FPRI, as well as with John Haines, Chris Miller, Maia Otarashvili, FPRI president Alan Luxenberg, and the rest of the FPRI staff. FPRI has given me many opportunities to speak on and enrich my own knowledge of these topics and the audience for them in and around Philadelphia. Similarly, I wish to thank the Center for European Policy Analysis in DC, Larry Hirsch, Wess Mitchell, Jakub Grygiel, and Peter Doran, for the opportunity to work with you for several years and learn from your perspective and events on Central Europe. In addition, I am indebted to my many friends and colleagues in the DC think tank community, who generously shared their expertise on Russian and East European international affairs. I would particularly like to acknowledge Samuel Charap, Derek Chollet, Daniel Hamilton, John Herbst, Fiona Hill, David J. Kramer, Marc Plattner, Alina Polyakova, Matt Rojansky, Blair Ruble, Steven Stoltenberg, Steve Szabo, Kurt Volker, and all the participants and speakers in the conferences you sponsored and hosted that enhanced my understanding of the foreign affairs of Russia and Eastern Europe. The United States is lucky to have such a terrific expert community, and I have been lucky to have the opportunity to learn so extensively from it. I am also grateful for the opportunity to serve on the board of an EU research project, EU-STRAT: The EU and Eastern Partnership Countries, organized by Professor Tanja Börzel of Free University Berlin and her two terrific former PhD students, Esther Ademmer and Julia Langbein, whose books and articles—as well as those of the many fine participants in this project—have taught me so much about Russian and EU influence on the lands in between.

I would also like to thank my colleagues at the University of Pennsylvania, in particular those in Russian and East European studies, and the Philadelphia-area Europeanist network, who have helped me in so many ways through their critical engagement with this work, including Osman Balkan, Richard Deeg, Cristina Dragomir, Kristen Ghodsee, Julia Gray, Orfeo Fioretos, Peter Holquist, Benjamin Katzeff-Silberstein, Ayse Kaya, Dan Kelemen, Julia Lynch, Ben Nathans, Kevin Platt, Mark Pollack, and Peter Steiner. Thanks also to the team at the Perry World House at the University of Pennsylvania, especially Director William Burke-White, John Gans, LaShawn Jefferson, Lisa Jourdan, and Michael Horowitz, for organizing so many events that have enabled me and the rest of the Penn community to stay on top of the issues this book addresses.

Finally, thanks to David McBride at Oxford University Press and his team, including Holly Mitchell, and Cheryl Merritt at Newgen UK, for helping this book along to publication. It has been a pleasure to work with you. Likewise, I would like to thank Gideon Rose and the young editors at *Foreign Affairs* for working with me to publish a number of short articles on various aspects of the conflict in the region and to my co-authors on some of those articles, Hilary Appel, Bojan Bugarič, Attila Juhász, Dan Kelemen, Péter Krekó, and Kálmán Mizsei. Special thanks also to Dimitar Bechev, Ecaterina Locoman, Elizabeth Sherwood-Randall, and several anonymous reviewers who kindly read drafts of the book prior to publication.

ABBREVIATIONS

CEE	Central and East European
DCFTA	Deep and Comprehensive Free Trade Agreement
EU	European Union
IMF	International Monetary Fund
LNG	liquefied natural gas
NATO	North Atlantic Treaty Organization

INTRODUCTION

"DON'T WRITE A BOOK ABOUT Moldova. No one will read it." My wife gives me a lot of sage advice, which I too often ignore. So the first thing I want to say is this is not a book about Moldova. This is not a book about small, poor European countries nestled in between Russia and the European Union that seem, in the popular imagination of the West, to have been released from the Soviet Union only to aggravate us on geography exams, lengthen Olympic parades, and provide color to Eurovision song contests.

This is a book about something much more troubling and significant: why politics in the West is becoming a lot more like politics in Moldova or Ukraine—vulnerable countries situated on the front lines of an emerging conflict between Russia and the West. As more countries find themselves on the front lines of this geopolitical conflict fought with conventional and unconventional tools, such as cyberwarfare, hacking, money laundering, and the threat of nuclear war, they are experiencing political pathologies similar to those that the front-line states have been dealing with for years. As a result, these small, vulnerable countries have a lot to teach us about how bad politics can become—and what to do about it.

I am writing this book for a Western audience, because many of us in the West are suffering from an intense sense of dislocation in politics. If you feel that politics has suddenly gone crazy, this book is for you. In the United States and many

European countries, it seems as if politics is suddenly unfamiliar. Old rules have become meaningless, and many of us feel unmoored. It is hard to understand why. I have spent a lot of time being confused myself. Yet as a professor of Russian and East European studies, I realized that I had a special insight to share.

Politics in Europe and the United States increasingly follows patterns well established in Moldova and other small, poor, and vulnerable countries about which most in the West know next to nothing. I have been teaching about these problems for years, and I thought that if I could explain to a general audience how the politics of hybrid war affects the lands in between, we in the West could better understand our own problems and perhaps address them more effectively. That is why I am writing this book. It is about the sudden and surprising relevance of East European politics to Western societies. That is why I am going to start with a short vignette about Moldova, before moving on. Please indulge me. This story will sound crazy at first, but I promise that, on further reflection, it will begin to sound all too familiar, and possibly like a mad parable about our own collective future.

In June 2017, the acknowledged kingpin of Moldovan politics, Vlad Plahotniuc, was invited to Brussels, the seat of the European Union and the North Atlantic Treaty Organization (NATO),[1] after a similar trip to Washington, DC, in May. Moldova is a small, predominantly agricultural, country nestled between Ukraine and Romania. Plahotniuc is Moldova's leading oligarch. His business empire consists of many official holdings, including Moldova's two leading TV stations, Prime and TV 2 Plus,[2] but also allegedly illegal businesses and scams. Some of Plahotniuc's businesses appeared in the Panama Papers, and he has been accused in the Moldovan press of laundering money from various schemes and investing the receipts in legitimate companies.[3] Some suspect him of stealing a good share of the

European Union funds that come to Moldova to promote development. Others allege that he got his start in human trafficking, selling Moldova's young women into bondage in the brothels of Western Europe and Turkey.[4] The very model of a corrupt oligarch in Eastern Europe, Plahotniuc spent 2017 trying to rehabilitate himself in the West. And, by all reports, he succeeded. In December 2017, he published an opinion piece in the *Wall Street Journal* stating that Moldova needed the West's help against an aggressive Russia.[5]

One Romanian member of the European Parliament was quoted as saying in May 2016, "I think he is perceived as rather . . . part of the solution than a part of the problem [in Brussels]. At some point, he said that the problem of Moldova is that the evil is black, but that the angels are not white. There is some truth behind that."[6]

In 2016, Plahotniuc's Democratic Party, which he chairs and funds, became the largest political party in the 101-seat Moldovan parliament—not only by winning 19 seats in 2014 elections, but by flipping 22 other members elected as representatives of other parties, presumably through various inducements. Following a damaging scandal in which $1 billion disappeared from the Moldovan banking system, the ruling Alliance for European Integration (of which the Democratic Party was a part) reshuffled the government, and Plahotniuc's Democratic Party became the lead party. Plahotniuc put himself up for the position of prime minister, but was rejected by Moldova's then-president for lacking integrity and because he was "generally disliked by the majority of the people."[7] After that, Plahotniuc ruled Moldova by proxy through Prime Minister Pavel Filip, but it was Plahotniuc who led Moldova's delegation to Brussels and Washington in 2017.

Plahotniuc was welcomed in these Western capitals because he positioned himself as the most powerful pro-European politician in Moldova. Without him, the Alliance for European Integration would be replaced by the pro-Putin Socialists under President Igor Dodon. Dodon became known as the "czar's doormat" after he distinguished himself as the only world leader to attend Russia's World War II Victory Day military parade on May 9, 2017. He earned a rebuke for his sycophancy even from President Putin, who likened him to an infamous court jester.[8] Yet Dodon was rising in popularity as citizens in Moldova became fed up with their corrupt pro-European government. While approximately one-quarter of Moldovans supported an alternative (and presumably less corrupt) pro-Europe alliance led by Maia Sandu, a plurality of voters in early 2018 wanted a pro-Russian party to govern. Meanwhile, Plahotniuc's Democratic Party was struggling to achieve the 5 percent support required to enter parliament, at least in public opinion polls.

In this context, it was surprisingly easy for Plahotniuc to win Brussels and Washington to his side. "Après moi, le déluge," as French king Louis XV said, "After me, the deluge." Brussels and Washington both realized that they were fighting tooth and nail with Russia for influence in the lands in between. In Moldova, it was widely felt that parliamentary elections in 2018 or 2019 would be a turning point from which the country might never turn back. Companies put business plans on hold, and pro-European citizens considered fleeing to Romania, Moldova's EU neighbor, in case of a Russian takeover. Politicians were tense as they geared up for an election that many suspected might be the country's last. The political scene sharply polarized between those willing to cast their lot with Russia and those determined for Moldova to join Europe. Parties advocating a third way, a "pro-Moldovan" option of balancing both sides, saw their public support dwindle. In this context, Plahotniuc positioned himself as the essential figure on the pro-Europe side, someone you may not like or respect, but who was necessary to fend off a Russian takeover. Hence he rehabilitated himself in the West.

Given that, it may be surprising to learn that Plahotniuc was not only the essential leader of the Alliance for European Integration, but also a covert ally of the pro-Russian president Dodon and his Socialist Party, which enthusiastically advocates a pro-Russia and pro-Putin line. The Socialist Party and Plahotniuc's Democratic Party teamed up in 2017 to revise the electoral system in Moldova to make it easier for the Democratic Party to gain representation in parliament. While they frequently attack one another in public, this public mudslinging is regarded by savvy analysts of Moldovan politics as a show that benefits both sides. "A constant battle along geopolitical lines is to Plahotniuc's advantage as it allows sceptical voters to support him in his attempts to halt the pro-Russian groups. . . . The more ostentatious Dodon is towards the Kremlin, the stronger the reaction of the Moldovan government."[9] So, having a powerful pro-Russia party create anxiety helps Plahotniuc to solidify his position as the pro-European savior. Analysts cite a number of instances besides electoral reform of cooperation between the seemingly opposed parties.

Plahotniuc's ability to bridge the two sides of the geopolitical divide in Moldova extends to his business operations. Plahotniuc, while decrying Russian influence, has made a fortune rebroadcasting Russian channels on his TV stations, along with their political propaganda. He is the leading rebroadcaster of Russian propaganda, owning the rebroadcasting rights to the leading Russian TV channel, Perviy Kanal.[10] Yet, in 2018, his party advocated banning these rebroadcasts in an effort to reduce Russian influence in the upcoming elections. He held this up to Brussels and Washington as evidence of his tough stance on Russia. Plahotniuc's businesses and political enterprises profit handsomely from both Russia and the EU.

Politics in the lands in between present a compelling paradox. On the one hand, the geopolitical conflict between Russia and the West has sharpened polarization.[11] It has forced countries to confront what many view as a "civilizational choice," to cast one's fate either with Western or with Russian civilization. This has had the effect of intensifying conflict between people on either side, and forcing political parties to identify clearly as pro-European or pro-Russian. Both Russia and the West exacerbate this divide by rewarding parties and individuals that support their objectives.

Yet at the same time, in this intensely polarized political environment characterized by "civilizational" conflict, the top power brokers benefit by working both sides. The lands in between frequently elevate top leaders like Plahotniuc who are adept at profiting from both the EU and the United States, as well as Russia. From a purely rational perspective, it is easy to see why—when two enormous outside powers are offering rich rewards for loyalty, the strongest person will be the one who manages to take from both. In a polarized political environment, paradoxically, the greatest asset is not ideology but flexibility.

But what lessons does this hold for the West itself, aside from being a little more careful to whom we provide foreign aid? The lesson is this: as Western countries become a battleground in a broader geopolitical conflict between Russia and the West, the same rules of politics begin to apply. Politics becomes more polarized. People start to regard those cooperating with the other side as traitors to the country or to Western civilization. Extremist politics grows as parties gain funding and media support from outside sources. And yet, paradoxically, the greatest benefits accrue to those who position themselves to win payoffs from both sides in this geopolitical competition. The most effective power brokers are not just shills for Russia. They depend on their strategic positions within Western power structures. They manage to draw resources as brokers of influence between two camps. They have a clear interest in accommodation *and* in the conflict that requires it. I will illustrate these lessons with examples, and I promise that when you understand this paradox of politics in the lands in between, the seemingly upside-down politics of the West today will snap into focus.

The plan for this book is simple. To begin, I lay out the nature of the geopolitical conflict that is threatening Western politics. The questions of whether and to what extent this conflict exists and whose fault it is have become so politically controversial that it is important to set the record straight. In the first chapter, I examine the nature of Russia's hybrid war on the West, why it started, its methods and objectives. In the second chapter, I explore the West's responses, with emphasis on military responses through NATO and national militaries, as well as economic responses from the United States and the European Union, Russia's largest trading partner and geopolitical rival. In the third chapter, I turn to describing the nature of politics in the lands in between—Moldova, Ukraine, Belarus, Georgia, Armenia, and Azerbaijan—to demonstrate how the politics of polarization and power brokers works in the lands in between. In the fourth chapter, I show that these trends not only affect these vulnerable countries between Russia and the West, but also new member states of the European Union and NATO in Central and Eastern Europe. The fifth chapter brings the argument home to the West, to explore how the politics of polarization and power brokers also affects core Europe and the United States. Finally, I conclude with some reflections on what is to be done. This book is not intended to be exhaustive, but rather to provide a general introduction to and a distinct perspective—from a scholar of Russian and East European studies—on a political trend that is shaping the modern world and that everyone needs to know.

▼

RUSSIA'S HYBRID WAR

ON THE WEST

ON JULY 16, 2009, A group of twenty-two Central and East European (CEE) leaders, mainly former presidents, prime ministers, and liberal intellectuals, penned "An Open Letter to the Obama Administration from Central and Eastern Europe." Václav Havel and Lech Wałesa, two symbols of the 1989 revolutions that ended communism, were among the signatories. The letter responded to the new US administration's attempt to "reset" relations with Russia. The CEE leaders warned that

> Russia is back as a revisionist power pursuing a 19th-century agenda with 21st-century tactics and methods. At a global level, Russia has become, on most issues, a status-quo power. But at a regional level and vis-a-vis our nations, it increasingly acts as a revisionist one. It challenges our claims to our own historical experiences. It asserts a privileged position in determining our security choices. It uses overt and covert means of economic warfare, ranging from energy blockades and politically motivated investments to bribery and media manipulation in order to advance its interests and to challenge the transatlantic orientation of Central and Eastern Europe.

The signatories called for strengthening NATO and greater US commitment to European affairs.[1]

This appeal appeared to fall on deaf ears.

The Obama administration continued to prioritize improving relations with Russia over CEE security. Even after the Russo-Georgian war of August 2008, the Obama administration and many West European governments believed that Russia was turning in a liberal direction under President Dmitry Medvedev.[2] The US administration believed it could achieve arms control agreements and win Russia's support for its wars in the Middle East by easing tensions with Russia in Europe. On September 17, 2009, the Obama administration announced that it was dropping plans for a missile defense system in Poland and Czechia, in what Republican presidential candidate Mitt Romney later called a "gift to Russia."[3] The timing was unfortunate, as it corresponded with the seventieth anniversary of the Soviet invasion of Poland in 1939. This episode seemed to show that the Obama administration paid little mind to the open letter's warnings and regarded CEE leaders as alarmist.

In fact, the West ignored the appeals of CEE leaders at its own peril. Most Western policymakers tended to view East Europeans as a bit paranoid on the topic of Russia. Traumatized by Russia in the past, these countries appeared unusually sensitive to the Russian threat, even obsessed.[4] Yet today their perspective seems prescient. Their close awareness of the Russian threat was a result of their being colonized by Russia or the Soviet Union or both. But that experience made them into canaries in the coal mine for the West, a valuable early warning system that, unfortunately, was not heeded.

It was clear to many CEE leaders by 2009 that Russia had launched an all-out hybrid war on their region, hoping to detach it from the West. This war was pursued in a limited and often covert fashion in order to escape notice. Its methods were largely deniable, such as hacking, media manipulation, and covert funding for political parties. Yet the goals of this hybrid war were broad and ambitious. It targeted not only the

NATO military alliance, aiming to divide Central Europe from Western Europe and the United States from its European allies, but also the European Union, a trading bloc and political union seen as a guarantor of peace in Europe, by stoking the flames of anti-Europe, xenophobic sentiment. Ultimately, Russia sought to divide Western liberal institutions, promote xenophobic extremism, and destabilize Western democracies. This was not a marginal activity for Russia, or a byproduct of a range of self-interested actions, but a strategy for hybrid war that addressed what Russia saw as an existential threat from the West.

For the West, the realization that Russia was serious about its hybrid war came much later, after a five-year delay. This failure to recognize what was going on put the West on the back foot in dealing with the Russia challenge. In particular, three events changed the minds of Western policy-makers and caused them to realize that the West was under a determined attack from Russia. Those were the re-election of Vladimir Putin to the Russian presidency in 2012, the invasion and annexation of Crimea in 2014, and the US presidential election of 2016, with its allegations of Russian meddling. Between 2007 and 2012, however, Russia pursued an all-out, mainly covert, political war on the West without much notice or reaction.

Even after these dramatic events, some in the West do not believe, or would prefer not to believe, that we are subject to a determined attack from Moscow.[5] The issue has become massively politicized. Therefore, any examination of the effects of Russia's hybrid war on the West needs to start by describing its very nature. What does Russia want? Why did Russia turn against the West in 2007? Why did it begin to wage a hybrid war against Western institutions including not only NATO, but the European Union? What are its methods? And does it really make a difference?

WHY RUSSIA TURNED AGAINST THE WEST

One of the most controversial issues in analyzing Russia's hybrid war with the West is the question of who started it. Lots of words have been spilled on this question, and the best scholars and analysts have produced many potential explanations. However, it is hard to know which one is true.

One possible explanation lies with Russian president Vladimir Putin. As opposed to Russia's pro-Western leaders of the late 1980s and 1990s—Mikhail Gorbachev and Boris Yeltsin—who sought closer relations with the West after years of Cold War enmity, Putin was a horse of a different color. Putin publicly mourned the loss of Russia's Soviet empire. He personally defended the Soviet Union in its last days from the KGB office in East Germany, preventing German citizens from ransacking the KGB building as the Berlin Wall fell.[6] Later, Putin appears to have become enthralled with visions of Russia greatness proposed by Russian fascist thinkers and Eurasianists such as Ivan Ilyin and Alexander Dugin.[7] In this analysis, Putin always, or eventually, opposed the pro-Western orientation of his predecessors and sought to rebuild Soviet Union 2.0, in one form or another.[8] This project was always bound to generate conflict with the West. As David Satter put it, after the Maidan revolution in Ukraine, "The West was suddenly faced not with a masquerade but with the Russia that had existed all along, that somehow had been overlooked by many Western policy makers and observers." Russia was a kleptocratic, mafia state that was fundamentally disappointed with the collapse of its empire and determined to reconstruct it.[9]

From my own experience, there is a certain plausibility to the idea that Putin was the author of these changes. At the very beginning of the Putin era in 2000, I was living in Moscow and working at Moscow State University, reputed to be the leading university in Russia. Already, in the first year of the Putin presidency, the faculty and students of the university, under a new, Putin-appointed rector, were in the process of throwing out their pro-Western orientations and adopting nationalist official rhetoric. In a broader sense, we know that Russia's shift from pro-Western partner to geopolitical opponent occurred during the Putin presidency, so it makes sense to blame Putin, who directed this reorientation from the top.[10]

Another possible explanation, however, is that the West pushed Russia into a corner with NATO expansion and, by creating a sense of insecurity in Moscow, forced Russia to respond to a perceived Western threat.[11] In this view, the West should have known of and respected Russia's threat perceptions, rather than aggravating them by expanding the anti-Russian NATO alliance into Eastern Europe and even admitting former republics of the Soviet Union after the end of the Cold War. By choosing to override Russia's perceived zone of influence, the West generated a predictable reaction from Russia. In this perspective, the conflict between Russia and the West is rooted in what international relations scholars call a "security dilemma." In a classical security dilemma, the security of one country is challenged by the reasonable security precautions of another. So, for instance, when the West acts to prevent a security vacuum in Eastern Europe by admitting vulnerable former Russian satellites into NATO, Russia feels challenged, and when Russia launches military exercises or modernizes its armed forces to confront this challenge, the West feels insecure. When NATO places forward troop deployments to deter a Russian invasion, Russia responds by nuclear saber-rattling, and so on.

There is no doubt in my mind that Russia and the West are locked in a security dilemma. And the strong implication of a security dilemma is that both sides are to blame for one another's sense of external threat.[12]

Another possible explanation that has gained currency is that Russia is a "bad" state, too large, too insecure, too ambitious for its means, and with too much of a history of imperial expansion to ever fit in with the West. A break was inevitable from the beginning, and it should be no surprise that Russia has adopted a policy of assertiveness against the West, as it has for many centuries. There are many versions of this type of argument that ground Russia's foreign policy behavior in its deep history, rather than in the actions of contemporary leaders like Putin. Some argue that Russia's foreign policy is "honor" based and that slights to its perceived sense of honor can cause radical changes in how Russia treats the West.[13] Others argue that Russia has always been an imperial state and is today either "neoimperial," "postimperial," or "transimperial," in one way or another still trying to digest the loss of the Soviet empire.[14] In these explanations, Putin is the unsurprising result of Russia's loss of empire after 1991 and the unique linkage between politics and geopolitics in the Russian imagination.

There is most likely some truth to all of these explanations by my academic colleagues. No doubt, some combination of Russia's history as a state, its mindset and culture, its interactions with the West, and the elevation of Putin to the presidency in 1999 are responsible for the current predicament. At the same time, it remains very hard to say which of these potential explanations is the silver bullet that explains everything.

All we know for sure is that in 1999, Russia was on the way to closer relations with a West that it emulated in economics and politics, but by 2007, Russia had decided to abandon the pro-Western direction of its foreign policy and launch an all-out political war on the West.

This about-face was surprising to many in the West because, until that time, Russia had followed a policy of progressive integration into Western security and economic structures. Foresightful analysts discussed the possibility of Russia joining

NATO.[15] Russia under President Yeltsin had been invited to join the G7, making it the G8, a club of leading democracies and economies, an organization representing the top table of the Western international system. Russia's decision to sharply oppose the West and its international system was so surprising that for many years, Western leaders and analysts failed to believe it was happening. Because of this, it is important to discuss when this transition happened.

THE TURNING POINT

While Russia's turning against the West may not have been sudden, but rather a process that began to unfold from the start of the Putin administration, my research indicates that the most important turning point occurred by 2007.[16]

In 2007, Vladimir Putin gave an important speech at the Munich Security Conference calling for an end to US unipolar leadership in the world. Putin remarked, "One state and, of course, first and foremost the United States, has overstepped its national borders in every way. This is visible in the economic, political, cultural and educational policies it imposes on other nations. Well, who likes this? Who is happy about this?" Putin advocated instead for a "multipolar" world in which other leading nations would be free to dictate their own foreign policy approach in their own neighborhoods. Putin referred to the dramatic growth of Brazil, Russia itself, India, and China (the BRICs) and commented, "There is no reason to doubt that the economic potential of the new centres of global economic growth will inevitably be converted into political influence and will strengthen multipolarity."[17] Later, Russia's actions seemed to back up these words with actions. In 2008, Russia sternly objected to NATO offering Georgia and Ukraine a path toward NATO membership and launched the Russo-Georgian war. In

2009, Russia objected strenuously to the announcement of the European Union's Eastern Partnership program that sought closer relations with former Soviet republics.[18] Russia's relations with the West had been souring for some time. Why was 2007 a turning point?

The most likely answer is Kosovo, a small Muslim country in Europe, a state that barely exists.

In 1999, NATO planes bombed Serbia to help bring the Yugoslav wars to an end. Russia objected strenuously, but unsuccessfully, against this attack on its historical ally, Serbia. As head of the Russian National Security Council at this time, Vladimir Putin witnessed Russia's inability to stop Western action firsthand. The bombing campaign ended successfully from a Western perspective, forcing Serbia to the negotiating table and leading to the Dayton Accords that forged a tense peace in the Balkans. Kosovo, a majority Muslim province of Serbia, remained a sticking point, however. In 2007, Finnish prime minister Martti Ahtisaari, acting on behalf of the United Nations, developed a proposal for "supervised independence" of Kosovo, with the aim of splitting it from Serbia, seeking to solve one of the remaining ethnic conflicts in the region. Russia again objected strenuously, pointing out that the UN mandate gave little basis for intervening in domestic matters of member states. Russia insisted that supporting the secession of Kosovo from Serbia was against international law and would open a can of worms. Russia threatened to retaliate by recognizing the secession of pro-Russian ethnic enclaves in a number of former Soviet states. Western powers noted Russia's objections, but pushed ahead regardless, encouraging Kosovo's unilateral declaration of independence in 2008.[19]

Russia made good on its threat by invading neighboring Georgia in August 2008, just a few months later. After the conclusion of the Russo-Georgian war, Russian president Dmitry Medvedev wrote an op-ed in the *Financial Times* entitled, "Why

I Had to Recognize Georgia's Breakaway Regions."[20] He made clear that Russia regarded its invasion of Georgia as a tit-for-tat response to Western recognition of Kosovo independence. He wrote, "Ignoring Russia's warnings, western countries rushed to recognize Kosovo's illegal declaration of independence from Serbia. We argued consistently that it would be impossible, after that, to tell the Abkhazians and Ossetians (and dozens of other groups around the world) that what was good for the Kosovo Albanians was not good for them. In international relations, you cannot have one rule for some and another rule for others."

In retrospect, Russian leaders frequently and publicly warned in 2007 that they had scrapped their pro-Western orientation in foreign policy and were ready to defect from the Western international system. Even so, Western countries— with the United States and Germany in the lead—refused to give up the hope that they could entice Russia to join the Western community of nations. Why?

There were a number of reasons, including the partly covert nature of Russia's assault on Western institutions, but the main reason was a failure of Western leaders to understand or respect Russia's worldview. Western leaders failed to see that Russia was worried not only about the project of NATO expansion, but by the entire Western project for a "Europe whole and free." For Russia, competition with the West had been reframed as an existential struggle. Limited in its ability to respond with traditional military means, Russia responded with a different kind of war.

THE WEST IN DISBELIEF

In 2007, while Russia had concluded that it was in a struggle to the death with the Western institutions that upheld the unipolar global order, Western leaders did not see it this way. Of course, it was widely recognized that Russia did not like NATO expansion. However, many in the West discounted Russian rhetoric on this point, since the supposed "encirclement" of Russia by NATO had taken place in conjunction with a major drawdown of US troops in Europe—from 300,000 to 30,000[21]—and a dramatic decline in military spending. With US troops leaving Europe in droves and European defense spending falling off a cliff, how could Russia feel threatened? By contrast, most European leaders believed that Europe would never experience a major war again. The Russian threat was gone and no other power seemed to have designs on Europe. With the European Union uniting the continent and security backstopped by NATO commitments from the Americans, Europe was at peace for the foreseeable future. NATO, seeking to justify its existence, primarily took up out-of-area operations, for instance in Afghanistan. Western countries had no intention of invading Russia and believed that their force posture showed this clearly. Russia should, therefore, have no indication of a threat from the West, and its concerns about NATO expansion had to be taken with a grain of salt.

What the West failed to realize was that for a Russian government determined to win back the former Soviet empire, the very existence of NATO and its security guarantees to member states constituted a threat. NATO was the embodiment of the unipolar world order that Putin castigated in 2007. Russia had begun not only to be concerned for its own security, but also to see itself locked in competition with NATO for influence over the lands in between—countries formerly part of the Soviet Union, but now independent, that Russia saw as part of its natural sphere of influence. An enlarged NATO alliance threatened Russia's attempts to establish itself as a great power with a legitimate sphere of influence.

In addition, Russia began to perceive a similar threat from the European Union (EU), the other major institution around which European security has been based in the post–World War II period. The EU is a trade bloc with a political purpose: to underpin peace in Europe through mutually advantageous international trade. The EU is so peaceful and so dedicated to the pursuit of peace that in 2012 it was awarded the Nobel Peace Prize for six decades of work helping to transform Europe "from a continent of war to a continent of peace." In his acceptance speech, EU Commission president Manuel Barroso stated, "It started with six countries and we are now 27, another one is going to join us next year and more want to come. So the EU is the most important project for peace in terms of transnational, supranational co-operation."[22] How could a zone of peace and prosperity ever be perceived as a threat? To Western leaders, it seemed nonsensical. And yet after the Maidan protests in Ukraine in 2013–14, it became clear to all that Russia views the EU—and not only NATO—as an existential threat.

THE THREAT OF EUROPE

To explain why, I turn to maps. I have always enjoyed looking at maps and imagining the many places in the world. But it was not until recently that I realized that all maps, if you stare at them long enough, reveal the political imagination of their designers. For example, consider figure 2.1. To Western eyes, the map in figure 2.1 looks like something one might encounter in a classroom, a common map of the European Union. Actually, it is an official map of the EU Council. The EU countries stand out in jaunty colors with each one represented by a brightly colored flag. Nothing objectionable here. Or is there? Let's think about this map for a moment from Russian eyes. A Russian might look at this map of Europe and note that Russia is absent. Or nearly absent. While other European countries such as Spain, Germany, and Malta, are celebrated with flags and colors,

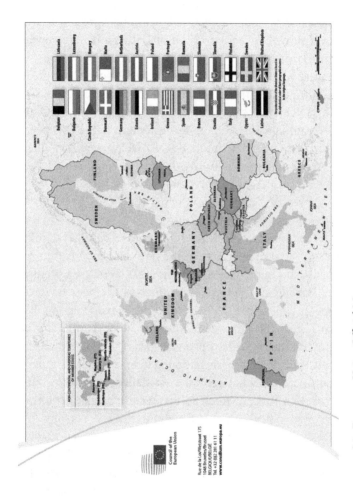

FIGURE 2.1: European Union Official Map. Source: © European Union, 2014. Reproduced with the kind permission of Lovell Johns, Oxford, UK, www.lovelljohns.com. Flag reproduced by Lovell Johns, Oxford, UK and authenticated by The Flag Research Center, Winchester, MA 01890, USA.

Russia, which occupies one-third of what is geographically recognized as Europe from the Atlantic to the Urals, is represented
as a tan mass on the periphery of the map. It does not even
justify a label or a border. Russia is a bland background to the
European Union's celebration of nations. Russia is barely even
part of this Europe.

That must sting. Russia has long identified itself as a great
power in Europe. Its cities, its culture, its history are deeply en-
twined with Europe. As recently as 1991, Russia controlled an
enormous empire in Europe, consisting not only of the European
states of the former Soviet Union, but also of Warsaw Pact allies
the Red Army occupied after World War II. Figures 2.2 and
2.3 paint a very different picture, one in which Russia is a very
substantial presence in Europe, during the Cold War and in
nineteenth-century imperial Europe.

Yet, in today's Europe, Russia occupies a peripheral role.
Consider one final map, a map of the new accession countries
of the European Union. The map in figure 2.4 creates a picture
of a tiered Europe. At the top tier are the core member states of
the European Union in 1995. A second tier is made up of CEE
states that joined the European Union in 2004. A third tier is
made up of Southeastern European laggards that joined the EU
in 2007. Russia, like Belarus, is relegated to fourth-tier membership of Europe, somewhat behind even stalled, long-term candidate states like Turkey, which at least receive brighter colors.

These maps speak eloquently about Russia's reasons for
wanting to overturn the EU project for Europe. Russia does not
imagine itself to be a peripheral force in Europe, but a great
power. Russia believes that, as a great power, it deserves a sphere
of influence in Europe. That sphere of influence is threatened
not only by NATO, but by the EU and its project of creating a
European continent dominated by a single trading bloc of democratic nation-states pooling sovereignty in Brussels, its capital.

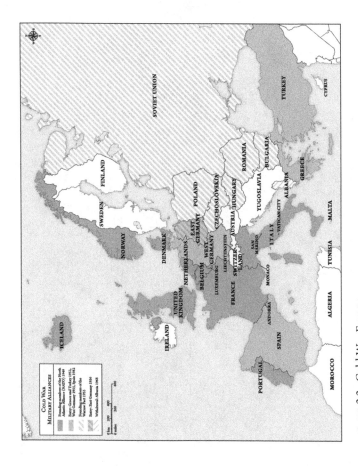

FIGURE 2.2: Cold War Europe

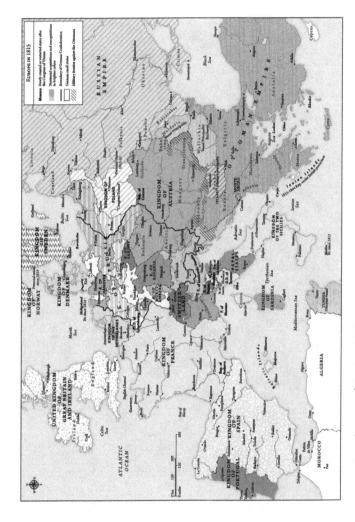

FIGURE 2.3: Concert of Europe, 1815

FIGURE 2.4: A Multitiered Europe. Source: © Nations Online Project.

A Political Threat

In the 2000s, Russia began to perceive the EU and NATO not only as threats to its geopolitical ambitions, but to the very survival of its authoritarian, kleptocratic political regime,[23] thanks to the West's democracy promotion efforts. The United States and the European Union share a strong belief that democratic governance fosters peace among nations, and the EU has made well-functioning democracy a requirement of membership. Trust in a "democratic peace" in Europe relies on a mountain of political science research, but also on a particular narrative of

European history. It is widely believed in Europe that the turn to dictatorship in 1930s Germany caused World War II and all its destruction. The lesson: dictatorships, lacking respect for individual rights, tend to use violence. Democracies, which give multiple groups and individuals a say in decision-making, tend to seek consensus and peace. Extending this logic, after the end of the Cold War, the United States and EU assiduously promoted democracy in former communist states. They made access to the enormous EU market, a huge driver of economic growth, contingent on creating strong democratic political institutions; and it worked. According to Milada Vachudova, a leading scholar of EU enlargement, "The European Union . . . may well be presiding over the most successful democracy promotion program ever implemented by an international actor."[24]

Yet there was one problem. Russia, after the color revolutions in Georgia and Ukraine, began to perceive EU democratic promotion in former Soviet states, including Russia itself, as an existential threat to the Putin regime.

It is easy to see why. Russia itself could be a target of prodemocratic protests and regime change. For while Russia holds periodic elections, it is not a democracy. As one of the leading Russian foreign policy analysts, Dmitri Trenin, puts it, Russia "is clearly authoritarian, despite the formal trappings of democracy."[25] Its elections do not meet the standard of "free and fair," as the playing field in these elections is not level, but rather decisively tipped toward progovernment candidates.[26] Candidates who have a realistic possibility of challenging President Vladimir Putin, the linchpin of Russia's dictatorial system of government, are regularly imprisoned (as in the case of Alexei Navalny), shot (as in the case of Boris Nemtsov), or otherwise excluded, often in creative but ruthless ways.[27] The Kremlin often runs its own pseudo-opposition candidates to soak up votes and create an appearance of freedom, as in the case of Ksenia Sobchak in 2017–18. In addition to carefully controlling who runs through a sophisticated campaign of official harassment and even assassination, the Kremlin owns or controls most of the media in the country. It regularly blacklists or humiliates opposition politicians, starving them of positive media coverage, or plunging them into scandal, especially on television. By contrast, Vladimir Putin is portrayed as a great leader and receives a full complement of positive news coverage on a daily basis. In 2018, state TV channel Rossiya 1 launched a new show devoted entirely to praising Putin, entitled, "Moscow. Kremlin. Putin."[28]

Putin's authoritarian regime resembles a mafia-type organization in which the president is a kind of *capo di capi* controlling the major oligarchs, the politically connected business leaders who own most of the country, as well as chieftains within the state bureaucracy.[29] The regime has many skeletons in the closet, including alleged terrorist attacks against its own people.[30] As a result, the Russian regime would be existentially threatened by the transparency that democratic governance would bring. Since a single electoral defeat would be seen as a sign of weakness and result in a disruption of the entire system, the regime in Moscow cannot countenance democratic elections. It keeps a tight lid on political communication as well. Even democratic successes in former Soviet states might give Russians the idea to promote democracy at home. As a result, Russia feels threatened by democratization in its "near abroad." EU and US support for democratization in countries like Ukraine appears to Russia to threaten the very existence of the regime in Moscow.

The Kremlin further believes that Western powers, specifically the EU and United States, use prodemocracy movements to undermine the Russian government. They see prodemocracy street protests in their own country as Western-sponsored attempts to launch a coup. For instance, Russia has accused the West of supporting a "coup" in Ukraine by unseating elected leader Viktor Yanukovich through street protests, although these protests were an indigenous Ukrainian action. Nonetheless, Russia blames former US secretary of state Hillary Clinton, former assistant secretary of state Victoria Nuland, and European leaders for sponsoring the protests and for Yanukovich's removal from power. Determined to divide the United States from the EU by feeding resentment of the United States in Europe, Russia often suggests that the EU is simply a tool of the United States. The Kremlin uses similarly divisive rhetoric to diminish public support for democratic protests, by claiming that protesters are paid by the West. Putin fears that such protests could break out in Moscow—an existential threat against which he is constantly vigilant. Putin viewed the Bolotnaya protests in Moscow in 2011 as a Western-sponsored "color revolution" and believes that the West deploys such tactics to unseat him.[31] Therefore, it is no exaggeration to say that the Kremlin perceives US and EU democracy promotion activities in former Soviet states to be an existential threat. Where the West sees democracy promotion as a strategy for promoting peace in Europe, Putin sees it as an act of war against Russia and his regime in particular.[32]

An Economic Threat

Strangely, Europe's strategy for building friendly ties between nation-states based on economic trade, mobility, and investment also has been perceived as a fundamental threat to Russia, since its economy operates in a very different way. The political economic system that Putin has built is, in many ways, incompatible with the law-based system of the EU, based on treaties and courts and independent judiciaries. Russia's corrupt economy cannot operate in the way it does while complying with EU rules. Applying EU laws would effectively undermine the patronage principles that lie at the heart of Russian crony capitalism—and vice versa. For this reason, the extension of EU rules to Russia began to be perceived as an existential threat to the regime in Moscow. European scholars have found that "any attempts to formalize the EU's interdependence with Russia can only lead to greater friction,"[33] since Russia has such different ideas about what integration and rule of law mean.

Margot Light's study of Russia's attempts at economic integration with the EU found that an accumulation of perceived economic and administrative incompatibilities may have caused Russia to turn away from the EU in the mid-2000s. After more than a decade of working closely with the EU, she contends, Russia realized that it continually faced difficulties in negotiating agreements with the EU on basic free market treaties such as an open skies agreement with the EU. While the EU sought time and again to eliminate overflight tariffs for EU airlines over Russia (and Russian airlines over EU states), Russia could not see why it should allow free access to its airspace. As a result, the EU canceled a planned aviation summit in Russia in 2007, believing that Russia had limited ability to become part of the European economic space. After a number of similar problems failed to be resolved during the 2000s, Russia turned decisively against the EU. In Professor Light's view, "Russians do not understand how the Brussels bureaucracy works and they complain bitterly about its 'rather woolly decision-making procedure.' A lack of experts in EU negotiations means that Russia is often at the receiving end of EU proposals, rather than making its own proposals, adding to frustration."[34]

Around the same time, Russia also decided that EU efforts to integrate neighboring states more closely with the EU constituted a threat. If former Soviet states joined or signed association agreements with the EU, their economies would become incompatible with Russia's modus operandi as well.[35] When Putin announced the creation of a Eurasian Economic Union in 2014, it amounted to a declaration of war against the EU that would be fought through competition for economic spheres of influence in a shared European neighborhood. The Eurasian Economic Union (EEU) has not been terribly successful, but Russia clearly conceives of it as a Eurasian competitor to the European Union, with one key difference. Since Russia is by far the most dominant economy in the post-Soviet space, Russia sees the EEU as an instrument of ever-closer economic and po-litical control over its neighbors. By encouraging its neighbors to join the Eurasian Economic Union rather than the European Union, Russia seeks to draw a clear demarcation line against EU economic influence in its "near abroad."

A Cultural Threat

Interestingly, Russia has also come to view liberal European values as a threat to its culture, as it promotes its own conserva-tive values worldwide. Russian media and political figures mock-ingly label the EU as "Gayropa" and object to expanding rights to homosexuals and transgender people. Opposition to gay rights has become a convenient symbol for Kremlin opposition to Western values of democracy and human rights across the board. Russia has sought to use the Russian Orthodox Church to deliver cultural and political messages throughout the Orthodox world. It has used a stern defense of conservative values to de-velop alliances with conservatives in core Europe and the United States as well. In doing so, Russia plays upon its long-standing claim that Moscow is the "third Rome" within Christianity, after the fall of Rome and Constantinople, and a tough defender of the traditional nuclear family, religious practice, a subordinate role for women, and opposition to sexual and gender minorities.[36]

Russia also plays on fears of Muslim immigration in Europe, making common cause with xenophobic and anti-immigrant governments and parties.[37] It supports European states like Hungary in their attempts to preserve a conservative national culture through opposition to immigration,[38] though this is a touchy issue in Russia itself, with its large, multiethnic popula-tion and sizable immigration from Central Asia. Regardless, as Russia attempts to build a strong nation-state led by Russians, it perceives, or at least purports to perceive, EU values of mul-ticulturalism and tolerance as a fundamental threat.[39] By con-trast, Western institutions see individual and minority rights as key aspects of their democratic peace project and seek to promote these values in Russia.

A Zero-Sum Game

At least since the mid-2000s, Russia has felt threatened by Western democracy promotion, economic integration projects, and culture. While Western leaders regard all three elements as building blocks of peace and prosperity in Europe, Russia sees them as attempts to expand the EU's zone of influence and as existential threats. It wasn't always this way. While Russia was always concerned about NATO enlargement, especially the placement of nuclear weapons closer to Moscow, or missile shields that might enable nuclear strikes, EU enlargement was seen as relatively innocuous or even as an opportunity. Since the EU has negligible armed forces and a complex decision-making structure, Russia tended to view the European Union as a sideshow to or a vehicle of the European great powers: Germany, France, and Britain. However, with the enlargement of the EU in the 2000s, Russia began to view the EU as a competitor for influence in its "near abroad." Moreover, the Kremlin observed that no CEE country joined the EU without joining NATO first. Therefore, to accede to EU membership was akin to agreeing to join NATO. By 2007, Russia had decided to oppose EU membership—and even visa free travel to the EU—for former Soviet states.[40] The Western project of a "Europe whole and free" poses an existential threat to the Putin regime. Therefore, Russia regards the battle for influence in the lands in between as a zero-sum game, to be won or lost.

RUSSIA'S HYBRID WAR

Russia, perceiving an existential threat from the West, responded by launching a hybrid war. Russia's strategy is frequently referred to as the "Gerasimov doctrine" of hybrid war, though some have argued that Russians do not use these terms, but instead refer to it as a campaign of "strategic deterrence," "reflexive control," or "new generation warfare."[41] However one chooses to label it, Russia's objectives are to polarize, disable, and ultimately destroy the European Union and NATO without incurring too great a reaction from the West, and ideally to replace them with a new European and international system. Destroying, or even substantially weakening, the EU and NATO would halt their attempts to integrate former Soviet republics and satellite states and strengthen Russia's hand with its former imperial subjects in Central and Eastern Europe. Second, Russia wants to secure its position as Europe's preeminent supplier of oil and natural gas, and a growing presence in nuclear power generation. Russia is currently Europe's largest source of hydrocarbons, but it faces competition from Norway, the Gulf States, North Africa, and the United States. Russia wishes to hamper its competitors' access to European markets and ensure dominance over pipeline routes that make Russian gas a cheaper, easier choice. Third, Russia wishes to weaken Europe's ties with the United States. US support has been crucial to the EU project of creating a zone of peace and prosperity in Europe, including through NATO. The United States sees EU enlargement as a way of extending this zone of peace and prosperity to a greater share of the European continent. Russia wants to limit US involvement and make EU states more reliant on Russia in security matters.

In this war against the West, Russia has used a wide range of tools: spying and active measures, cyberwarfare, funding for anti-EU political parties, media campaigns and disinformation, support for nongovernmental organizations and pro-Russia paramilitary organizations, and military interventions against countries signing association agreements with the EU, such as Ukraine. In addition, Russia uses relations with Russian nationals abroad, leverage over gas resources, and conservative cultural appeals to exercise influence over other countries. The following sections provide a brief overview, rather than an exhaustive examination, of the techniques Russia has used in its war on the West and how they result in political polarization and destabilization from within.[42]

Covert Action

The first thing to know about Russia's war on Europe and the United States is that it is largely covert. While Russia has sometimes used direct military force, as in the Russo-Georgia war or Ukraine, it has more often masked its actions and intentions through covert action, computer hacking, and use of proxies and state-run entities to achieve plausible deniability and keep its opponents confused and off guard. In 2009, Janusz Bugajski observed that "Russia is operationally stealthier than the Soviet regime was prior to its collapse. Without declaring any ideologically motivated global mission and by claiming that it is pursuing pragmatic national interests, the Kremlin engages in asymmetrical offensives by interjecting itself in its neighbor's affairs, capturing important sectors of local economies, subverting vulnerable political systems, corrupting or discrediting national leaders, and systematically undermining Western unity."[43]

Because of these stealth methods, uncovering the full range of Russian actions in its hybrid war with the West has taken some time. The full extent of Russia's actions may not be known, and what is known is probably incomplete. Still, progress has been made, and much of what is known is in the public domain. I rely almost entirely on what the intelligence community would call "open-source intelligence," meaning publicly available information, supplemented by some off-the-record interviews with investigative sources. At this point, the public has access to a very rich array of information about Russian strategy, tools, and tactics. Unfortunately, there are still many in the West who ignore this information—as in 2009—or prefer not to look at it or believe it.[44]

Western intelligence agencies have been sounding the alarm about Russia's hybrid war for some time. According to Belgian intelligence chief Alain Winants, Brussels, the capital of the European Union, where the EU institutions and NATO are based, has become "one of the big spy capitals of the world," a major target of Russian intelligence and influence operations.[45] Winants reports that "in Belgium, espionage, Russian espionage and from other countries, like the Chinese, but also others, [is] at the same level as the Cold War. . . . We are a country with an enormous concentration of diplomats, businessmen, international institutions—NATO, European institutions. So for an intelligence officer, for a spy, this is a kindergarten. It's the place to be."

Beyond reports carefully redacted and made public by European spy agencies, it is very difficult to know exactly what this spying consists of. However, my own discussions with EU officials over the years make clear that officials believe that Russia hears everything that goes on in Brussels—even in closed meetings of top EU councils. There are no secrets. While some of this may be due to wiretaps and other signals intelligence, much of the information is generated by EU officials themselves, who freely communicate with Russian intelligence agencies and their surrogates, such as the Belarusian authorities, often on an informal basis. Many EU officials believe that the Russians should be informed of EU actions and discussions to prevent misunderstandings—or that they are potential allies. EU ambassadors frequently use insecure forms of communication, such as cell phones. So the EU bureaucracy is enormously leaky. Russians have ears everywhere. It is very likely that Russia deploys information operations in Brussels in an effort to discredit or mislead EU and NATO officials.

One of the most successful operations to mislead Western officials was the election of Dmitry Medvedev as Putin's successor as president in 2008. Serving one term from 2008 to 2012, Medvedev portrayed himself as a Western-leaning leader. EU and member state officials were seduced by Medvedev's plans for economic modernization, especially creating a Russian high-tech center in Skolkovo, near Moscow, plans that never came to fruition and were most likely designed to deceive Westerners into turning over vital technology in the belief that Russia was a modernizing, Westernizing power. Many European and US officials believed that Medvedev indicated a modernizing direction for Russia, failing to recognize that he was only a convenient front for Vladimir Putin, who had exceeded the term limits under Russia's constitution and had to step aside. Yet after a constitutional change that Medvedev pushed through, Putin returned to the presidency in 2012 for two additional six-year terms. This ruse should have been evident to observers, but some preferred to believe that Medvedev stood for modernization and liberalization. Medvedev's presidency disarmed the West for years as Russia pursued a hybrid war against the West. He was, in many senses, a modern false Dmitry, pretender to the Russian throne.[46]

Agents of Influence

In addition to simple intelligence-gathering and information operations, Russia also deploys "agents of influence" against the West. These are people who not only trade in information, but also undertake operations on behalf of Russian spy services to undermine Western institutions. I reported with Hungarian analyst Péter Krekó on one such case a few years ago in *Foreign Affairs*: the case of KGBéla. Béla Kovács is a member of the European Parliament from Hungary and a representative of the far-right Jobbik Party. He was investigated by the Hungarian parliament and had his parliamentary immunity lifted by the European Parliament, where he was also investigated for spying for Russia. The exact nature of the charges against him were never made public. However, his background and dossier make for very interesting reading. Kovacs grew up in Japan, where his foster father worked in the Hungarian embassy as a building superintendent; his foster mother was a cook. He was apparently recruited into the KGB, spent years working in business in Russia, and then returned, wealthy, to Hungary to become the treasurer of Jobbik. Jobbik enjoyed a sudden rise to power with extensive new financial resources. Simultaneously, it adopted a pro-Russian (and pro-Iranian) foreign policy stance, positions that were not typical of the Hungarian Far Right. In World War II, the Hungarian Far Right was pro-German and aligned with the Nazis, not the Russians. After winning election to the European Parliament, Kovács became treasurer of a small far-right group that promoted the views of extremist parties from across Europe. He was photographed in regular meetings with Russian intelligence services and frequently visited Moscow, but no further information was released to the press. His wife was revealed to have several other husbands, including a Japanese nuclear scientist and an Austrian mafia boss, and to have worked as a courier for Russian intelligence.[47] Kovács became a leader of an extremist faction in the European Parliament, as well as contributing to the rise of Jobbik in Hungary.

Funding Extremist Parties

As with Jobbik in Hungary, it has become clear in recent years that Russia has funded and promoted far-right and far-left parties throughout the European Union whose programs seek to undermine, destroy, or pull their countries out of the Union.[48] The parties Russia has supported seem to have two things in common: they have taken a pro-Russia political stance in their official platforms and they offer explicit support for the Russian annexation of Crimea and other controversial Russian foreign policy objectives. While proof is often lacking, it is fair to assume that European political parties that echo controversial pro-Russia foreign policy positions—such as support for Russian annexation of Crimea—receive financial and other assistance from Russia. Why else would they adopt policy positions that are irrelevant to most European voters? This is the quid pro quo that Russia demands for its support.

Take the case of Marine Le Pen's National Front. In 2014, it was widely reported that her presidential election campaign was financed by a Kremlin-connected Russian bank. During the last stages of her election campaign, she made a prominent state visit to Russia and met with Vladimir Putin. She also voiced her support for Russia's annexation of Crimea.[49] It is not clear how supporting the annexation of Crimea helped her in her bid for the French presidency. Articulating support for controversial Russia foreign policy positions may have helped her, however, to obtain financing from a Russian bank. Numerous other far-right and far-left parties in Europe have vocally come out in support of Russia's annexation of Crimea, even sending observers to validate the Crimean annexation referendum in 2015. Parties that sent observers to validate the Crimea referendum include the Austrian Freedom Party, Alternative for Germany, Ataka (Bulgaria), Change (Poland) (whose leaders are now in prison in Poland), Italy's Northern League, the Serbian Radical Party, the Czech Freedom and Direct Democracy Party, and the UK Independence Party.[50] Russia supported the Brexit referendum, most likely with substantial financial assistance, in a successful effort to divide the EU and destabilize UK politics.[51]

In addition to financial support, Russia also provides opposition research (in the case of its social media trolls and bots active in supporting the Trump campaign, for instance), and media support for parties that take an anti-EU, anti-NATO, and pro-Russian foreign policy stance. Russia's media campaigns became famous after the massive disinformation campaign in the US presidential election in 2016. But they have been going on for a long time in many countries. Within Russia itself, Russian state media maintains a powerful propaganda machine, combining high-quality entertainment television and pro-Kremlin political propaganda. People mostly watch the state-owned or state-connected channels in Russia for the great entertainment TV and imbibe political messages along the way.

Propaganda and Disinformation

It is hard to understand Russian propaganda without first getting a taste for how it works in Russia, where international news stories often are turned on their heads, and fantastical, made-up news regularly dominates the airwaves. For instance, the downing of Malaysian Airlines MH-17, which Dutch investigators found was shot down by a Russian missile in territory controlled by Russian-supported rebels in Ukraine, was reported creatively in Russian media. Russian news channels reported a variety of conspiracy theories, including that a Ukrainian government missile brought down the plane after mistaking it for Putin's own plane, that the Dutch government loaded the plane with corpses and downed it intentionally in Russian territory, and that a Ukrainian jet shot it down in a "false flag" operation to pin blame on Russia. Russian propaganda extends beyond Russia itself since Russian speakers in countries of the former Soviet Union often watch Russian state TV and imbibe these propaganda messages. Agnia Grigas writes of Russian influence in the Baltic States that "Russia has been particularly successful in creating a virtual community involving not only the Russian diaspora but also a segment of the Baltic population that remains linked culturally, linguistically and ideologically to Moscow."[52] Tim Snyder suggests that Russian media intentionally lie to create a fictitious world for a malleable audience willing to be lied to and enthralled with Kremlin power. Its information war is "designed to undermine factuality while insisting on [Russian] innocence."[53] Russia must always portrayed as the innocent victim, since this justifies any aggressive action Russia might take as self-defense.

In addition to broadcasting propaganda to Russian speakers at home and abroad, Russia has also invested in foreign-language broadcasters, which offer a digestible version of the same messages. Russia Today is the seemingly respectable flag-ship of Russian foreign-language TV propaganda, available in more than one hundred countries in Arabic, English, Spanish, Russian, German, and French. It is accompanied by the less respectable Sputnik radio, which peddles a *National Enquirer* brand of trash journalism on the Internet. Both outlets mix propaganda with reasonable reporting on social issues in the West, designed to win readers and render them more trusting of the more fantastical fare. Russia Today and Sputnik often manu-facture stories out of whole cloth. The US Office of the Director of National Intelligence report on the 2016 US presidential elections found that RT published such fantastical stories as "an exclusive interview with Julian Assange entitled 'Clinton and ISIS Funded by the Same Money.' RT's most popular video on Secretary Clinton, 'How 100% of the Clintons' 'Charity' Went to . . . Themselves,' had more than 9 million views on social media platforms. RT's most popular English-language video, called 'Trump Will Not Be Permitted to Win,' featured Assange and had 2.2 million views."[54]

As the US director of national intelligence found, the impact of these fake news stories is magnified by a network of right-wing news sources in all Western countries that broadcast Russian disinformation to a much larger audience. Russian propaganda messages also are "amplified on social media, sometimes by computer 'bots' that send out thousands of Facebook and Twitter messages." Russia has famously used Twitter bots to disseminate defamatory information about political candidates as well as an army of trolls who seek to influence debates in a variety of so-cial media settings. Trolls generally make harsh and negative comments to discredit views that they do not like. Moscow employs hundreds of trolls at a "troll factory" in St. Petersburg, Russia.[55] According to the CEO of the US Broadcasting Board of Governors, John Lansing, Kremlin messaging is "really almost beyond a false narrative. It's more of a strategy to establish that there is no such thing as an empirical fact. Facts are really what [is] being challenged around the world."[56]

As Clint Watts, a fellow of the Foreign Policy Research Institute, pointed out during the US presidential election campaign, Russian "active measures" propaganda and disinformation was distributed and amplified by candidate Donald Trump and his campaign team, in an unusual episode of collusion. "Part of the reason active measures have worked in this US election is because the commander in chief has used Russian active measures at times against his opponents," Watts, a former FBI agent, testified to the US Senate Intelligence Committee on March 30, 2017. Watts cited several instances in which the Trump campaign deployed false Kremlin propaganda stories to attack opponents.[57]

Regardless of their limited audience ratings, Russian news channels provide a useful outlet for extremist politicians in many countries.[58] Since extremists often do not get much media coverage at home, the publicity that Russian channels provide can mean a lot. For instance, before the UK Independence Party (UKIP) was taken seriously in Britain, its leader, Nigel Farage, appeared repeatedly on Russia Today, and became a regular, paid commentator for the station, effectively an employee of the Russian state.[59] In the United States, Russia Today broadcast the Green Party presidential debate in 2012 and 2016. The 2016 Green Party candidate Jill Stein visited Moscow during the presidential election campaign for an RT event and made glowing statements about Russian foreign policy. RT has sought to defend Jill Stein from a supposed "smear campaign" against her examining the Russia ties of her campaign.[60] Russian intelligence knows that fringe parties can have a real impact on elections, by drawing away support from mainstream parties and, in the case of the US elections, tipping the Electoral College in certain key states.

One of the key objectives of Russian disinformation in Europe has been to spread fear of Muslim immigration, in an effort to worsen perceptions of the EU's immigration crisis. Former Hungarian counterintelligence officer Ferenc Katrein accused Russian intelligence of aggravating a perceived migration crisis by spreading false stories or exaggerating real ones, such as the sexual assaults of young women at a New Year's party in Cologne, where the offenders were described as recent migrants.[61] By exacerbating the immigration crisis and shaping negative perceptions of it, Russia has hoped to destabilize European governments, raise awareness of Russia's position as a defender of European values, and undermine support for democratic institutions and the EU. The "Lisa" case in Germany is one instance, where Russian news outlets spread the false story of a young girl who was supposedly gang-raped by Muslims. Russia even organized protests in Germany by Germans of Russian origin against supposed German government inaction over this fake event.[62] Such attacks have a direct impact on the domestic politics of affected countries, furthering political polarization.

Cyberattacks

In addition to propaganda and disinformation campaigns using TV and social media, Russia has deployed cyberattacks against opponents in Europe and the United States. Some of the worst have been unleashed against Ukraine. These encompass both computer hacking designed to gather and release damaging information about political figures as well as attacks designed to disrupt public infrastructure, such as shutting down the electric grid.[63] Russia's computer hacking is well known. One of the most disruptive incidents occurred during the 2004 presidential election in Ukraine, when Russian hackers gained access to the Central Election Commission and changed the vote in favor of

Viktor Yanukovich.[64] This led to a massive protest requiring international intermediation, which resulted in a decision to rerun the election. In the rerun, Yanukovich was defeated by opposition figure Viktor Yushchenko. Similar hacking attempts have occurred in Europe, where Russian hackers connected with various intelligence agencies hacked the accounts of the Christian Democratic Party in Germany, temporarily took over the French TV5 television channel,[65] and stole the emails of French president Emmanuel Macron, among other disruptive and embarrassing feats. Often, Russia has chosen to release hacked information through Wikileaks, which appears to be a paid agent of Russian intelligence. In 2018, The *Guardian* reported that Russian diplomats offered to spirit Wikileaks founder, Julian Assange, out of the United Kingdom, where he faces sex crimes prosecution and has been holed up in the Ecuador embassy.[66]

In 2014, Russian hackers attempted to breach Ukraine's election computers to declare victory for a marginal right-wing candidate Dmytro Yarosh, who actually received 1 percent of the vote. Yarosh's "victory" was reported on Russian TV. As Peter Ordeshook, a California Institute of Technology political scientist told the *Christian Science Monitor*, "We've seen vote fraud before in Ukraine, including a rigged computer system in 2004. But this wasn't an effort to steal the election outcome, so much as to steal the election itself—by entirely discrediting it in the eyes of key segments of the population in Ukraine and in Russia, too." The attack was narrowly averted by Ukrainian cybercrime investigators.[67] In 2016, Russian hackers—for the second time—shut down Ukrainian power plants, proving that they could use malware to disable critical infrastructure. Ukrainian president Petro Poroshenko stated that these attacks were performed with "direct or indirect involvement of secret services of Russia, which have unleashed a cyberwar against our country."[68] While Russia has often used Ukraine as a testing ground for its cyberwar capabilities, it has the capacity to attack

Western countries as well. In September 2017, a Russian attack penetrated the US power grid, demonstrating the possibility that hackers could produce blackouts in the United States.[69] In a separate attack in 2017, suspected Russian hackers also targeted nuclear power plants and manufacturing facilities in the United States, trying to gain access to control systems.

MILITARY INTERVENTION

Nothing is more polarizing than war. And in addition to various efforts to hack and sabotage European and US elections and disable critical infrastructure, inflaming and polarizing opinion, Russia has also deployed covert and direct military and paramilitary intervention in Western and non-Western states. While Russia's interventions in Georgia and Ukraine are well known, less well known has been its funding for paramilitary organizations in Central and Eastern Europe—and in the West itself. These paramilitary organizations seek to subvert established governments, create a chaotic security environment, and give Russia some cards to play in Europe's internal security. Russia provides direct assistance to paramilitary organizations in EU member states and places its spies within these organizations, giving Russia an armed base of operations within Europe. In Hungary, it was revealed that Russian embassy officials provided military training to the Hungarian National Front, a neofascist organization, participating in airsoft drills. This came to light after Hungarian National Front leader István Györkös shot and killed a police officer who was trying to exercise a search warrant on his house. The Hungarian National Front had previously disseminated Russian disinformation during the Ukraine war, alleging incorrectly that Hungary, a NATO ally, had been sending tanks to Ukraine.[70]

Russian-funded and trained paramilitaries are common throughout Central and Eastern Europe. The Hungarian liberal think tank Political Capital issued a series of reports showing that Russia has supported far-right and paramilitary organizations in Czechia, Slovakia, and other EU countries. During 2013 to 2015, a number of far-right paramilitary organizations were founded in Czechia with pro-Russia foreign policy stances and Facebook pages, including the Czechoslovak Soldiers in Reserve and National Home Guard, whose leaders visited the Donetsk People's Republic. Starting in 2010, a number of Slovak paramilitary organizations began to align themselves with Russia, and new organizations were founded. One of their main activities has been to spread Russian propaganda and disinformation through their websites and Facebook pages. Poland's Minister of Defense Antoni Macierewicz of the Law and Justice Party, who supported the development of nationalist paramilitary organizations in Poland, was accused of ties to Russia before being dismissed in a government reshuffle in 2018.[71]

Russia has intervened militarily in a number of countries, including Georgia in 2008, and maintains troops in Transnistria, a breakaway republic of Moldova where Russia prevented Moldova from exerting control in a short war in 1991. Russia also created and supported local militias in Ukraine to rebel against the government in Kiev after President Yanukovich fled the country in 2014. Russia recruited volunteers to fight in Ukraine and also deployed its own troops to prop up the Donetsk and Luhansk breakaway republics when they looked like they might be defeated by the Ukrainian national government in 2014. Russia appears to have provided direction and leadership for these movements, appointing and apparently dismissing or killing its leaders at will. Russia also sent its troops without insignia into Crimea to secure and annex the peninsula. Direct military action sends a strong message to other countries that Russia is not afraid to use military force to exert control in its sphere of influence.

Russia has also used limited force against the United States and United Kingdom. Russia deployed GRU military intelligence to launch a nerve agent attack on a former spy, Sergei Skripal, in the United Kingdom in 2018, a highly unusual deployment of chemical weapons in Europe. The United States announced it has evidence that Russia launched an unusual sonic or microwave attack on its embassy staff and their families in Cuba and China that resulted in brain damage.[72] These attacks are meant to warn and frighten Western states while maintaining a façade of deniability.

Energy Blackmail

Russia has also deployed energy diplomacy and threats of gas cutoffs to exert control over European countries. In 2006 and again in 2009, Russia cut off gas supplies to Europe during a payments' dispute with Ukraine. These gas cutoffs forced the European Union to question whether Russia was a reliable supplier. Since that time, Russia has seen Ukraine as an unreliable transit country and has sought to build pipelines that circumnavigate Ukraine. These include the North Stream pipeline that directly connects Russia and Germany under the Baltic Sea, the proposed North Stream II that adds capacity along this route, as well as South Stream, now Turkish Stream, which seek to enhance Russian dominance of supply routes for Caspian and Central Asian gas to Europe. Construction of new pipelines has angered CEE states along the existing supply routes, such as Poland, Belarus, and Ukraine, which feel vulnerable to Russian gas cutoffs and resent the reduction in transit fees.[73] Russia uses pipelines and other energy projects to create networks of high-level business and political allies within the countries in which it operates, both enriching them and making them complicit in corrupt deals.[74]

Trojan Horses in the EU

Russia has sought to subvert Western decision-making processes from within by developing relations with "Trojan horse" governments, friendly governments with direct access to EU institutions.[75] Many of these relationships appear to be connected to energy partnerships, traditional religious ties, organized crime networks, or ideological similarity of the governments in question. For instance, Russia has forged a strong partnership with the government of Viktor Orbán in Hungary primarily on the basis of energy and ideological ties. The relationship is cemented by an energy partnership that includes not only promises to make Hungary a key distribution point in the planned South Stream pipeline, but also Russian financing and construction of a new nuclear power station. It is further underpinned by Orbán's pro-Russia foreign policy stance—for instance his support of Hungarian irredentist groups in Ukraine during the recent crisis, and general similarities between Orbán's authoritarian government style and that of Putin. In Bulgaria, Russia tried and succeeded in buying support for the South Stream project in the government and parliament, only to have its pipeline route vetoed by the EU due to failure to follow EU procurement procedures.[76]

Russia seeks to use Trojan horse governments to break European unity on policy toward Russia, particularly the sanctions regime. Hungarian and Greek leaders, for instance, have frequently spoken out against EU sanctions on Russia. In May 2016, for example, Greek prime minister Alexis Tsipras told reporters, "We have repeatedly said that the vicious circle of militarization, of Cold War rhetoric and of sanctions is not productive. The solution is dialogue."[77] Nonetheless, Russia's Trojan horses within the EU have consistently voted in favor of sanctions within the EU Council—despite their public opposition. The reason is simple: although EU voting in many instances is formally based on a unanimity principle, a lot of horse-trading occurs. For smaller states reliant on EU financing, it can be very costly and painful to vote against a large majority. It could mean the loss of EU funds that countries like Hungary or Greece rely upon. Smaller countries can still be used by Russia to articulate its foreign policy positions within the EU. However, Russia has learned that, in order to subvert EU institutions from within, it will require more powerful Trojan horses. This explains why, in 2017, it targeted election campaigns in France and Germany. These major states have the capacity to shift EU policy on vital foreign policy matters.[78]

So, in addition to support for far-right fringe parties and paramilitary organizations, Russia also relies on relationships with top government leaders from mainstream parties, such as Czech president Miloš Zeman, to provide multiple, reinforcing levers with which to influence national politics. As one think tank report put it in the case of Czechia, "While these actors have little political significance on their own, together they amount to a loud pro-Russian lobby demanding Czechia's secession from the EU and NATO and the recognition of the unlawful secession of Crimea."[79]

Tools of Hybrid War

In summary, Russia has developed a wide range of tools, from covert operations to media influence campaigns, to cyberwarfare to military action, to undermine the European Union and NATO, to deter them from exerting influence in lands in between, and to divide Europe from the United States. Starting in the mid-2000s with the gas cutoffs to Ukraine, the Russo-Georgian war, and particularly after Russia's covert invasion of Ukraine in 2014, many tools and techniques of Russian influence have come to light. Overall, however, Russia's hybrid war has been designed in a way to evade detection and to create a facade of plausible deniability. For instance, Russia did not create populism in the West, xenophobic nationalism, anti-immigrant sentiment, or resentments between Hungarians and Ukrainians. It has simply inflamed these divisions in Europe and North America, using a variety of techniques. Russia's hand is hidden, and many doubt whether it exists and whether it really matters. Still, the effect of Russia's hybrid war has been to polarize politics along a number of fault lines, to destabilize, and to control.

Knowing what we know now about Russia's "political war" on Europe, it is hard to regard it as anything but an all-out assault on Western institutions, conducted largely by covert methods in order to escape notice and avoid provoking a strong response. Intelligence expert Mark Galeotti argues that, while Russian efforts to undermine the West are often decentralized and give off a somewhat disorganized air, they are in fact centrally coordinated, most likely by President Putin himself. A wide array of Russian agencies are involved, with limited central control and a lot of room for experimentation. To some extent, agencies compete with one another to please the boss. They also pursue different objectives and priorities in different states. Yet Galeotti writes that "insofar as there is a command-and-control node, it is within the Presidential Administration, which is perhaps the most important single organ within Russia's highly de-institutionalised state." He recommends that "Europe must nonetheless address its own vulnerabilities: 'fixing the roof' rather than simply hoping the rain will stop."[80]

The West is just at the beginning of a process of understanding and addressing the determined Russian assault on our institutions of government and international relations. In the next chapter, I will show why the West has responded so slowly, but also suggest that, once the danger became known, Western institutions have responded more vigorously than expected, presenting a remarkably united front in the face of newly perceived Russian threats. The EU and NATO have been no passive victims of Russia's political war, but have retaliated in ways that have been extremely painful for Russia. The outlines of a Western response have become clear, though its mobilization has taken a long time.

THE WEST'S BELATED

RESPONSE

THE WEST'S RESPONSE TO RUSSIA'S hybrid war was slow in coming. While the Russian invasion of Georgia in 2008 gave ample warning that Russia would oppose, by military force if necessary, Western attempts to integrate countries in its near abroad, it was not until 2012 that Western leaders began to realize that Russia had launched a major assault on Western institutions. During the Medvedev presidency from 2008 to 2012, many Western leaders believed that Russia was moving in a liberal direction. The covert nature and plausible deniability of Russian attacks enabled this perception, playing into the West's unwillingness to come to terms with an unpleasant reality. However, when Putin returned to power in 2012, and particularly after the Crimea invasion in 2014, things changed. A powerful Western multilateral response finally began to materialize. The West deployed its vast economic superiority, as the United States and EU coordinated economic sanctions on Russia and the EU pushed for energy diversification in Europe. NATO deployed rapid response battalions in Central and Eastern Europe to signal that it would mobilize to prevent another invasion. And in terms of values and objectives, it is notable that the West never gave up on its vision of a Europe "whole and free." The result of this relatively decisive action, however, has not been to scare Russia off, but rather to deepen a geopolitical divide in Europe and intensify a game of tug of war between Russia and the West over the lands in between.

DELAYED REACTION

The most striking success of Russia's hybrid war on the West has been the failure of Western leaders to recognize it from 2008 to 2012. The West "missed the warning signs" that it was facing an all-out political offensive from Russia.[1] It ignored evidence that Russia was pulling back from economic integration with the EU.[2] The George W. Bush administration ignored Russia's cyberattack on Estonia in 2007.[3] Western leaders surely noticed the gas cutoffs to Ukraine in 2006 and 2009 that limited supplies to some home markets. They heard President Vladimir Putin's Munich Security Conference speech in 2007 that railed against a unipolar world led by the United States[4] and experienced the Russo-Georgian war of 2008. Yet, in face of these realities, many Western leaders continued to believe that Russia remained on a path toward political and economic modernization. Germany, in particular, whose leaders suffered from a deep sense of guilt toward Russia for the crimes their country committed against Russia during World War II, continued to feel that the best way to deal with Russia was to invest in a "modernization partnership." Over time, they believed economic partnership would win out as Russia modernized its resource-dependent economy,[5] and moved toward a Western-oriented liberal politics and peaceful coexistence with the West. This was reflected in the EU's approach to the Russo-Georgian war, which was to accept Russia's annexation of Georgian territory while offering ineffectual EU peacekeepers, papering over the conflict after a visit from French president Nicolas Sarkozy. Europeans did not want to rock the boat, assuming that the long-term trajectory was positive.

Why did it take so long for the West to realize that Russia had launched an offensive against the Western international system?

It is possible that Western leaders suffered from "end of history" thinking, a perception that the forward progress of Western capitalism and liberal democracy was inevitable.[6] Many in the West did not believe that Russia would reject the Western orientation that Russian leaders Mikhail Gorbachev and Boris Yeltsin had adopted and revert to a former Soviet outlook. Few took Putin literally when he said that the collapse of the Soviet Union was the greatest geopolitical catastrophe of the twentieth century. Fewer still thought that he wanted to create Soviet Union 2.0. "The West found it easier at the time to disregard [warning signs] and indulge in the fantasy that Russia was progressing toward a liberal-democratic model with which the West felt comfortable."[7] From a business perspective, it certainly seemed as if Russia remained Western oriented. Western companies flooded Russia with investment in the period 2010–14, never imagining that they were feeding an enemy determined to destroy the West. In one extreme example, German security firm Rheinmetall built a $140 million combat simulation training center in Russia in 2011 to train Russian special forces, never thinking that these same forces would be used to annex Crimea or fight against Western interests in Syria. Germany pulled out of this relationship only in 2014, as its "modernization partnership" backfired spectacularly.[8]

A second factor was Western leaders' failure to see through the misleading optics of the Medvedev presidency from 2008 to 2012, discussed earlier. Medvedev was a smooth operator with good language skills; he knew how to talk to Western leaders and was welcomed warmly in the West. Although Western governments realized that Putin wielded power from the sidelines, US president Barack Obama, German chancellor Angela Merkel, and other Western leaders treated Medvedev as the real president of Russia, in the hope that he would one day sideline Putin and encourage Russia to progress in a more liberal direction. Yet Putin remained firmly in charge. Medvedev got his start as Putin's assistant;[9] and his assistant he remained.

A third factor in the West's failure to see Russia's hybrid war has been the plausible deniability created by Russia's use of disinformation and covert methods. Many in the West believed Russia's contention that it had invaded Georgia in a defensive operation designed to protect the South Ossetians. In fact, Russia intentionally provoked the war by using South Ossetian militias to bomb Georgian towns. Georgia unwisely responded to this provocation and Russia invaded as planned.[10] Yet after the war, Russia managed to convince French president Nicholas Sarkozy, representing the European Union, to support Russia's peace plan for the region. Similar disinformation tactics were used in the Crimea invasion in 2014, which was conducted by "little green men" with no insignia who were not readily identifiable as Russian military until after they had gained control of the peninsula. As one Dutch think tank report put it, "The Georgia War was not a one-time exception. It turned out to be just a step in President Putin's campaign to restore the international grandeur of Russia."[11] Western leaders did not fully appreciate this at the time.

Finally, there is the question of self-interest. Western countries faced powerful economic incentives to improve and deepen relations with Putin's Russia. Few in the West wanted to acknowledge the existence of a hybrid war that would disrupt business and force countries to increase military expenditures. Many Western companies piled into Russia, a fast-growing, emerging economy, just as Russia was ramping up its hybrid war on the West. Inward investment into Russia boomed in the 2000s.[12] Russia used Western eagerness to participate in Russian growth to raise money for its companies through minority stock offerings and to develop close relations with powerful business people and interest groups in the West. Russia created business councils in Germany, France, and many other Western countries that could be deployed to spread pro-Russia sentiments within Europe and bolster anti-Americanism.[13] Russia's strong links with European energy companies effectively turned their executives into "lobbyists for the Kremlin, leaning on their governments to put their national interests above a unified European energy strategy."[14] Russia used a cresting wave of foreign investment to fund its ambitious foreign policy agenda— with Western support.

For a variety of reasons, Western leaders fooled themselves about Russian intentions, ignored experts and analysts ringing alarm bells about Russia's political war on the West, and remained bullish on Russia and its prospects of integration with the West until 2012.[15] President Obama launched a hopeful "reset" of relations with Russia from 2009 to 2011, despite overwhelming evidence that Russia had abandoned the West and embarked on a Eurasian adventure.[16] German chancellor Angela Merkel remained committed to the modernization partnership with Russia until 2012.[17]

THE END OF PARTNERSHIP

This changed when Vladimir Putin returned to the presidency in 2012. After Russian parliamentary elections in 2011 appeared to be rigged, thousands of protesters appeared on the streets in Moscow and St. Petersburg demanding fair elections and calling for an end to the Putin regime. Putin's reaction was to tighten control and work harder to rig the 2012 presidential election. He developed a deep resentment toward Secretary of State Hillary Clinton, whom he accused of organizing and supporting the protests.[18] For Western leaders who had embraced the view that Medvedev represented a more liberal future for Russia, Putin's "return" to power came as a shock. In May 2012, *Der Spiegel*, the leading German magazine, wrote that Chancellor Angela Merkel "felt hoodwinked. She was forced to realize that the man she had placed such great hopes in was merely a Putin puppet."[19] Led by Germany, the EU began to re-assess its approach toward Russia.

Even then, few in the West were prepared to believe the out-landish claim that a relatively poor, weak Russia was attempting to destroy the European Union and NATO and divide the United States from its European allies. During the 2012 US presidential election campaign, President Obama mocked his Republican opponent, Mitt Romney, for labeling Russia America's greatest strategic enemy in response to a debate question. During the third presidential debate in 2012, President Obama jested that "the 1980s are now calling to ask for their foreign policy back because the Cold War's been over for 20 years."[20] Obama won re-election on a policy of not worrying too much about Russia. Though he imposed sanctions on Russia after the 2014 invasion of Crimea, the Obama administration appeas to have underesti-mated the Russian threat through the 2016 election campaign, despite evidence of a massive influence operation waged by Russian intelligence.[21]

It was only after the Maidan protests in Ukraine in late 2013 and the Russian invasion of Crimea and the Donbas in 2014 that most European Union leaders began to see Russia as a "strategic problem" rather than a "strategic partner," in the words of EU Council president Donald Tusk, a former Polish prime minister.[22]

The troubles really began in 2013, when Russia pressured Ukraine's president, Viktor Yanukovich, not to sign a Deep and Comprehensive Free Trade Agreement (DCFTA) with the EU at a summit to be held in Vilnius in November 2013. Yanukovich's government had painstakingly negotiated this agreement over a two-year period and gave every appearance of being ready to sign, ushering Ukraine into a new era of economic prosperity with greater access to EU markets and investment. Yet, having vetoed Ukraine's progress toward NATO membership in 2008, Putin wished to veto Ukraine's economic integration into the West as well. Shortly before the summit, Yanukovich was summoned to Moscow and promised $15 billion in emergency economic assistance as well as lower gas prices if Ukraine canceled its participation in the Vilnius summit where the EU free trade agreement was to be signed.[23] Yanukovich complied, setting off street protests in Kiev's Maidan square to demand that the government keep Ukraine on a path to European integration. Called the "Euromaidan," protesters waved EU flags, exhibiting a stunning belief in the economic benefits of EU integration at a time when the EU suffered from a sovereign debt crisis and a crisis of confidence.

After repeated attempts over several months to disperse the protesters and tear down their barricades, spawning street battles that captured international media attention, the Yanukovich government decided to fire on protesters on February 18, 2014, in a botched attempt to use overwhelming force. At the same time, armed opposition grew and EU leaders stepped in to negotiate between the two sides and prevent a civil war. The French, German, and Polish foreign ministers brokered a deal on February 21, 2014, for President Yanukovich to resign after six months and make way for a transitional government and new elections.[24] However, this deal collapsed soon after it was inked, when President Yanukovich fled to Russia, worried for his personal safety and no longer commanding the allegiance of the armed forces.[25] Russia declared that Yanukovich had been removed in a "coup" and decided to invade Crimea a few days later, right after the closing ceremony of the Sochi Olympics, when President Putin returned to Moscow.[26] "Little green men" appeared on the streets of Crimea. Russia used its Sevastopol naval base in Crimea, home of Russia's Black Sea fleet under a long-term lease agreement with Ukraine, to take over the peninsula in a rapid and well-planned military operation. Western leaders, shocked by the invasion—and then annexation—of part of a sovereign European state, responded by imposing economic sanctions on Russia.

In total, thirty-seven countries representing 55 percent of world GDP imposed sanctions on Russia, starting in March 2014.[27]

THE WEST PUSHES BACK

At that point, the West finally acknowledged that something had changed in Russia and began to push back. Russia, which had not met much resistance before then, was taken aback, particularly by the German reaction. Germany had long been an advocate of treating Russia with kid gloves. According to one 2015 report published by a Russian government think tank, the Russian International Affairs Council, "Germany's position with respect to Russia's policy proved to be much tougher than expected," and, as a result, Europe achieved an unexpected level of unity on sanctions against Russia.[28] Why did the West respond so much more vigorously to an annexation of part of Ukraine than to a similar de facto annexation of parts of Georgia in 2008? Perhaps because Ukraine was a large state, more centrally located in Europe. Perhaps because of the extensive media coverage of the Maidan protests, which reminded viewers of the revolutions of 1989 and received emotional support. Perhaps because this was Putin's war, not Medvedev's. Whatever the reason, something broke in Russia's relations with the West in 2014. And it only got worse after revelations of Russian involvement in elections in France, Germany, and the United States in 2016.

At that point, the West began to respond in earnest to what a growing chorus of leaders believed was a hybrid war by Russia on Western political and international institutions to debilitate the West from the inside. US and EU economic sanctions seriously jolted the Russian economy. EU "third-energy package" regulations began to bite as the EU sued Gazprom, Russia's state-owned gas company, to enforce market rules that would ensure supplies without disruption. A re-energized NATO took measures to shore up its defensive posture in the Baltic States and Central Europe. And the West continued to support democratization and Western integration for the lands in between.

Meanwhile, Russia continued to intensify its own efforts, leading to a sharpening of geopolitical conflict after 2014.[29] Thus began a battle to the finish. Either Western institutions would collapse, giving a victory to Putin's Russia, or they would outlast his regime. The pressure building up between the two sides was felt most acutely in the lands in between Russia and the West, the small, vulnerable states of the former Soviet Union that were caught between two worlds at hybrid war.

Sanctions

By far the most important element of the Western response to Russia's hybrid war has been economic sanctions. Since the West controls a far greater share of world gross domestic product than Russia, it can impose serious costs on Russia without much worry of retaliation. By contrast, military engagement must be avoided due to Russia's status as a nuclear power. As a result, in March 2014, Western countries imposed a first wave of sanctions on Russia in response to its annexation of Crimea, rather than responding by military means. Since that time, scholars and analysts have debated how effective economic sanctions have been and whether they have worked to deter Russia. This is a complicated debate, with many aspects to consider, but in brief, the evidence suggests that sanctions have had a significant impact on the Russian economy, that they sent a strong signal to Russia about Western resolve, but have not persuaded Russia to back down. To the contrary, painful Western sanctions have only intensified Russia's determination to undermine Western institutions.

Western sanctions against Russia can be divided into two different types: sanctions that punish specific individuals thought to be involved in Russia's annexation of Crimea, invasion of Eastern Ukraine, or other aggressive actions, and sectoral sanctions that retaliate against specific sectors of the Russian economy, such as finance, weapons production, or oil drilling. The first type seeks to deter Russia by making individuals in Putin's inner circle think twice about supporting an aggressive foreign policy. The second type is meant to have a long-term impact on the Russian economy, forcing the population to reckon with the costs of aggression.

For the most part, the Crimea sanctions were of the first type. A long list of Western countries (plus Japan), led by the US and EU, imposed sanctions on a list of Russian officials connected to the Crimea invasion, freezing their assets and banning them from travel to the West. Additionally, the Crimea sanctions banned Western companies from doing business in occupied Crimea and stopped cruise ships from docking at Crimean ports. Visa and Mastercard withdrew from Crimea, among other companies.

When these sanctions failed to prevent Russia's invasion of Eastern Ukraine in 2014, Western countries coordinated to impose sanctions on specific sectors of the Russian economy, helping to send the Russian economy into recession in 2015–16. These sectoral sanctions banned leading Russian banks from accessing international markets, limited Western companies' investment in Russian oil and gas exploration, and banned trade and investment in military equipment and services. These sectoral sanctions caused a sharp decline in Western investment and business activity in Russia. Inward investment into Russia declined precipitously from $53 billion in 2013 to $12 billion in 2015.[30]

While the West did little to deter Russia's hybrid war prior to 2014, these sanctions were the first sign of a determined Western response. But were they enough? Did sanctions achieve their intended result?

Certainly, sanctions sent a strong signal. Russia had not anticipated that Western sanctions would be as severe as they were, as coordinated, or as long-lived.[31] While the EU had considered imposing sanctions on Russia in the wake of the Russo-Georgian war in 2008, it ultimately rejected this option when Russia threatened to cut energy supplies to the European Union.[32] Russia expected a similarly frail response in 2014. In particular, many observers believed that the European Union—Russia's largest trade and investment partner—would not be able to maintain coordinated sanctions on Russia for any substantial length of time. All twenty-eight member states had to vote to renew sanctions every six months, and it was widely known that several EU countries had become Russia's "Trojan horses" within the EU, representing Russia's views within EU councils and openly opposing the sanctions regime.[33] Yet despite Russia's supporters within EU governments, EU sanctions endured for years, with US support and encouragement.

Europe's sanctions endured because smaller states that opposed sanctions deferred to the Big Three powers in the European Union—Germany, France, and the UK—on foreign policy matters. All of the Big Three had come to realize the seriousness of the Russian threat by 2014. Britain had long accused the Putin regime of assassinating émigrés in London, for instance Alexander Litvinenko, who was poisoned by the radioactive isotope polonium-210. Its radioactive trail was traced back to Moscow.[34] As a result of this and other conflicts, Britain had long had a poor relationship with Russia and was skeptical of the Putin regime. France and Germany had taken a softer line toward Moscow prior to 2012, but Chancellor Angela Merkel and other German leaders grew increasingly concerned with Russia's return to authoritarian rule. German leaders objected strenuously to Russia's crackdown on human rights, antigay legislation, and harsh imprisonment of members of the Russian protest rock group Pussy Riot. After the annexation of Crimea, Germany made clear that "no partnership can work without a core set of shared values."[35] Merkel was disillusioned that President Putin, with whom she had frequent phone conversations, had lied about key facts, including whether Russia had troops in Crimea. She told President Obama that Putin appeared to have lost a grip on reality and was living "in another world."[36] In 2014, Germany rallied European support for economic sanctions. French president François Hollande also condemned Russia's annexation of Crimea in March 2014 and promised a "strong and coordinated" EU response.[37]

Leaders of other EU states followed, either because they did not want to be seen as spoilers of a common European foreign policy, or because they were subject to pressure and logrolling by the Big Three. Greece is a case in point. Despite holding a press conference in Athens with President Putin on May 28, 2016, and calling sanctions "not productive," Greek prime minister Alexis Tsipras's government voted to renew sanctions on Russia a few days later, under threat of losing a vital EU rescue package for Greece's ailing economy. In 2018, a far-right Italian government came to power also criticizing Russia sanctions. In October 2018, Italian prime minister Giuseppe Conte labeled Russia a "strategic partner," invited Putin to Italy, and called for "dialogue" to replace EU sanctions.[38] It remains to be seen whether Italy too will trade compliance with EU sanctions policy for economic assistance.

Another reason for the united European sanctions response was the downing of Malaysian Airlines flight MH-17 on July 17, 2014. En route from Amsterdam to Kuala Lumpur, MH-17 was shot down over rebel-held territory in Eastern Ukraine by a Russian-made BUK missile. The death toll of 298, mainly Dutch passengers and crew members, included many top scientists traveling to an international AIDS conference in Melbourne, Australia.[39] MH-17 brought home to Europeans that there was a war raging in Europe that could not be ignored. It cast Russian-supported rebels as the bad guys. Footage of rebels sifting through passengers' personal effects in the debris while failing to secure the crash site or allow access to investigators left a very bad impression in the West, as did President Putin's denial of responsibility for deploying the BUK missile that brought down the plane. More than anything previous, this episode severed trust between Russian and European leaders.

It had a particular effect on the Netherlands, Russia's largest trading partner in the EU. Much of Russia's oil is refined in Rotterdam and shipped from there to the world. Although the Netherlands had been very reluctant to support a hard line against Russia in the past due to its strong business interests in Russia, MH-17 forced the Dutch to support the call for sanctions against Russia. As Dutch foreign minister Frans Timmermans blamed Russia for the missile attack and made an emotional appeal for justice at the United Nations,[40] the United States, EU, and other Western nations imposed sanctions targeting key Russian enterprises in the financial and energy sectors. These "sectoral" sanctions banned the export of arms and dual-use technologies to Russia, restricted the issuance of financial instruments on behalf of Russian companies, and placed controls on oil-drilling technology exports to Russia. They effectively isolated Russia from Western banking institutions and had a far more severe impact on the Russian economy than the limited and targeted sanctions over Crimea. The Western community of nations displayed a common front, something Russia had not anticipated.

After this second round of sanctions in July 2017, Russia's previously fast-growing economy sank into a sustained recession. Following years of dynamic economic growth, the Russian economy grew by only 0.7 percent in 2014 before shrinking by 2.8 percent in 2015 and 0.2 percent in 2016. Capital flowed out of the country. Net outflows totaled $152 billion in 2014, $59 billion in 2015, and $15 billion in 2016, exceeding the amount of capital that flew out of Russia during the global financial crisis in 2009. The Russian ruble devalued by 50 percent versus the US dollar in 2015, and inflation jumped from 6.8 percent in 2013 to 15.5 percent. Russia's government budget deficit widened from 0.9 percent in 2013 to 3.2 percent in 2015, forcing it to tap international reserve funds, which dropped from almost $500 billion at the start of 2014 to $368 billion at the end of 2015. Overall, the 2014–16 recession had a more enduring impact on Russia than the global financial crisis of 2009. The sanctions regime forced analysts, investors, and Russian officials to question whether high growth would return.[41]

Russia responded to the 2014 sanctions with counter-sanctions of its own. Unable or unwilling to retaliate against its major customer, the European Union, with an oil and gas cutoff, Russia instead retaliated with a ban on the import of food and agricultural products. The worst-affected states were neighboring countries that exported a high proportion of their agricultural products to Russia. Polish apple farmers, Danish and Latvian dairy farmers, and Norwegian fisheries were badly hit.[42] Products such as French cheese, Norwegian salmon, and Hungarian salami quickly disappeared from Russian shops to be replaced with Belarusian or Russian substitutes. Russia undertook dramatic enforcement actions against smuggling, destroying tons of imported food that made their way into Russia after the sanctions were imposed. President Putin stated that the sanctions would be good for Russian domestic producers, helping to build local industry. He later invested in import substitution projects throughout the economy.[43]

However, Russian countersanctions also had a devastating impact on Russian household budgets. According to one group of Russian academic researchers, food prices rose dramatically in 2014 and 2015, and "household spending associated with the acquisition of food and non-food products, transport, medical care, [and] housing services have risen sharply." As a result, consumers focused their spending on essential items and saved any additional funds.[44] While inflation in Russia peaked at 15.5 percent in 2015,[45] prices for some food items rose much more dramatically. Overall, food inflation reached an average of 21 percent in 2015.[46] As a result, discretionary spending plummeted. The number of Russians in poverty rose by 3.1 million to 19.2 million in 2015, a total of 13.4 percent of the population.[47]

Western sanctions hit Russia at the same time as oil prices dropped sharply when Saudi Arabia decided to punish Russia for failing to reach an agreement on limiting oil production. In response, the Saudis flooded world markets in an attempt to win market share. Prices plummeted from approximately $100 in July 2014 to $40 per barrel in February 2016. These simultaneous shocks damaged the Russian economy. Economists have estimated that approximately two-thirds of the damage was done by oil prices and one-third by sanctions. The IMF estimated that sanctions were costing the Russian economy about 1.0–1.5 percent of gross domestic product per year, or a total of 9.0 percent over the medium term, or approximately $123 billion.[48] President Putin stated in November 2016 that the sanctions are "severely harming Russia" in terms of access to international financial markets, although the impact was not as severe as the decline in energy prices.[49]

In the United States, Russia's intervention in the US presidential election in 2016 led to a third round of sanctions from the United States alone. Congress in 2017 passed tough new sanctions on Russia, Iran, and North Korea. New legislation gave the US president sweeping powers to sanction any company worldwide doing business with a sanctioned Russian company. Among other things, the law enabled the president to sanction companies involved in new gas pipeline deals with Russia. Europeans opposed these sanctions, worrying about their effect on the vital energy trade with Russia and, in particular, the North Stream II pipeline project. In 2018, the United States added Putin-connected oligarchs and their companies to the list of sanctioned entities, including Oleg Deripaska and his company Rusal, the dominant force in Russia's aluminum industry and exports. This extension of the sanctions regime to Putin-connected oligarchs and their companies further damaged Russia's reputation and changed perceptions about whether Russia's economic ties with the West would recover. A leading Putin aide, Vladislav Surkov, wrote that "Russia's epic journey toward the West" was over, marking an end to its "repeated fruitless attempts to become a part of Western civilization" over four centuries.[50]

Despite the surprising unity shown by Western states and the economic impacts of sanctions, many analysts have questioned whether sanctions have effectively altered Russia's behavior. Opponents of sanctions point out that Russia has not left Ukraine. Therefore, it would be impossible to say that Russia has been deterred by sanctions in any meaningful way. Some argue that sanctions only hurt innocent Russian civilians and blocked opportunities for trade and investment that may benefit the West.[51] Some contend that a military response would have been more effective. However, sanctions advocates point out that while Russia has not pulled out of Ukraine, it may have been deterred from further aggression. For instance, Russia abandoned its campaign for "Novorossiya." After launching a public relations campaign to combine the Donetsk and Luhansk republics and possibly other parts of Ukraine in a newly established territory of Novorossiya, the Kremlin appears to have canceled or shelved this campaign.[52] Therefore, just because

Russia has not left Ukraine does not mean the sanctions had no effect. Sanctions may have created a disincentive for further military action. Sanctions certainly contributed to the stagnation of the Russian economy between 2014–16 as foreign direct investment dried up. These economic costs may have a long-term impact on public evaluations of government policy. But they have not caused Russia to re-evaluate its hybrid war on the West. Russia appeared to accelerate and intensify its interventions in democratic elections in many Western countries after 2014.

While the debate on sanctions rages in the West, it must be noted that sanctions are not the only measure Western governments and institutions have taken to respond to Russia's hybrid war on the West. Russia also was kicked out of the G8. Yet one set of EU counter-measures has nearly escaped notice: Europe's renewed push to unify its energy markets and ensure the security of its gas suppies. These measures have had a tremendous impact on Russia's business relationship with the West, limiting Russia's ability to use energy to exert political leverage on EU states.

Third Energy Package

The great irony of Russia's assault on the EU and NATO is that Russia is almost completely reliant on Europe for its foreign trade revenues. Europe is Russia's largest market for hydrocarbons, particularly for natural gas, since natural gas is distributed primarily through pipelines to contiguous territories. Nearly 80 percent of Russian gas is sold in the EU, with most of the rest going to Turkey and former Soviet states in Eastern Europe. Russia is even dependent on the EU for its crude oil exports, much of which is refined in the Dutch port of Rotterdam before being exported to the world. Russia supplies approximately 30 percent of the EU's crude oil and natural gas and is Europe's largest energy supplier. However, Russia's dependency on the EU is far greater than the other way around. This dependency motivates, but also complicates, Russia's ability to project power over EU states through energy geopolitics.[53]

Russia's strategy to address its dependence on European markets has been to divide and rule. Russia understands that if the EU ever banded together in a buyers' consortium, it would have tremendous pricing power. Therefore, Russia prefers to make special deals with individual countries, bypassing common EU regulation. Russia realizes that "a common EU policy would foster diversification of sources and unbundle national utilities, in the process cutting profit margins and reducing Gazprom's incentives to buy European companies. It would also weaken bilateral special relationships with Russia."[54] Some European countries are more dependent on Russian gas than others. Finland and some East European countries depend almost entirely on Russian gas for home heating; and Russia has used its power in these markets to charge higher prices. Until recently, European countries have paid very different prices for Russian gas, based on their specific relationship with the Kremlin and other political criteria.[55]

However, Russia's gas disputes with Ukraine in the mid-2000s caused alarm bells to ring in Europe and pushed EU policymakers to take steps toward an EU-wide energy market. In 2006 and 2009, Russia cut off gas supplies to Ukraine in a dispute over back payments. Since most of Europe's pipeline gas traveled across Ukraine to European markets, these cutoffs threatened the energy security of the European Union, the world's largest economy. Several EU member states faced supply disruptions and some were forced to tap reserves or ration gas. To the corporate captains of EU industry, this was an intolerable situation. EU leaders realized they needed to protect their economies from excessive reliance on Russian gas.[56]

A direct result of Russia's gas cutoffs to Ukraine was the passage of an EU "third energy package." The third energy package mostly consisted of measures that had previously been proposed in Brussels, but had met with stiff opposition from German and French energy companies that wanted to protect their dominant positions in home markets. Russia's gas geopolitics, however, generated a consensus long lacking in Europe to further integrate EU energy markets to limit price differentials and ensure energy security.

While the individual regulations of the "third energy package" make for incredibly dense reading, their essence is pretty simple. I will summarize. The third energy package employs two basic methods to respond to Russia's attempts to divide and rule European energy markets: first, connecting European energy grids and gas pipeline networks to enable resource sharing across national boundaries, and second, developing alternative supplies and ensuring that no country is dependent on any individual supplier. In a 2014 statement, EU energy commissioner Günther Oettinger declared, "We want a uniform gas price in the European common market. The game of 'divide et impera' (divide and rule), or a game of this type proposed by Moscow cannot be and will not be accepted by EU member states."[57]

The first revolutionary, yet disarmingly simple, innovation of the third energy package was to build *interconnectors* between European gas and power networks. These projects were relatively inexpensive, but had a massive impact on countries that had previously relied on a single source of gas or electricity, such as Finland and many CEE countries. Overreliance on one supplier was potentially disastrous in a crisis and opened countries to energy blackmail. Russia's 2009 gas cutoff to Ukraine had forced Bulgaria, an EU member state, to cut off gas supplies to industrial users. Under the third energy package, Bulgaria sought to remedy the situation by enabling reverse flows at the

Greek border and building an interconnector with Romania under the Danube River. After delays in construction, the project was taken over by an Austrian company in 2016.[58] In contrast, Czechia was quicker to build interconnectors that both enabled it to survive the 2009 cutoff and caused a dramatic drop in prices. In 2014, gas prices at Czechia's main hub were 30 percent higher than in the Netherlands. By 2017, prices had dropped and converged. A similar process took place across the EU. Now, nearly all EU pipelines, as well as those running through Ukraine, can handle reverse flows. Building interconnectors "changed the status quo forever." Increasingly, pipeline gas in Europe is priced in connection with "spot" markets, not long-term contracts.[59] One study showed that the variance of gas prices between EU countries in 2017 dropped to one-quarter of 2014 levels, largely because of the third energy package.[60] Russia's ability to punish or reward countries with higher or lower gas prices was greatly diminished, eliminating a key tool of Russian geopolitical strategy and strengthening the hand of EU institutions.

A second feature of the third energy package has been to diversify supplies by constructing new pipelines and liquefied natural gas (LNG) terminals at strategic points around the continent. Liquification enables natural gas to be loaded into tanker ships and transported from Qatar, North Africa, the United States, and elsewhere to Europe. While Spain and other southern European countries already had LNG terminals, countries reliant on cheaper Russian pipeline gas initially had none. This is because LNG is more expensive than pipeline gas thanks to the high costs of compressing gas at supercold temperatures and transporting it in special tanker ships. However, an LNG terminal ensures continuity of supply, which can be invaluable. Lithuania and Poland were the first East European countries to build new LNG terminals after 2009 with EU support. Lithuania pointedly named its terminal "Independence."

Finland, also reliant on Russian gas, developed plans for several terminals.[61] As EU gas networks became increasingly interconnected, terminals could serve neighboring countries as well. Building LNG terminals diversified EU gas sources, causing a dramatic change in EU gas markets. Whereas before, most gas was sold through long-term contracts with pipeline suppliers, most gas in certain West European markets now is sold on spot markets, dramatically reducing suppliers' control over prices.

In addition to interconnecting networks and diversifying supplies, the third energy package included powerful antimonopoly regulations. The third energy package required companies to "unbundle" electricity and natural gas production from supply and distribution. Russia perceived this as a direct assault on Gazprom's strategy of vertical integration. Gazprom had bought up pipeline networks and distribution companies in European countries in order to control the entire business from gas extraction to supplying the end user. As a result, when the EU's third energy package was announced in 2009 and implemented in 2011, Russia launched an open campaign against it.[62] As Ukrainian Opposition Bloc lawmaker Yuliya Lovochkina put it in 2017, "The third energy package is seen as a threat to Russia."[63] The third energy package also invalidated clauses in existing contracts that prevented recipient countries from re-exporting gas.

Russia raised several objections. First, Russia felt that, as a nonmember of the EU, its companies and pipelines should not be bound by EU rules. Second, it argued that an unbundling of supply, transit, and distribution companies was discriminatory against Gazprom. Third, Russia insisted that it had long-term contracts with gas consumers that should be enforced and that the prices specified in them were legal. Fourth, it insisted that Russia, as a large supplier, needed preferential access to pipelines in order to uphold its own contract commitments. Therefore, Russia could not abide by the letter of open-access laws.[64]

The first test of the antimonopoly provisions of the third energy package came when Lithuania took Gazprom to court to force it to sell its Lithuanian pipeline network as part of "unbundling." Lithuania had suffered from damaging and politically motivated Russian gas cutoffs in the past.[65] Though Gazprom protested, it ultimately agreed to sell its Lithuanian assets, not wanting to fall afoul of EU regulations and jeopardize access to its biggest market. This is something that Lithuania could never have achieved on its own. EU regulations hit Russia even harder in 2014 when the EU forced Bulgaria to cancel construction of Russia's South Stream gas pipeline. Russia launched a countersuit with the World Trade Organization. However, ultimately, Gazprom decided that it made more sense to follow EU law than to become a pariah in its largest market. There is little doubt that this shift harmed Gazprom's profitability, which dropped sharply after a postcrisis decline in world oil prices and the conclusion of the Iraq war.[66]

After starting to divest Gazprom of some of its European pipeline assets, the EU announced its intention to sue Gazprom in 2013 over price gouging in gas contracts with Lithuania and other CEE markets that relied on Russia as their primary supplier.[67] The priciest gas was found in countries where Gazprom dominated the market and Russia had political disagreements with ruling parties. The EU-Gazprom case dragged on for several years, but was ultimately settled in May 2018 after Gazprom agreed to drop discriminatory pricing in Europe and eliminate clauses that banned the re-export of Russian gas to third parties.[68] Gazprom acceded to the EU's main demands in exchange for unfettered access to the EU market. Gazprom announced the sale of its Latvian network assets in 2016.

The third energy package did not seek to replace Russia as Europe's largest energy supplier, but rather to create common rules for companies operating in European markets. The EU balanced the objectives of achieving energy security and maintaining access to an abundant supply of inexpensive Russian gas. Therefore, the EU allowed Gazprom to negotiate privileged access to some pipelines. The EU also exempted new infrastructure projects from some antimonopoly rules, in order to encourage new investment. This is the context for understanding EU actions regarding the proposed North Stream II pipeline.

North Stream I and II have been controversial within the EU, with transit countries like Poland disputing the necessity of increasing reliance on Russian gas by constructing new pipeline capacity and placing existing transit countries at risk of energy blackmail.[69] Some have accused the EU and German companies in particular of caving to Russian pressure. However, the EU's third energy package was never intended to reduce reliance on Russian gas, only to regulate it. While the EU prevailed over Russia on most regulatory points, it also wished to spur new investment. This reflected a fine balance between the EU states that were more dependent on Russian gas and those that were less dependent and wanted to ensure cheap supplies. The third energy package enabled Russia to continue to sell into the EU market, but made it more difficult for Russia to exert leverage over European countries through gas geopolitics.[70]

While the EU's third energy package forced Russia to obey EU rules in a key market and limited its ability to use energy as political leverage, it did not reduce Russia's will to conduct a hybrid war on Europe. If anything, the third energy package strengthened Russia's resolve to undo the EU institutions that imposed such a high cost on Gazprom and Kremlin energy policy.

Countering Russian Propaganda, Disinformation, and Hacking

In contrast to the gas wars in Europe, in which the EU arguably came out on top, Western countries have faced greater difficulties in countering Russian propaganda and disinformation. As democracies, it is nearly impossible for Western countries to ban media sources, even if they distribute Russian government propaganda. Within the EU and United States, almost any speech is protected by laws on press freedom and freedom of expression. Ukraine has banned Russian television and social media and even some journalists from its territory for national security reasons, but it is not a member of the EU, where such actions most likely would be struck down by the European Court of Justice, if not by national courts.

The EU has responded to Russian propaganda instead by trying to shore up cyber defenses, identifying propaganda through public education campaigns, and trying to debunk it. For instance, when Germany was hit with Russian hacking in advance of its parliamentary election in 2017, Chancellor Angela Merkel warned that the election would be undermined by Russia. Hans-Georg Maassen, head of Germany's domestic intelligence agency, announced in 2017, "There's increasing evidence of attempts to influence the election" by Russia. "We expect another jump in cyber-attacks ahead of the vote," after Russian hackers had tried to gain access to computers belonging to political party-connected think tanks. Hackers connected to Russian intelligence previously gained access to the computer system of the German parliament. Russia's objective was clear: to damage the electoral chances of Angela Merkel, Russia's main opponent in Europe, to bolster the Alternative for Germany and other anti-EU parties, and to decrease confidence in elections. According to press reports, Germany responded forcefully.

> Merkel's Christian Democratic Union (CDU) is calling for a law that would allow the country to "hack back" and wipe out attacking servers. The BSI [Federal Office for Information Security] this year is hiring 180 people—from lawyers to coders—and will

embed experts with the election watchdog to protect the vote. The agency has set up cybersecurity response teams to clean up after attacks and help infiltrated government agencies keep computer systems from collapsing. In May the BSI held talks with counterparts such as France's online security agency to gather information on thwarting attacks like one that targeted the presidential campaign of Emmanuel Macron.[71]

After Russia's hacking of the US presidential elections in 2016, EU governments began to take Russian covert intervention in elections far more seriously. France's presidential election produced a decisive win for candidate Emmanuel Macron, despite Wikileaks dumping his emails days before the election.

In order to call out Russian propaganda and dispel myths, the EU created a strategic communications strategy in 2016. The European Parliament resolution "notes with regret that Russia uses contacts and meetings with EU counterparts for propaganda purposes and to publicly weaken the EU's joint position, rather than for establishing a real dialogue." It further alleges that "the Russian Government is employing a wide range of tools and instruments, such as think tanks and special foundations (e.g. Russkiy Mir), special authorities (Rossotrudnichestvo), multilingual TV stations (e.g. RT), pseudo news agencies and multimedia services (e.g. Sputnik), cross-border social and religious groups, as the regime wants to present itself as the only defender of traditional Christian values, social media and internet trolls to challenge democratic values, divide Europe, gather domestic support and create the perception of failed states in the EU's eastern neighbourhood."[72]

To counteract this, the EU proposed a wide variety of measures, including the creation of an EU Strategic Communication Task Force and the dissemination of its publication "Disinformation Digest," which aims to counter Russian propaganda by challenging its veracity. The EU seeks to raise public awareness of propaganda and to develop the ability to discern propaganda from regular news, to encourage quality journalism and journalism training, and to monitor social media and other media sources to encourage good journalism practices. While the EU is still groping toward a comprehensive strategy to counter Russian and other propaganda (from ISIS, for instance), it has begun to take concerted action.

The United States has also taken some initial steps in the public domain, and may have covert plans as well. The US foreign news agency, Radio Free Europe / Radio Liberty, has engaged in antipropaganda actions, regularly debunking Russian disinformation. However, the Trump administration has failed to spend $120 million allocated to the State Department for increasing such efforts.

Public companies such as Facebook have come under pressure to regulate political advertisement and prevent the spread of fake news, particularly sponsored by foreign sources. In 2018, Facebook began requiring political advertisers "to state who is paying for the message," and said that "it will verify the identity of the advertiser," making it harder for anonymous trolls to disseminate political messages on the widely used social media site.[73] These efforts remain in their infancy, but there is no doubt that much can be done to strengthen the information space in Western countries and make it less vulnerable to outside attack during election campaigns, while upholding principles of free speech.[74]

Military Responses

Since Russia poses a military threat to Europe, Western countries also have responded to Russia's increasing aggressiveness since 2014 through increased military spending, preparedness, and coordination. To a large extent, Russia's war on the West has not been pursued by traditional military means. Under the so-called Gerasimov doctrine of hybrid war, Russia hopes to achieve its objectives by influencing or destabilizing the politics of its opponents with minimal use of direct military force.[75] However, direct military action has always been part of the equation. Russia used military force to invade Georgia and Ukraine, where its overmatched opponents had little chance of resistance and casualties remained low.[76] Russia also threatens nuclear warfare and frequently reminds the West of its capabilities, as well as its doctrine of limited nuclear use to deter conventional war, but shows little sign of wanting a massive conflagration. Instead, Russia uses military threats to intimidate opponents, force them to bargain with Russia, respect its prerogatives, and fear the Russian state.

All of this has made NATO states feel less secure, particularly after the Ukraine invasion in 2014. NATO has responded with a range of measures designed to increase confidence in the West's ability to confront a renewed Russian threat. NATO created a Readiness Action Plan that aims "to convey a strong message: that NATO will stand by its members if and when these are threatened—or actually attacked." In 2014 and 2015, NATO devoted sixteen fighter jets to air policing in the Baltic States, began air surveillance flights over eastern NATO territory, sent more patrol ships to the Black, Mediterranean, and Baltic Seas, deployed ground troops to eastern NATO states on a rotational basis, conducted hundreds of NATO/national exercises, created a Very High Readiness Joint Task Force of several thousand troops to respond to an invasion of a NATO state within a few days, and built permanent national command and control stations in the most vulnerable eastern NATO states.[77] Together, these measures were not intended to return to the days of the Cold War, when hundreds of thousands of US troops were stationed in Europe to counter a massive Russian invasion. Nor were they intended to enable NATO to invade Russia. Instead, they were intended to send a clear message that NATO would respond if one of its member states were invaded by Russia and give Russia the impression that, in that case, it would be fighting NATO militaries, rather than a single national army, as in Georgia or Ukraine. Though one could criticize these responses as doing the bare minimum to deter an invasion, they did demonstrate that NATO has the ability to act in unison when it feels threatened.

NATO's response, however, has been hampered by a decline in military spending in Europe after the end of the Cold War. During the 1990s and 2000s, most European countries believed that they faced no military threat. While the United States dropped its military spending from 6 percent of gross domestic product (GDP) in 1989 to 3.6 percent in 2017, European NATO allies reduced spending from an average of 3 percent in 1989 to 1.5 percent in 2017, below the 2 percent threshold set by NATO.[78] Since 2000, the United States has criticized European states' unwillingness to spend the 2 percent that NATO advocates as a minimum for member state expenditures. US president Donald Trump stepped up that criticism to new levels, threatening that the United States would not support the alliance unless European countries pay up.[79] At the same time, the emerging conflict with Russia began to change European threat perceptions and average defense expenditures have crept up since 2014, particularly in countries like Poland, the Baltic States, and Romania that feel most exposed to Russian aggression.[80] Other countries have come face to face with their lack of preparedness. For instance, after a presumed Russian submarine invaded Swedish waters in 2014, non-NATO Sweden realized that it could not adequately respond to such a threat because it had scrapped its antisubmarine helicopter program and reduced its fleet after the end of the Cold War.[81] Sweden and Finland began to consider joining NATO.

Increased threat perceptions in Europe have partly to do with the Crimea invasion, but also with Russia's direct military actions against EU and NATO states themselves. Russia has repeatedly penetrated the airspace of the Baltic States, sent submarines into European and North American waters, flown its long-range bombers into UK and US airspace, and buzzed NATO warplanes and warships in the Baltic and Mediterranean Seas. In 2014, shortly after the United States and Canada welcomed Ukrainian president Petro Poroshenko and the United States promised $46 million in nonlethal aid to the Ukrainian military, US and Canadian fighter jets were forced to intercept Russian nuclear-capable long-range bombers flying toward North American airspace.[82] In 2015, Russia threatened to target Danish warships with nuclear missiles if Denmark joined a NATO missile defense program.[83] Since 2014, Russian nuclear-capable bombers have repeatedly flown by or into UK airspace, forcing the Royal Air Force and other European air forces to scramble jet fighters. Russia also sailed an aircraft carrier through the English Channel in 2017.[84] As a result of these and hundreds of other threatening military actions, many European countries are bolstering their defense preparedness after decades in which they believed they faced no serious adversary.[85]

In addition to increasing preparedness for a Russian invasion of a NATO state, NATO has continued to offer membership to CEE states, despite concerted Russia opposition. After Albania and Croatia joined in 2009, NATO made Montenegro a member state in June 2017. A small nation of only 622,000 inhabitants, Montenegro occupies a strategic location on the Adriatic Sea. Russia fought hard to prevent Montenegro from joining NATO. It is estimated that Russian politicians and oligarchs own 40 percent of the real estate in Montenegro. In 2015, Russia sought an agreement in 2015 to use Montenegrin ports to refuel and maintain its navy. When this agreement was refused and elections in October 2016 threatened to bring a new government to power that would join NATO, Russian intelligence operatives helped to plan an election-day coup. The coup failed, however, and Montenegro joined NATO in 2017.[86]

In the face of increasing Russian aggression, NATO has continued to take in new East European member states and bolster its ability to deter a Russian attack. However, these actions have only further aggravated Russia and encouraged it to intensify its hybrid war on the West, with a host of negative consequences for front-line states. As described in chapter 2 earlier, Russia and Europe are locked in a classical security dilemma. The more one side takes actions to shore up its perceived security needs, the more the other side feels threatened.

A Europe Whole and Free

Throughout this period of increasing tensions, the EU has continued to deepen relations with former Soviet republics, such as Ukraine, Moldova, Belarus, Georgia, Azerbaijan, and Armenia.[87] The EU launched its Eastern Partnership in 2009 after two waves of enlargement in 2004 and 2007 brought in ten new member states in Central and Eastern Europe. All of a sudden, the EU had a host of new neighbors in the former Soviet states. The EU did not wish to offer membership to these relatively underdeveloped states, but rather to support their economic integration with the EU over the long term. The EU offered deep and comprehensive free trade agreements (DCFTAs) to all the Eastern Partnership states.

Russia sharply opposed the Eastern Partnership program from the beginning, seeing it as an unwanted intrusion into its own zone of influence. Yet the EU refused to be deterred by Russia, either before or after its intervention in Ukraine. Emboldened, perhaps, by the Euromaidan movement, the EU signed a DCFTA with Ukraine in 2015 that came into force on September 1, 2017, after a year's delay sought by Russia. The EU reached similar DCFTAs with Georgia and Moldova that came into force in 2016.[88] Belarus, Armenia, and Azerbaijan chose not to conclude DCFTAs with the EU in the face of determined opposition from Russia. By contrast, Armenia concluded a "comprehensive and enhanced partnership agreement" with the EU in 2017, after it joined the Russia-sponsored Eurasian Economic Union.[89] In all Eastern Partnership countries, the EU also monitors and encourages progress on democratization and human rights.

The EU's persistent projection of its economic and democratization projects in the Eastern Partnership countries continues to aggravate Russia. Yet the EU persists because it views Russia's objectives as neoimperialist and illegitimate. The EU maintains a vision of peace through economic interconnectedness and wishes to strengthen political and economic relations with countries on its periphery. In this way, the EU has stood up to Russian aggression. Thus Europe today is defined by two competing integration projects. In the following chapter, we will explore how the lands in between Russia and the European Union—countries like Ukraine and Moldova that are neither colonies of Russia nor member states of the European Union—have coped with the pressures and opportunities presented by both sides.

CONCLUSIONS

Though Western leaders failed to understand the full nature of Russia's hybrid threat from 2008 to 2012, Western institutions began to respond starting in 2012, but particularly after the invasion of Crimea in 2014. Since that time, Western institutions have shown considerable unity and presented a strong but measured response. NATO appears to have done enough to make Russia think twice before invading one of its member states. And while Russia has treated the EU as an organization without teeth, a Venus compared to the martial nations of the United States and Russia, the EU has exhibited surprising strength in opposing Russia's new imperialist aggression, primarily in the economic realm. The EU has hit Russia where it is vulnerable, in its weak, resource-dependent economy. Whereas Putin sought to use Russia's oil and gas resources as a geopolitical asset in the 2000s, the European Union fought back successfully, forcing Russia to obey EU regulations and thwarting the tactics of its powerful eastern neighbor. The West still struggles to counter Russian propaganda, and efforts have only begun to protect the integrity of Western electoral systems. Yet Western leaders have taken steps to bolster its cybersecurity and military infrastructure to withstand a Russian assault. The EU has also continued its policy of economic integration of former Soviet states in between Russia and the European Union, in the face of determined Russian opposition. In short, the West has reacted more strongly than commonly recognized.

Yet Russia has not backed down. Still reeling from the twin impact of sanctions and lower energy prices after 2014, Russia nonetheless redoubled its efforts to undermine Western institutions and Western elections, hoping for a breakthrough in its struggle to disable Western opponents from within. Russia has moved from quiet support of extremist parties to blatant undermining of EU and Western elections, to sow as much chaos as possible. These attacks are taking place not because the EU is weak, as commonly suspected, but rather because Russia perceives the EU to be too strong. Unable to rely on small, malleable, Trojan horse governments in Cyprus, Greece, and Hungary, Russia now aims to recruit politicians and dismantle support for the EU in one of the Big Three member states of the EU. Brexit was a major victory for Russia—and investigations have begun in the UK Parliament to determine how far the Brexit campaign and UKIP leader Nigel Farage were funded by Russian sources. With the chaos caused by Brexit, Russia has sought to elect a pro-Russian government in France or Germany or the United States and throw these core political systems into chaos. Russia has not succeeded in dismantling Western institutions yet, but has succeeded in transforming every European election into a high-stakes referendum on the future of democracy and the international system.

With the stakes raised, Russia and the West are entering a dangerous time in their relations. They are engaged in a pitched battle to determine the political future of Europe. Either the West's vision of a rule-bound, liberal order or Russia's vision of a great-power Europe dominated by authoritarian rulers will prevail. Nowhere is this conflict felt more than in the lands in between Russia and the EU, which sit literally on a knife's edge balanced between two competing geopolitical zones.

THE LANDS IN BETWEEN

IN MARCH 2016, BELARUS'S DICTATOR, President Aleksander Lukashenko, addressed the geopolitical forces dividing his country. "If the partners which we're in dialogue with try to insist that we have to choose between Russia, Poland or the EU, we don't want to be put in this position," he said. At that moment, Belarus, closely aligned with Moscow, was in talks with the Washington, DC–based International Monetary Fund for a $3 billion loan to bolster its currency reserves in exchange for implementing a raft of liberal economic reforms.[1]

Lukashenko, frequently demonized in the West, has become a virtuoso at managing his country's reliance on Moscow while talking to the West when needed. Belarus defers to Russia when necessary. For instance, Lukashenko chose not to sign a Deep and Comprehensive Free Trade Agreement (DCFTA) with the EU when it became clear that this would incur sanctions from Russia. However, when Russia tries to force Lukashenko to take actions that would compromise Belarusian sovereignty or independence, for instance to sell a strategic enterprise to a Russian oligarch or to host a permanent Russian military base, he leans toward Brussels and Washington. Lukashenko will make an agreement with Western institutions that angers Moscow, demonstrates his independence, and puts money in the state coffers. In the words of one analyst, "Rejection, resistance, oscillation and 'non-commitment' have defined Lukashenko's regime."[2] In a similar vein, he has positioned himself as an honest broker between Russia and the West by hosting the Minsk talks that seek to end the conflict in Ukraine. While remaining primarily reliant on Russia, Lukashenko takes every opportunity he gets to remind Russia that he is not a lapdog and to rehabilitate himself in Western eyes.

Lukashenko embodies the political paradoxes that haunt the lands in between. Caught between two powerful neighbors pulling in different directions, politics in these countries has become sharply, intensely polarized. Some talk of a "civilizational choice" between East and West, a battle between a world of Orthodox, post-Soviet fellowship and a European Union future of liberal democracy. In the lands in between, people and political parties are sharply divided into pro-European and pro-Russian camps. Each watches its own television stations, lives in its own media and information bubble, and feels threatened by the other. Some work and study abroad in Europe; others in Russia. It often seems that two different civilizations exist in the same place. No wonder some scholars have called Eastern Europe the "shatterzone of empires."[3]

Yet the paradox is this. While political parties and public media fight a pitched battle for the hearts and minds of the population, seeking to drag their country to the East or West, things look different at the pinnacle of power. There, many of the key power brokers in these societies share one important characteristic: an ability to profit from both sides—and from the conflict that divides them.

In some cases, these power brokers are presidents, who may align primarily with Russia or the West, but are always careful to hedge bets and maintain room for maneuver in order to protect their own sovereignty. In other cases, these power brokers are not presidents but oligarchs, leading business people with substantial political influence. For instance, most Ukrainian oligarchs have proven enormously flexible, enriching themselves under the pro-Russian Yanukovich regime before switching their support to the pro-Western Poroshenko regime. Oligarch Victor Pinchuk is famous for having opposed NATO membership for Ukraine before supporting it when a new regime came to power in Kiev. Needless to say, he does not seem to be a man of principle. Pinchuk was a close associate of the Clintons who later switched allegiances and donated to Donald Trump's election campaign. He is a man who knows how to stay close to power.[4] As noted in the introduction to this book, Moldova's Vlad Plahotniuc has maneuvered himself into the leadership of his country's governing pro-EU alliance while profiting from rebroadcasting the main Russian TV stations and their political propaganda. Georgia's Bidzina Ivanishvili entered politics on a platform of closer ties with Russia, while also maintaining Georgia's pro-EU direction. The paradoxes are endless and hard to comprehend.

Yet there is a simple explanation. In countries where mass politics is extremely polarized—fought out between media and political forces that are fiercely pro-EU or pro-Russia—the greatest power and wealth flows not to ideological partisans, whose gains are often partial and transient, but to the power brokers who position themselves to profit from the enormous passions and insecurities of both sides. In a war such as this, there is always a catch-22—and a Milo Minderbinder armed with greed, instincts of self-preservation, and flexibility who deftly manages to transcend it.

This politics of polarization and power brokers is most visible in the lands in between, vulnerable states caught up in a geopolitical struggle between two "civilizations"—West and East. However, the same type of politics is becoming increasingly important in the West as well. As Western countries are caught up in Russia's hybrid war, their politics become more vulnerable, and the lessons of the lands in between become more relevant. The lands in between are often seen as poor, backward states. But on this dimension, their greater vulnerability to Russian influence puts them ahead. They are the canaries in the coal mine and have much to teach us about the disorienting politics of hybrid war that we in the West are experiencing today.

VULNERABILITY TO RUSSIA

The lands in between are highly vulnerable to Russian influence: military, economic, and cultural. This greater vulnerability sets them apart from the CEE states that joined the European Union and NATO in the 2000s and from the developed Western countries of Europe and North America.

On the military side, many of the lands in between have suffered Russian military intervention in recent years. Georgia, Moldova, and Ukraine all have parts of their territory occupied by the Russian military or by breakaway republics under the protection of Russia. While other European countries may be concerned about Russian military threats, the lands in between live with the reality of being small, weak states in Russia's backyard and in many cases with the reality of occupation. This threat has persisted since the end of the Soviet Union in 1991.

Moldova's experience of occupation dates from 1991, when its attempts to exercise military control over its entire territory were repulsed by the Soviet Fourteenth Army stationed in Transnistria, a sliver of land across the Dniester River from the rest of Moldova. The Soviet Fourteenth Army fought to keep Transnistria—with its larger Russian-speaking population—independent from a newly sovereign and mostly Romanian-speaking Moldova. This short war ended with a frozen conflict between Russia and Moldova and the creation of the Transnistrian Moldovan Republic, propped up by a small 1,500-troop Russian occupation force to the present day.

Georgia was invaded by Russia in 2008 and has been forced to cede control of two territories to the Russian army: Abkhazia and South Ossetia.[5] Ukraine was invaded in 2014 by Russian forces that annexed Crimea and occupied the Donbas region, establishing breakaway republics in Donetsk and Luhansk.

While the rest of the lands in between have not experienced occupation directly, the possibility of Russian military intervention remains an ever-present reality. Armenia hosts a Russian military base and has a close security relationship with Russia. For instance, after prodemocracy protests in Armenia overturned a dictatorial, pro-Russian government in 2018, the new prime minister, Nikol Pashinian, felt compelled immediately to reaffirm the "strategic alliance" between Russia and Armenia.[6] No surprise here. Armenian leaders believe that a close relationship with Russia deters neighboring Azerbaijan from invading and retaking the territory of Nagorno-Karabakh. Armenia seized Nagorno-Karabakh, formerly an Armenian enclave within Azerbaijan, in a war in the 1990s. Yet as Azerbaijan grew wealthy as a result of oil revenues, it overtook Armenia in economic development and now wishes to retake Nagorno-Karabakh.[7] It probably would be capable of doing so were it not for Russia's military support for Armenia. Belarus, while it has fought off Russian efforts to establish an airbase in its country to preserve its national independence, hosts a Russian radar station and naval communications base.[8] It hosted large-scale Russian military exercises in 2017. Azerbaijan has no Russian military base and tries to maintain good relations with both Russia and the West. However, its territorial demands on Armenia are effectively kept in check by the Russian army.

Economically, these countries are heavily dependent on Russia, as they are relatively small countries bordering the much larger Russian economy. In most cases, Russia is one of their largest trading partners. Moreover, this trade dependence is "asymmetric": they depend on Russia far more than the other way around.[9] This gives Russia the ability to use trade sanctions to severely punish (or reward) the lands in between.

For instance, in the case of Moldova, Russia halted the import of Moldovan wine in 2006–7 and 2013–17 and other food products in order to punish it for increasing ties with the EU.[10] Belarus fell afoul of Russia when it violated Russian countersanctions against the EU in 2014–15.[11] As a result, Russia intercepted and destroyed suspected (often rebranded) EU products moving through Belarus to the Russian market. These enforcement actions occurred despite Belarus's membership in the Eurasian customs union with Russia. Russia also imposed a series of trade sanctions on Ukraine in 2013–14, declaring all imports from Ukraine "high-risk" and justifying extensive scrutiny that effectively shut down trade for several weeks, among other more targeted sanctions on particular industries and companies.[12] Russia blocked imports of Georgian agricultural products in 2006, after the Rose Revolution that brought Mikheil Saakashvili to power, and only relaxed this trade embargo in 2013.[13] Despite its supposed commitment to free trade within the Eurasian Economic Union and the World Trade Organization, Russia frequently uses trade embargoes and sanctions against the lands in between, forcing them to reckon with their economic vulnerability to Russia.

Culturally, the lands in between are also exceptionally vulnerable to Russian influence. As former Soviet republics, all have substantial Russian-speaking populations, a legacy of Soviet imperialism that provides an entry point for Russian state media and political propaganda.[14] Russian state media creates an alternative worldview for its spectators. Many aspects of its virtual reality are distorted. Conspiracy theories abound. Enemies are identified and berated. Facts are covered up. Heroes—especially Russian president Vladimir Putin—are built up. The Kremlin controls the content of news stories and metanarratives on a daily basis.[15] Its intent is to create a population that believes Russian narratives—including seeing America and the EU as enemies and Russia as an innocent victim—and to use this group to influence the politics of target countries.

As a result of this information warfare, Ukraine, one of the biggest targets of Russian propaganda, banned the broadcast of Russian TV channels and prevented certain Russian journalists from entering Ukraine. Similarly, Ukraine banned Russian social media websites, which the government said were being used to transmit Kremlin propaganda messages to Ukraine's large Russian-speaking population.[16]

While Russia's media campaigns have gained enormous attention in the West, its use of the Orthodox Church as a mechanism of foreign cultural influence has not. Yet not only do most of the lands in between share the Orthodox faith, but their churches have been under the direct control of the Moscow patriarchate of the Orthodox Church, which deploys its priests to deliver political messages, particularly at election time. In Ukraine, Moldova, and Belarus, Russia has enjoyed direct control over one of the most trusted institutions in the country.[17] Russia uses the church to emphasize conservative family values, anti-EU and anti-US messages, and to encourage parishioners to vote for (pro-Russian) political parties that espouse these views, while emphasizing a common Orthodox culture in the lands in between.[18]

In order to counter this influence, Ukraine founded a Kiev patriarchate of the Orthodox Church, separate from Moscow. The Kiev patriarchate rapidly gained ground, establishing thousands of churches and parishes throughout the country attended by approximately 15 million Ukrainian parishoners, compared to 10 million for the Moscow patriarchate in 2017. Many Ukrainians regarded both as legitimate Orthodox churches. Yet there was one important difference: the Kiev patriarchate declared itself firmly in favor of Ukrainian national independence and sovereignty.[19] In 2018, Orthodoxy's world center, the Patriarchate of Constantinople, finally recognized the Kiev patriarchate as sovereign in Ukraine, despite protests and threats of retaliation from Moscow. Moscow retains an important influence through the churches of the Moscow patriarchate.[20]

In summary, Russia has a number of tools of geopolitical influence in the lands in between that it does not have elsewhere in Europe or in North America. The lands in between are significantly different from countries that have joined the European Union, where the EU now constitutes a stronger countervailing cultural and economic influence. The lands in between are former Soviet republics that did not seize the opportunity to join the EU and NATO after the collapse of the Soviet Union in 1991. They are divided between those who see a European future for their countries and those who wish to remain in a more familiar Russian sphere of influence. Because of Russia's greater military, economic, and cultural influence in the lands in between, most people in the West feel there is little to learn from these countries. However, now that Russian influence has begun to affect all countries in the West, the experience of lands in between has become more relevant.

EUROPEAN UNION INFLUENCE

While Russia has been a major influence on the lands in between for many years, since 1991 these countries have opened to the West and found that their prosperity depends on integration with Western economies. As a result, the lands in between embraced neoliberal economic reforms in the 1990s and 2000s, to varying degrees.[21] As their CEE neighbors joined the EU in the 2000s, these countries all of a sudden found themselves bordering on the EU and wanting or needing closer ties with the massive EU common market. In some cases, the lands in between required a closer economic relationship with the EU just to maintain preexisting trade and investment relationships with neighboring countries that had joined the EU. For instance, Moldova and Romania, which share a common language and history, suddenly found themselves on opposite sides of the EU customs union border. Just to maintain preexisting relationships meant that the lands in between needed closer relations with the EU.

The EU responded by launching the Eastern Partnership program in 2009. According to the official EU website, "The Eastern Partnership aims at building a common area of shared democracy, prosperity, stability and increased cooperation." While the EU does not offer a prospect of membership to the Eastern Partnership countries, it does offer a closer economic and political relationship for countries willing to adopt EU practices and institutions. On the political side, the heads of state or government from the six Eastern Partnership countries convene at summit meetings with their EU counterparts twice per year. The EU also sponsors civil society, local and regional government, parliamentary, and business partnership meetings. Since the Eastern Partnership is part of a wider European Neighborhood Policy, the partner countries and the EU produce "action plans" and "progress reports" on integration on a yearly basis. These provide an opportunity for countries to set integration objectives and for the EU to critique progress toward integration.

On the economic side, the EU sought to conclude DCFTAs with all Eastern Partnership countries in 2014, agreements that offered substantial access to EU markets in exchange for regulatory harmonization with EU rules. Because of Russian opposition, Armenia, Azerbaijan, and Belarus declined to sign such agreements—as did Ukraine under President Yanukovich. However, Georgia, Moldova, and ultimately Ukraine, after the Maidan revolution, concluded DCFTAs with the EU in 2016 and 2017.[22] Armenia joined Russia's Eurasian Economic

Union, but also signed a more limited partnership agreement with the EU in 2017. At the 2015 Riga Summit, the Eastern Partnership countries decided on four "priority areas of cooperation": stronger governance, stronger economy, better connectivity, and stronger society, mirroring the requirements of EU membership. In addition, the EU provides significant financial support to the Eastern Partnership countries, amounting to 2.8 billion euros from 2014 to 2017,[23] and the prospect of visa-free travel to the EU, a major incentive for citizens who seek to study or work abroad.

The EU also exerts significant influence over the lands in between as a major trading partner and model of economic prosperity and good governance. Many citizens of the lands in between see that EU membership dramatically boosted the economic prospects of neighboring countries in Central and Eastern Europe, including Poland and Romania, whose wages have been converging with those in the European Union.[24] They want the same for their countries. Some analysts believe that the incentives for change would be far higher if the EU had offered the prospect of membership to the Eastern Partnership countries.[25] Still, it is clear in the lands in between that while Russian influence works primarily through cultural and military means, EU influence works primarily through the attraction of its enormous and highly developed economy. This may explain why EU integration seems to appeal to different groups in the population, primarily those best positioned to take advantage of the economic opportunities it offers.

Countervailing influences of Russia and the West have left people in the lands in between divided. Some prefer a pro-Russian direction for their countries, while others advocate for rapid integration with the EU. Overall, Georgia, Ukraine, and Moldova have taken the most pro-EU perspective, while Armenia, Belarus, and Azerbaijan have shown less enthusiasm for a European path. Yet in each country, these choices have

spawned sharp divisions that have become sharper still as geopolitical conflict between Russia and the EU grows.

THE POLITICS OF "CIVILIZATIONAL CHOICE"

Between the threat of Russian military intervention, trade sanctions, and foreign media influences in the lands in between, and
the EU's push to integrate countries through DCFTAs and political steps toward a prosperous and democratic Europe, it should
be no surprise that politics in these countries is increasingly
polarized. In Moldova and Ukraine, many politicians feel that
their countries are at a crossroads and speak of a "civilizational
choice," between the EU and Russia. For instance in 2017, the
prime ministers of Ukraine and Moldova held a press conference to reaffirm the European direction for their countries.
Ukrainian prime minister Volodymyr Groysman stated, "A
stable political situation in Moldova and preserving the course
of Chisinau towards European integration poses great interest
for Ukraine. Successful realization of our joint civilizational
choice shall facilitate the stability and security in the region, the
effectiveness of our cooperation and the prosperity and development of our peoples."[26] Similarly, on the brink of Moldova's
2014 parliamentary election, Moldova's prime minister, Iurie
Leancă, told the *Financial Times*, "This election is critical and
crucial for the future of the country. Do we want to move the
country forward? It is a civilizational choice."[27]

When each election becomes a referendum on a
"civilizational choice" between Russia and the EU, it is hard
to find an in-between position. On the one hand, the lands in
between can choose closer relations with the EU, a huge and
successful market characterized by rule of law, freedom of
speech, anticorruption campaigns, visa-free travel, educational

opportunities, and a path toward Western prosperity, but at the risk of high inequality and increasing internationalism. On the other, they can choose to be part of the new Russian empire, where they share a common culture and history, speak the same language, and benefit from long-standing trade and employment ties, but also suffer from a top-down system of corruption, a weaker economy, and a state propaganda machine that feeds a debilitating belief in conspiracy theories.

Given the stark nature of this choice, it is not surprising that geopolitics has become the number-one political issue in these countries. Not left versus right, which has been the dominant political cleavage in Western countries for hundreds of years. Nor liberal versus conservative. Not even the divide between former communist and anticommunist opposition, though these divisions sometimes overlap. The main issue in national politics is whether to rejoin Soviet Union 2.0 or to achieve national independence in an EU framework. Because this is the most fundamental issue for voters—one that will determine their economic futures, their life chances, and the manner in which their country and economy is governed—political parties tend to provide a clear choice. At election time, politicians remind voters what is at stake and beg them to forgive minor transgressions, such as endemic corruption, in service of a greater good.

"Civilizational choice" has thus become a defining issue for political parties. As one analyst puts it, "Most of the elections in Ukraine's recent political history have not only been hotly contested but have also manifested the clash between two visions for the country's future, one anchored on the European political model of liberal democracy and the other associated with Russia and its illiberal political tradition of state paternalism and centralized leadership."[28] Voters in these countries first look at the overall direction of a party, then secondarily at its positions on domestic policy issues. In other words, geopolitics dominates politics in the lands in between. For countries caught in the middle of an intensifying geopolitical competition, it is hard to find middle ground, even though, for many politicians, "This is not the position we want to be in."[29] Many politicians would rather debate the substance of domestic political issues or economic development rather than an abstract civilizational choice.

While the whole idea of "civilizational choice" may seem abstract to some, both the EU and Russia consciously promote their own visions of European civilization. While the EU presents a world of "European values," prosperity and human rights, Russia emphasizes traditional values that it believes are shared by the lands in between, as a result of a common connection to the Orthodox Christian Church. In Ukraine, "Patriarch Kirill I of the Russian Orthodox Church, a true spokesperson of Kremlin political worldviews, has . . . persistently emphasized the cultural and spiritual unity of Russians and Ukrainians."[30] Russia wants Ukraine, Moldova, Belarus, and other Orthodox countries to remain part of a common Orthodox civilization centered in Moscow.

Russia's appeal to the existence of a common Orthodox civilization and the language of "civilizational choice" and the "Russian world" has become a key aspect of Russia's attempts to influence the lands in between. On the eve of the Ukraine conflict, for instance, Vladimir Putin attended an Orthodox Church conference on the "civilizational choice" facing Ukraine and underlined Ukraine's and Russia's common heritage in the medieval state of Kievan Rus. Putin said, "We know today's reality of course, know that there are the Ukrainian people and the Belarusian people, and other peoples too, and we respect all the parts of this heritage, but at the same time, at the foundations of this heritage are the common spiritual values that make us a single people. The Ukrainian Orthodox Church leaders spoke about this today. It would be hard to deny this. We can only agree with it. . . . We must remember this brotherhood and preserve our ancestors' traditions. Together, they built a unique system of Orthodox values and strengthened themselves in their faith."[31]

In this perspective, joining the EU undermines this Orthodox tradition by adopting corrupt Western values of individual freedom and self-expression. Gay marriage is often deployed as the greatest symbol of Western wrongheadedness and decadence. Russian leaders often refer to Europe as "Gayropa." And increasingly the Russian leadership no longer considers Russians European, but Eurasian. As Kremlin aide and thinker Vladislav Surkov put it, Russia's culture is a "mixed breed" that incorporates elements of both the East and the West, like "someone born of a mixed marriage. . . . He is everyone's relative, but nobody's family. Treated by foreigners like one of their own, an outcast among his own people. He understands everyone and is understood by no one."[32] In short, Russians are not European, but from a different civilization.

Armed conflict, or the threat thereof, only makes these political divides more intense. Instead of choosing between civilizations, people in the lands in between often feel that they have to decide which side to fight on.

THE FRONT LINES

Ukraine

The hottest war in the lands in between is of course the one in Ukraine. And there is nothing like war to sharpen political polarization at home. Prior to 2014, the median voter in Ukraine wanted closer relations with the EU and Russia simultaneously and did not worry if these goals were mutually exclusive.

Ukrainians simply wanted good relations with both sides. Knowing this, pro-Russian president Viktor Yanukovich negotiated a DCFTA with the EU throughout 2012 and 2013 in pursuit of a "multivector" foreign policy that would allow Ukraine to balance between Russia and the EU, as many Ukrainian citizens desired at the time. However, when Russia grabbed Crimea and Eastern Ukraine in order to prevent Ukraine from joining the EU, it pushed a majority of Ukrainians into the pro-EU camp and made them see Russia as an enemy. Geopolitical orientation and nationalism became firmly aligned.

Russia's invasion in 2014 convinced the median voter in Ukraine that Russia was an aggressor, not a friend, and that Ukraine's future lies with the West. The old political middle ground was suddenly gone. It was replaced by a pro-Western majority that believes an independent Ukraine must ally with the West. In public opinion polls conducted in September 2014, a few months into the conflict, a vast majority of Ukrainians supported joining the EU for the first time, with 59 percent in favor compared to 17 percent for joining Russia's Eurasian Economic Union.[33] Russia's annexation of Crimea forced Ukrainians to make what appeared to be a civilizational choice. A significant majority of Ukrainians chose the West. As a result, Ukrainian national identity now means independence from Russia.

However, there remains a minority of the Ukrainian population that cannot abide Ukrainian nationalism and wants to remain part of Russian civilization, or at least not too distant from it. Ukrainian nationalists view this pro-Russian population as traitorous. It is subject to marginalization and attacks. Since the war broke out, any hint of cooperation with Russia can be construed as evidence of treason. This has forced political parties that represent pro-Russian Ukrainians to make a point of declaring their support for Ukrainian national independence, the Ukrainian state, the EU, and, to some extent, hiding or obfuscating their support for pro-Russia policy positions.

War has made life particularly difficult for the Opposition Bloc, the successor to President Yanukovich's Party of Regions, the largest party representing the views of pro-Russia Ukrainians. The Opposition Bloc previously gained a great deal of its support from Crimea and Eastern Ukraine, two areas that no longer vote in Ukrainian elections, since they are no longer administered by the Ukrainian government. The Opposition Bloc represents many Ukrainians who identify with Russia, but insists that it is not pro-Russian but rather pro-Ukrainian. It opposes extreme forms of Ukrainian nationalism, favors treating Russian as an equal state language, and advocates for the rights of Russian-speaking Ukrainians. The party believes that the nationalist perspective on Russia is counterproductive and that, were the Ukrainian government more flexible in fulfilling the Minsk agreements, for instance, it could end confrontation with Russia and get Ukrainian territory back. There is every reason to believe that the Opposition Bloc wants Ukraine's occupied territories back—both Crimea and Donetsk were strongholds of its party. Still, despite its frequent attestations of allegiance to a multinational Ukraine, many nationalists regard the Opposition Bloc as too willing to cater to Moscow and possibly disloyal. Its politicians sometimes face physical attacks by extreme nationalist groups.[34]

Politics in Ukraine is now perceived as a life-or-death issue. For instance, in Odessa, the events of May 2, 2014, in which street clashes between nationalist and pro-Russian groups escalated into the firebombing and death of forty-two pro-Russian protesters inside a trade union building, has left a legacy of violence and fear in the city. Nationalists believe that their actions kept Odessa, a port city along the Black Sea, from sliding into the same kind of chaos as Donetsk and Luhansk. Many citizens who identify with Russia or speak only Russian, however, feel persecuted. They worry that Ukraine will pass a language law that will eliminate Russian as a state language, force them to communicate in Ukrainian, and result in long-term discrimination. On the other side, Ukrainian nationalists in Odessa worry that those who identify with Russia represent a dangerous fifth column. People are fearful of deportation, invasion, and their sons and daughters dying at the front. In such circumstances, it is hard to trust the other side. Polarization produces political choices that appear to be starkly pro-Ukrainian or pro-Russian.

For many Ukrainian nationalists, articulating a pro-Russia line is tantamount to killing Ukrainian soldiers. Joining the Eurasian Economic Union means abandoning hopes of national independence. By contrast, when Ukrainian president Petro Poroshenko celebrated the launch of visa-free travel in June 2017 for Ukrainians into the EU, he hailed it as a "final break" with the Russian empire and quoted a famous poem by Russian poet Mikhail Lermontov, stating, "Farewell, unwashed Russia."[35] The middle ground that many Ukrainians once occupied, of being friendly to both the EU and Russia, now seems like a practical impossibility.

Belarus

Belarus, the former Soviet republic to the north of Ukraine, has chosen a different path. And given Ukraine's travails, many Belarusians believe they made the right choice. Belarus has remained clearly aligned with Russia since the 1990s, even joining together with Russia in a "union state." EU influence in Belarus has been minimal. However, politics in Belarus is also polarized between those who support a pro-Russian direction and those who would like to see Belarus move closer to Europe.

President Aleksander Lukashenko's regime in Belarus rests on two pillars: a repressive security apparatus that is closely aligned with Russia, and a liberal intelligentsia that provides a modicum of good governance and holds out the hope of closer relations with the West. Belarus also has a small but active opposition movement made up of Belarusian nationalists who oppose subservience to Moscow and liberals who wish to see Belarus integrate into the European Union. Many Belarusian opposition members live or work in Lithuania or Poland, EU member states a few hours' drive from the Belarusian capital, Minsk. Since both nationalists and liberals perceive Moscow as the greatest threat to Belarus, opposition politicians in Belarus are almost uniformly pro-EU. As in Ukraine, to be in favor of national independence means to be anti-Russia and pro-EU.

Meanwhile, the Lukashenko regime adopts much of Russia's anti-EU propaganda, railing against "Gayropa" and in favor of conservative cultural values. Belarusian state ideology emphasizes that Belarus has always been vulnerable to invasion from the west. The government uses its disastrous experience as a battlefield between the Nazi and Red armies during World War II as a justification for why Belarus needs authoritarian rule, to protect Belarus, promote stability, and prevent war.[36]

Moldova

Similarly in Moldova, politics has become increasingly polarized, breaking down into clearly identified pro-Russia or pro-EU camps. President Igor Dodon's Socialist Party advertises itself as pro-Russian and seeks to bring Moldova into the Eurasian Economic Union. It is supported by pro-Russian television and makes no secret of its links to Russia. During the 2016 election, Dodon promised to rule "like Putin" and declared that Crimea is Russian territory.[37] Dodon is opposed by an Alliance for European Integration that wants to see the country integrated with the EU. Approximately 10 percent of the population would like to see Moldova merge with Romania, which they see as a fast track to EU membership, since Romania is already an EU member. The Moldovan language is Romanian, and many Moldovans qualify for Romanian passports, which provide entry into the European Union for work or travel. However, non-Romanian ethnic minority groups tend to distrust Romania and feel safer with Russia. A majority of Moldovans wish to preserve their country, and many support integration into the EU as an independent state. In 2016, the pro-EU camp voted for Maia Sandu, a former World Bank employee and minister of education who came second in the presidential election, running on a "Pro-EU Action" platform.

The battle between pro-EU and pro-Russia forces in Moldova has intensified since the Ukraine conflict, with Russia and the EU pushing hard for their domestic allies with monetary and media support. According to one analyst, "Playing on the East-West geopolitical divisions within society represents the favorite and most effective way to manipulate atomized public opinion in Moldova."[38] In 2018, these conflicts appeared to be coming to a head. Moldovans tensely await parliamentary elections in 2018 or 2019 that many believe could determine Moldova's geopolitical orientation for a long time to come. Pro-EU liberals believe that if Moldova were to elect a pro-Russia government (in addition to a pro-Russia president), Moldova would integrate into Soviet Union 2.0 as a subsidiary of the new Russian empire. A pro-EU government would continue Moldova's troubled path toward European integration, with visa-free travel and greater possibilities of work and study, but also greater competition and opportunities from the massive EU economy. Approximately equal shares of the population support both options.[39]

Unfortunately for the West, while the Alliance for European Integration that governed Moldova from 2009 to 2018 promised progress toward EU trade, travel, and eventual membership, it presided over extreme corruption. In one notorious case, $1 billion went missing from the Moldovan banking system. A preliminary report from the US security firm Kroll found businessman Ilan Shor culpable, but he was never charged.[40]

However, former Moldovan prime minister Vlad Filat, head of a pro-EU government, was sentenced to nine years in jail for taking bribes from Ilan Shor.[41] EU funds allegedly also were stolen. The result has been that many voters have been turned off to the EU integration coalition.

In Moldova, parties that campaigned on a "multivector" approach to Russia and the West were once popular, but as the conflict has deepened, these parties have been sidelined. For instance, Renato Usati's Pro Patria Party, which identifies itself as pro-Moldovan and seeks to avoid being identified too closely with either Russia or the EU, has seen its support wither in recent years. In a political spectrum sharply divided between pro-EU and pro-Russian forces, voters want to know which side parties are on. And Pro Patria has increasingly been identified with Russia, since Renato Usati returned to Russia after being threatened with arrest in Moldova and is rumored to have links to Russian secret services. Ethnic parties face the same problem of being forced to identify as either pro-EU or pro-Russia. As Daniel Cadier and Samuel Charap write, "The Ukraine crisis seems to have reinforced the tendency to approach the region through a binary geopolitical lens, which is detrimental to political and economic reform. . . . Worse, this binarization of regional politics exacerbates internal divides in the countries of the common neighbourhood and allows elites to instrumentalise competition among external actors to their benefit."[42]

In sum, the intensifying geopolitical conflict between Russia and the West has forced political parties and voters in the frontline states to choose. Either their country can seek prosperity and freedom in the European Union, with all the good and bad that entails, or they can join the Eurasian Economic Union, which offers closer political and economic integration with Russia. Geopolitics seems to have overwhelmed politics. While in most countries, politics revolves around domestic issues such as jobs, economic growth, healthcare, and public services, in the lands in between the big question is, what civilization do we belong to?

POLARIZATION AND POWER BROKERS

This sharp polarization, however, creates a paradox. In this context of geopolitical competition, sharp polarization, and "civilizational choice," the big winners are the ones who play both sides. This is a dangerous game. Some win and some lose. All play it differently. But the ability to profit from both sides is a surprisingly common feature of the power brokers who dominate these divided societies.

Here is how it works. In polarized politics, competing sides offer different ideological visions. In the case of pro-Europe camp, it is the vision of a state ruled by law, individual freedoms, and self-expression. In the case of the pro-Russian side, it is a vision of traditional Christian culture, family values, and Orthodox spirituality. External actors—the European Union or the Russian state—encourage and reward those who support these value systems. Obviously, individual interests come into play. Those who speak European languages and have a higher degree of education may support pro-EU parties. Those who live and work in Russia may support a pro-Russian orientation. However, both sides in this struggle combine an appeal based on values with an economic message: Believe in Europe and enjoy prosperity. Believe in a unity of Slavic or Orthodox people and enjoy the patronage of the Russian state.

Yet in polarized societies neither side can thoroughly dominate.[43] There is always a significant minority that is aggrieved. This introduces a certain volatility into political life. To maintain control, the most successful politicians—or business people—do not pin their flag to one side or another, but find a way to diversify their appeal and cater to all sides. Think of it this way: if you were running a company that wanted to dominate the media market in the lands in between, it would be helpful to own newspapers and TV stations on opposite sides of the civilizational divide. To take a pure ideological position would be to cede market share to someone else. The same is true in politics. The most successful politician is the one who wins votes—or campaign contributions or economic support—from both sides. This requires sacrificing ideological consistency.

While political parties traffic in ideas—selling the idea of a Ukrainian, Georgian, or Belarusian nation or the ideals of rule of law or good government—power brokers prioritize material concerns. They are concentrated on achieving real gains in the here and now. As David Cadier and Samuel Charap point out, both Russia and the EU share a "willingness to subsidize political loyalty."[44] Russians pay good money for compliance with their wishes and desires. The EU also devotes substantial sums to supporting programs of international development that bring these countries closer to Europe. In the polarized politics of "civilizational choice," many politicians and party leaders gravitate to one side or the other out of deeply held beliefs. However, paradoxically, the leading politicians and businessmen in this environment are the ones who win resources from both sides by pursuing a dangerously ambiguous or flexible approach.

There are plenty of fascinating examples in the lands in between. Each is characterized by distinctive characteristics, strategies, and circumstances. While the Western media tend to focus on its pro-Western heroes like Mikheil Saakashvili, who imposed liberal reforms on the Republic of Georgia, before later losing power and even his Georgian passport, it has less to say about his successor as major domo of Georgian politics, Bidzina Ivanishvili. Yet Ivanishvili has dominated Georgian politics for many years and he is no hero.

Ivanishvili is the most powerful Georgian oligarch. He lives in a 108,000-square-foot modernist compound situated on a hill above the capital city of Tbilisi. He made his money in Russia, starting in the 1990s as an importer of computer and phone equipment. He founded a bank and participated in voucher privatization, acquiring ore and metals companies and rising in the Forbes ranks of global billionaires. He is a Russian oligarch who, during his election campaign in 2011–12, made a point of arguing that Georgia needed to normalize relations with Russia after the 2008 Russo-Georgian war, which he blamed on Saakashvili. He told the British daily *Telegraph*, "The government encourages hysteria about Russian aggression. They want to frighten people, and use it [the Russian issue] as part of a political game. But we will be obliged to forge relations with Russia, whether we like it or not. We should not forget that Russia is our biggest neighbour and we should use that."[45]

However, Ivanishvili and his Georgian Dream Party did not mean to abandon Georgia's Western orientation, which many see as central to Georgia's future economic success. Instead, he emphasized that he would continue to seek closer relations with the EU and NATO, while at the same time improving relations with Russia. He told the *Guardian*, "Our policy is European and Euro-Atlantic integration. There is no substitute for NATO." While this may seem contradictory, Ivanishvili was able to put an end to the Russian embargo on Georgian agricultural products in 2013 and normalize business ties with Russia, despite continued Russian land-grabs and occupation of parts of the country. Personally, Ivanishvili sold most of his Russian holdings after entering politics, but retained a sizable share of Gazprom stock. He also showed up prominently in the Panama Papers as the holder of an offshore company. Yet Georgia has not relinquished its Western aspirations under his rule and signed a DCFTA with the EU in June 2014.[46] This seemingly contradictory set of policies is underpinned by public opinion. "Georgians overwhelmingly desire a good political relationship with Russia," and supported close relations with the United States (71 percent), EU (65 percent), and Russia (54 percent) in a poll conducted soon after the Russo-Georgian war in 2009.[47] Presumably, Georgians on both sides of the divide can find something to love and to hate about their leading oligarch, who, after winning election as prime minister in 2012, resigned in 2013 to once again stand behind the scenes. In 2018, he was forced to return to lead his Georgian Dream Party after a power struggle broke out within its ranks between the prime minister and mayor of Tbilisi. His chosen candidate, Salome Zourabichvili, won the presidency in 2018 with 60 percent of the vote.

Ivanishvili is one of the most dramatic examples of a power broker in the lands in between, in part because he lives in a James Bond–style futurist mansion and owns a $1 billion art collection, but he is not alone. Many leading politicians in the lands in between manage a similar balancing act, earning fortunes in business with Russia while running a pro-EU government, or vice versa.

These power brokers try to achieve the unachievable: attaining closer ties with the West while maintaining friendly relations with the regional superpower, Russia. For smaller states, it is sometimes said that agility and responsiveness are natural advantages as they seek to navigate the minefield of great-power politics.[48] It is not only a necessity, but an opportunity that may be richly rewarded. The EU provides billions of euros of assistance that can be channeled by leaders. Russia offers business deals and rich payoffs to its political allies. As geopolitics becomes more polarized and violent, the amount that the EU and Russia are willing to pay for compliance tends to increase, while careful balancing becomes more difficult to achieve for the lands in between. How do oligarchs, presidents, and other power brokers walk that line?

For power brokers in the lands in between, flexibility is the ultimate resource. In a recent academic take on this subject, Stanislav Markus and Volha Charnysh investigated the political activities of oligarchs in Ukraine.[49] In an article entitled "The Flexible Few," they found that oligarchs—superwealthy and often politically connected business leaders—benefit from flexibility. While some become governors (or presidents) and adopt political roles themselves, these positions do not enhance an oligarch's personal wealth. Oligarchs do best when they remain in the background, providing donations to one or more parties. This allows them greater flexibility to hedge their bets between different parts of the political spectrum or to change positions as circumstances change. Markus and Charnysh point out that many of the same oligarchs that fared extremely well economically under the pro-Russian Yanukovich regime also have fared extremely well under the pro-EU Poroshenko regime. Indeed, there has been very little change in the lineup of Ukrainian oligarchs between 2012 and 2016. Since the Crimea invasion, most oligarchs in Ukraine adopt pro-EU messages and promote pro-Ukrainian parties and even militias. However, this does not mean that they will do the same tomorrow. Their allegiance is, first and foremost, to their own power. Flexibility is a great asset in a highly polarized and volatile political climate.

In the introduction to this book, I discussed the fascinating example of an oligarch who supports pro-EU and pro-Russia positions simultaneously—Vladimir Planotniuc of Moldova. The richest man and most powerful oligarch in a small country perched between Ukraine and Romania, Planotniuc is leader of one of its major pro-EU parties, the Democratic Party. At the same time, he is reputed to be a supporter of the Socialist Party of President Igor Dodon, which has aligned itself with Russia. This enables Planotniuc to, on the one hand, curry favor with the EU and win financing for passing EU legislation in parliament, while on the other hand winning the support of pro-Russian voters and parties. Some say that his party and business networks benefit from EU contracts, effectively stealing money from the EU along the way. At the same time he also owns the most prominent Russian-language TV channels in Moldova, which regularly pump out Russian propaganda. He appears to be well compensated for this.[50] With cynical ideological inconsistency and a willingness to play both sides for the generous resources they offer to keep the other side at bay, Planotniuc walks a fine line. He balances the polarized political scene in Moldova, benefits from financial rewards from both sides, and builds his own power in the process.

President of Moldova Igor Dodon is another fascinating case. One of Putin's greatest allies in the region, Dodon made his career as a pro-EU reformer in the leadership of Moldova's Ministry of Economy and Trade from 2006 to 2009. In 2007, he advocated that Moldova sign an association agreement with the European Union that he now promises he will scrap if his Socialist Party wins a majority in parliament in 2019. Yet, as a member of parliament in 2012, Dodon was one of three members of parliament to cross party lines to support the Alliance for European Integration candidate for prime minister, Nicolae Timofti, ending a long deadlock.[51] Dodon abandoned the pro-EU parties when the political winds began to turn against them, and founded a political party funded by Moscow, espousing a pro-Kremlin line. Putin poked fun at Dodon when he became the only foreign leader to observe Russia's Victory Day celebrations in Moscow in 2017, calling him a court jester. Dodon subsequently made several moves to exhibit his own independence, including accepting US money to refurbish a military base close to Transnistria, the Russian-occupied breakaway region of Moldova.[52] Dodon appears to be a leader without strong or consistent values, but a keen sense of how to change tack to take advantage of the direction of the winds.

Azerbaijan too has carefully managed relations with both Russia and Europe. An oil dictatorship run by the Aliev family, father and son, Azerbaijan signed contracts with Western firms to exploit its oil resources in 1994. The country refused to join Russia's Eurasian Economic Union or the Collective Security Treaty Organization that includes both Moscow and Beijing. Azerbaijan forced the last Russian troops off its territory when it refused to extend a lease on a radar station in Gabala. However, it has also joined the Russian trans-Adriatic pipeline project, decided not to conclude a DCFTA with the European Union, and cooperated with Russian efforts to negotiate an end to the conflict in Nagorno-Karabakh. Amanda Paul calls this strategy "choosing not to choose" between the EU and Russia, a policy enabled by Azerbaijan's oil wealth, which gives it the resources to pursue an independent policy.[53]

Armenia likewise has sought to follow a path between Russia and the EU that is remarkable for its flexibility. While Armenia made great progress toward signing a DCFTA with the EU, it suddenly pulled out of negotiations in 2013 at Russia's insistence and joined the Eurasian Economic Union in 2015. It further granted Gazprom monopoly control over its pipeline network. Yet, soon after, Armenia began negotiating an amended trade agreement with the EU.[54]

LANDS IN BETWEEN?

What relevance does this experience have for the West in general? One might believe that this strange politics of polarization and power brokers afflicts the lands in between—small, vulnerable states on the front lines of great-power conflict in a geopolitical "shatterzone of empires."[55] But does it have anything to do with politics in the developed West?

More than you might expect. As Western countries have become vulnerable to and affected by Russia's hybrid war, the same politics of polarization and power brokers can be observed in the West as well. Of course, the lands in between remain more vulnerable, for all the reasons previously listed—their economic, cultural, and military closeness to Russia. Yet as Russia's hybrid war takes its toll through disinformation, political chaos, and encouragement of extreme parties, patterns of politics in the small, weak states in between Russia and Europe are increasingly reflected in the West.

I build this argument in the next chapter, which demonstrates that the politics of polarization and power brokers afflicts not only the lands in between, but CEE member states of the European Union. These countries were once seen as major success stories of transition, countries that escaped the Soviet sphere. Yet they are now caught up in this new conflict. They exhibit a growing polarization and the rise of cynical power brokers who, unbelievably, have created a problem of "civilizational choice" in countries where that decision appeared to be settled. A further chapter suggests that, to an extent, these same patterns are visible even in core Europe and the United States. Therefore, exploring the paradoxical politics of the lands in between can help us to better understand our own politics in an age of hybrid warfare and cultural transformation.

THE CONTEST FOR CENTRAL

AND EASTERN EUROPE

WOULD ANYONE HAVE IMAGINED IN 2008 that Czechia in 2018 would have a pro-Russian president? Or that this pro-Russian president would be the same leader who opposed the Russian invasion in 1968, brought his country into NATO in 2001 as prime minister, and negotiated the terms of the country's EU membership? Yet that is the case in one of the most economically successful of postcommunist countries.

Re-elected president in 2018 for a second term, Miloš Zeman is a fascinating figure with a long history in Czech politics who exhibits the same flexibility over time as some of the power brokers in the lands in between. Zeman first rose to prominence as a 1968er, a Czech Communist who favored economic reforms and opposed the Russian invasion of Czechoslovakia. Like other reform Communists, he suffered greatly in the years after the invasion. To this day, Zeman speaks out against Russian disinformation about the 1968 invasion.[1] After the collapse of communism, Zeman rose to be the leader of the Czech Social Democratic Party and, serving as prime minister from 1998 to 2002, helped negotiate Czechia's accession to the European Union and NATO. On the eve of Czech accession to NATO in 1999, he stated, "We have finally embarked on the path leading us to the Europe which is undivided and free. This year will be remembered as a turning point in our history. . . . the direction we have chosen is the right one. We consider it as a vote of confidence in our future, in the future of Central Europe and in the future of Europe." Yet after Zeman was deposed as leader of the Social Democratic Party and defeated in his run for the presidency in 2003, he began a period of soul searching, and a new Miloš Zeman emerged. Zeman became part of a wave of new populist politicians in Central and Eastern Europe, adopting anti-Muslim, anti-immigration, and pro-Russian political views. He was recruited to attend a pro-Russian Dialogue of Civilizations by Vladimir Yakunin, head of Russian railways. Zeman also acquired a close aide, Martin Nejedly, a Czech businessman with extensive Russian connections who used to run a subsidiary of Lukoil.[2] Nejedly has been accused in the Czech press of suspicious Russian ties. In 2015, when Nejedly was fined $1.4 million by a Czech court in a business dispute, Lukoil came forward to pay the fine.[3]

With this new financing and populist line, Zeman won the presidency in 2013. Since being elected president, Zeman has aligned himself with the European Far Right. He has lauded Russia's annexation of Crimea and stated that there are no Russian troops in Eastern Ukraine. During the Ukraine conflict, Zeman spoke out against Western sanctions on Russia. Zeman endorsed Russian actions in Syria and called for a "Czechxit" referendum on leaving the EU in 2016. In 2018, Zeman won his campaign for re-election against Jiří Drahoš, a pro-EU academic who was subjected to a massive trolling and disinformation campaign, similar to other Russian efforts at electoral manipulation. While the Czech president is largely a ceremonial post that has limited influence over government policy, Zeman has done a lot to legitimize Russia's foreign policy messages and business interests in Europe.[4] He has certainly made Czechia's belonging in the European Union more ambiguous and accommodated Russia's demands for influence, showing that there is a true contest today for the allegiances of Central and Eastern Europe. While it is impossible to know Zeman's true motivations, some suspect that he models himself on Hungary's Viktor Orbán, seeking to extend his power with Russian help, while milking resources and investment from the European Union.

With the success of Zeman and similar leaders, Central and Eastern Europe is now contested terrain in Russia's hybrid war with the West. Countries that had joined the European Union and seemingly made their civilizational choice in joining the West are now turning east. Political leaders in these countries do not necessarily seek to break from their EU membership and a primary Western orientation, but they see an opportunity to profit from the resources and opportunities Moscow offers and to accommodate Russian foreign policy demands. They understand that Russia is a weaker power, but also believe that it can and should be accommodated. For the West, it feels as if the ground has shifted under its feet.

As with the lands in between, Russia has many tools of influence in Central and East Europe, including energy policy, media, support for anti-EU parties, and military operations. While Central and East European states enjoy the protection and support of the EU, they are more vulnerable to Russian influence than the countries of core Europe. First, Central and East European countries have oil and gas infrastructures that make them heavily dependent on Russia for energy supplies. Second, they have populations that are sympathetic to Russian messages. Third, Russia has a long history of intervention in these countries and deep knowledge of domestic politics and economics that it can exploit in influence operations. Together, these factors have enabled Russia to undermine the EU from within using a variety of strategies, including energy geopolitics, funding for anti-EU extremist parties, and recruiting "Trojan horse" government leaders to advance Russia's agenda.[5]

Perhaps not surprisingly, this Russian campaign has affected the politics of Central and Eastern Europe in a way similar to the lands in between, exacerbating political polarization and playing into the hands of power brokers who seek to dominate the commanding heights of politics with the resources that they gain from both sides.[6]

ENERGY POLITICS

Energy has played an outsized role in the contest for Central and Eastern Europe. Lacking energy supplies outside of abundant coal, which is considered a dirty fuel by the European Union, Central and East European states are crisscrossed by pipelines bringing Russian oil and gas to the West. These transit states are almost entirely reliant on Russia for gas supplies, as well as transit fees. Not surprisingly, Russia's gas cutoffs to Ukraine in 2006 and 2009 demonstrated that most Central and East European member states were vulnerable to gas blackmail. These were not isolated events. Scandinavian scholars found fifty-five instances of Russian attempts to use energy blackmail for political ends before 2007.[7] Russia uses any type of reliance, as well as the promise of new gas pipeline routes and nuclear facilities, to exert pressure on Central and East European member states and tie them to Russian business interests.[8]

Of course, for CEE member states of the EU, membership exerts a powerful countervailing influence, enabling them to diversify energy supplies, as described in chapter 2. Most countries have taken advantage of these opportunities. Lithuania, hit hard by its own Russian pipeline shutoffs, became the first EU state to require Gazprom to "unbundle" production and distribution, forcing the sale of Gazprom's pipeline network in Lithuania. Russian president Vladimir Putin protested, calling it "uncivilized robbery."[9] Yet the EU gave Lithuania the legal basis and political backing to follow through. Similarly, Poland and Lithuania built LNG terminals on the Baltic Sea coast to facilitate import of Qatari and US natural gas.[10] Lithuania named its LNG terminal "Independence." With EU encouragement, most CEE countries have created interconnectors that enable them to receive gas imports from multiple sources, reducing reliance on Russia. A few countries, such as Bulgaria, proved slower to build interconnectors and diversify supplies, though even Bulgaria mostly completed a two-way connection with Romania in 2016 under the Danube River, with plans to link up with Serbia and Greece as well.[11]

Russia has tried to respond to EU attempts to diversify supplies with its own pipeline projects in Central and Eastern Europe. A key element of this strategy is the new South Stream pipeline. Like North Stream, which connects Russia directly with Germany, cutting out Poland and Belarus, South Stream seeks to replace Ukraine as a transit state for both business and political reasons. It is hard to be at war with a country that is the main conduit for your leading exports to the West. To build South Stream, Gazprom reached agreements on pipeline routes with a number of EU states, perhaps the most important being Bulgaria, where the pipeline was planned to make landfall after traveling from Russia (and now Crimea) under the Black Sea. However, Russia wanted to construct the pipeline without obeying EU rules on procurement, pipeline access, financing, and usage. To some extent, this was a business decision, but it also had a political dimension, to demonstrate that the EU is a paper tiger. As prominent Russian opposition figure and energy analyst Vladimir Milov put it, "The Kremlin, as always, is trying to achieve its goals and overcome European regulations through political means."[12] Russia bribed Bulgarian parliamentarians and government officials to take its side in these matters, causing the cost of the project to quadruple between 2008 and 2015.[13] However, after the 2014 annexation of Crimea, the

EU put down its foot and pressured Bulgaria into canceling the South Stream pipeline until Russia complied with EU regulations, thus saving Bulgaria from becoming "Gazprom's new preferred transit banana republic," in the words of Milov. Russia then moved its pipeline route to make landfall in Turkey.

Though Bulgaria is an EU member state, the EU had to fight hard to keep Bulgaria on its side.[14] Russia exerts considerable influence, as Russian companies and individuals have bought up a substantial share of the Bulgarian economy in recent years. Russian Duma deputy Piotr Tolstoy raised eyebrows in 2016 when he stated on Russian TV, "We will just buy out the entire [country]. Half of its coastline we have already bought." Bulgarians were offended at his "arrogance." Yet he is apparently right that Russian (followed by Armenian) investors are far and away the most important in Bulgaria. Russians own an estimated 500,000 mostly seaside homes in Bulgaria. Tolstoy, a great-grandson of novelist Leo Tolstoy, added that the EU needed deep reform and should abandon its policy of enlargement to countries in "Russia's zone of national interest."[15]

Russia also has sought to develop Hungary, another EU member state, as an energy ally and found a willing partner in Prime Minister Viktor Orbán. Russia promised to make Hungary a hub for South Stream gas in 2015, providing transit fees and most likely bribes or slush funds to Hungarian officials in the process.[16] Orbán has been open to Russian proposals and an enthusiastic partner, seeing it as an opportunity to increase gas supplies for the EU and to play an important economic role in Europe. Hungary also agreed to allow Russia to finance and build two new nuclear reactors at an estimated cost of some 12 billion euros at the site of an existing plant at Paks, 120 kilometers from the capital, Budapest. While this project proved controversial when Hungary awarded Rosatom, a Russian state company, a no-bid contract, normally a no-no in the EU, it managed to convince EU regulators to approve construction in 2017.[17] Orbán intends to broker the demands of Russia and the EU, profiting from the desire of Russia to bolster its energy market in Europe, while accommodating EU regulatory demands and remaining on the inside of the European Union. Russia sealed the deal with generous financing for the Paks project. In 2015, Orbán stated, "Whoever thinks that Europe can be competitive, that the European economy can be competitive without economic cooperation with Russia, whoever thinks that energy security can exist in Europe without the energy that comes from Russia, is chasing ghosts."[18]

The priority that the Russian state accords its energy diplomacy in Central and Eastern Europe is demonstrated by its use of its intelligence services to identify partners and win contracts. In 2014, the Czech Security Information Service (BIS) wrote in its annual report that "Gazprom, the major exporter of Russian natural gas, made efforts to exert maximum control over natural gas transit, storage and trade in Central Europe," attempting to advance business interests and exert political influence over the country. "Russia started perceiving Czech nuclear power engineering in a broader Central European context aiming to make good use of investments and efforts devoted to creating, managing, stabilizing and future exploitation of networks expanding Russian influence in Central Europe." Specifically, Russian intelligence attempted to influence "all entities even indirectly involved in fulfilling the goals of Czech energy policies" with a view to gaining or influencing control over Czech power plants, engineering companies, and supplies of nuclear fuel. Under President Putin, Russia has made no secret that it sees energy politics as a key to geopolitical influence and deploys its intelligence services to further its goals in this regard.[19]

Energy politics very often filters into normal politics because of its propensity to generate rents for top leaders. While there are rumors about extensive bribery of top officials and creation of slush funds for political parties across the EU, a *New York Times* investigation in Bulgaria showed how the system works. The *Times* reported that a Russian state-owned bank (VTB) "showered the country with politically strategic investments as Mr. Putin pushed the government to move forward on South Stream." Russia courted Bulgaria's far-right party, and a Russian Duma deputy (who also brokered a Kremlin loan to France's far-right National Front) came to Bulgaria and promised to make the deputy energy minister "very comfortable" if he would cooperate in the project. When Bulgaria awarded contracts for the construction of its portion of South Stream, they went to Kremlin-connected Russian companies in partnership with Bulgarian insiders.[20]

In sum, EU energy policy has enabled CEE member states to diversify supplies and reduce reliance on Russia. However, Russia has countered by offering profitable deals to governments willing to buck EU regulations and help Russia circumvent Ukraine and other transit states. Russia has threatened gas supplies and dangled the prospect of lucrative new energy deals, while developing cozy relations with CEE politicians, gaining allies, and seeking to undermine EU policies from within. While the EU has demonstrated the power to shut down Russian projects at will, as with the cancellation of South Stream construction in Bulgaria, the battle is far from over.

In 2018, attention turned to the proposed North Stream II pipeline, which would add capacity on a direct route between Russia and Germany, under the Baltic Sea. The German government approved the project despite objections from European Union partners such as Poland, who feared that it would increase reliance on Russian gas, cut out Central European transit states, and make Germany more vulnerable to Russian influence. Progress has been halting, particularly after the United States passed legislation that would allow sanctions on companies doing business with Russia and followed up by sanctioning a number of major Russian companies and oligarchs. North Stream II thus divided governments who wish to profit from cheap Russian gas from those who view dependency on Russia as a major security issue.[21]

POLITICAL INFLUENCE

In addition to the energy weapon, Russia has many other cards to play in the new EU member states of Central and Eastern Europe.

In some countries, particularly the Baltic republics of Estonia and Latvia, Russia uses large Russian-speaking minorities to exert influence on domestic politics. These Russian-speaking populations, made up of Belarusians, Russians, Ukrainians, and other, smaller, ethnic groups, have access to Russian-language media and thus are disproportionately influenced by Kremlin media messages. While most Russian speakers in the Baltics are pleased to live in the EU rather than in Russia, they are vulnerable to Russian propaganda: "In Estonia in 2007, following false reports in the Russian media about the destruction of a monument to Soviet soldiers in World War II, young Russian-speakers rioted and protested holding signs with slogans like 'USSR Forever.'" Whether or not Russian-speaking minorities believe Russian propaganda or act upon it, "Most Baltic Russian-speakers would qualify for protection as outlined in Russia's laws and compatriot policies," giving Russia an excuse for intervention whenever it judges the interests of Russians abroad to be violated. As a result, Baltic governments are on tenterhooks. Russia has sought to intensify its links to Russian-speaking populations in the Baltic republics by issuing them Russian passports and by many other measures. Agnia Grigas suggests that these are first steps in a process that has led to armed intervention in other parts of the former Russian empire.[22]

In addition, Russia has sought allies among fringe political parties throughout Central and Eastern Europe in order to destabilize domestic politics and governance. Strangely for a country that frequently portrays itself as an opponent of fascism, many of Russia's allies in Central and Eastern Europe hail from the far right of the political spectrum. The main criterion for Russian support of extremist parties is that they articulate anti-EU, anti-NATO messages and support controversial Russian foreign policy goals, such as the annexation of Crimea. While Russia certainly did not create far-right nationalism in Europe, Russia today is the greatest sponsor of neofascist and far-right parties across Europe. Russia supports the far-right Jobbik Party in Hungary, Ataka in Bulgaria, the Freedom Party in Austria, Golden Dawn in Greece, and many others. Russia provides financing, political advice, training, and technology to parties it supports, in exchange for adoption of a pro-Russia foreign policy platform and statements in support of Russian positions on foreign policy matters. Far-right parties legitimate Russia's discourse within the EU and destabilize mainstream parties that support the EU. Some analysts, like historian Tim Snyder, conclude that Russia's support for fascist parties is based on ideological affinity.[23] Others suggest it is a marriage of convenience and that Russia will support any party with an anti-EU ideology. Whatever the case, Russia's support for far-right European nationalists is part of its broader strategy to disable Western institutions from within.

Some CEE states take a hard line on Russia within the EU, particularly Poland and the Baltic States. For instance, Poland has supported Ukraine in its struggles against Russian intervention and opposed the Russian annexation of Crimea and the North Stream pipelines between Russia and Germany. Lithuania took Russia to court to force Gazprom to unbundle its energy assets in Lithuania under the third energy package. Both countries have been strong supporters of the Energy Union within the EU, the successor to the third energy package. Poland was a main author of the Eastern Partnership policy, together with Sweden, offering EU support to the lands in between. Poland and the Baltic States also support stronger NATO presence in their countries, with the vast majority of Poles regarding Polish-Russian relations as negative.[24]

This has not stopped Russia, however, from trying to recruit fringe politicians in Poland and elsewhere to toe the Russian line. Until his imprisonment in Poland on charges of spying for Russia, Russia was funding Mateusz Piskorski and his far-right Change movement. Like most far-right movements funded by Russia, Piskorski criticized Ukrainians as "fascists" and supported the Russian annexation of Crimea. Piskorski also helped to organize international observers for elections in various territories seized by Russia, such as Transnistria and South Ossetia.[25]

In addition to extremist parties like Change in Poland, Russia finances and helps to train far-right paramilitary organizations in many EU member states (and the United States). Its intelligence services sponsor fight clubs that teach the Russian style of hand-to-hand combat. These organizations are believed to be a recruiting tool for Russian military intelligence and a means of creating connections with far-right groups. For instance, the head of Slovakia's Facebook page promoting the "Russian fighting style" is also head of external relations of a Slovak far-right organization, the Slovak Revival Movement.[26] The Slovak Revival Movement articulates a pan-Slavic ideology and spreads Russian propaganda via its web presence. A similar group, the Slovak Conscripts, is "a paramilitary group providing military training combined with pan-Slavic and pro-Russian ideological indoctrination." The organization is basically a militia with units based in various parts of Slovakia. It is based on the model of Russian military-patriotic clubs and often invites visiting instructors from Russia to assist with training.[27] While small, these pro-Russian paramilitary organizations operate throughout Central and East Europe.

Far-right parties supported by Russia have enjoyed significant success in CEE politics in recent years, and Russia has stepped up support since the Ukraine crisis. In Slovakia, the pro-Russian, neo-Nazi People's Party—Our Slovakia, won 8 percent of the vote in parliamentary elections and 14 out of 150 seats in the Slovak parliament in 2016. Its leader, Marian Kotleba, was elected governor of the Banská Bystrica region. People's Party—Our Slovakia "labelled the Maidan revolution an act of 'terrorists' and . . . launched its petition to secede from the EU and NATO."[28] Hungary's far-right Jobbik Party has become the second largest party in Hungary after Viktor Orbán's FIDESZ, gaining 17 percent of the vote in parliamentary elections in 2010 and 20 percent in 2014. The party founded and supported a number of violent neofascist paramilitary organizations, including the Hungarian Guard, the Sixty-Four Counties Youth Movement, Army of Outlaws, Hungarian Self-Defense Movement, and the Wolves.

In 2014, one leader of Jobbik, Zoltán Lázár, wrote in support of a colleague accused of spying on the EU for Russia, "We stand for anti-globalization, we are Eurosceptic, anti-liberal and we believe in Eastern Opening. In that context, Russia doesn't appear to be all that threatening. In other words, if someone 'spies for them' on the EU, all we say is: hip-hip hurray." By supporting far-right parties in Central and Eastern Europe, like People's Party—Our Slovakia or Jobbik, Russia increases political polarization. Studies show that the share of the radical-right vote in Europe has increased in recent years, in part due to spiking illegal immigration into Europe in 2015–16. No doubt the Far Right existed in Europe long before Russia got into the game, but their recent successes have been fed, in part, by Russian propaganda, financial support, and actions in Syria, for instance, that have exacerbated the flow of migrants, or percep-tions of the harm they cause.[29]

TROJAN HORSES IN EU GOVERNANCE

While Russia's support for far-right parties and paramilitaries is surprising and attention-grabbing, given Russia's history with fascism, and has garnered much media attention, Russia also has sought to cultivate ties with mainstream and governing po-litical parties in Central and Eastern Europe, to develop sym-pathetic leaders and governments that it can use to fracture the EU from the inside. The most important case in this regard is Hungary, where President Putin has a close relationship with the authoritarian regime of Prime Minister Viktor Orbán, a power broker cut from the same cloth as those in the lands in between.

Orbán, who began his career as a democratic, anticommunist political activist, has made no secret of his Russophilia, which began suddenly in 2009 after a personal meeting between Putin and Orbán.[30] When he was elected prime minister in 2010,[31] Orbán promised an "Eastern winds" economic strategy that emphasized opportunities in the East as well as the West. While seeking to remain a player within the European Union, Orbán has pushed the boundaries of what the EU will accept from its CEE member states through his authoritarian constitutional changes, close relations with Russia, and frequent statements against the EU sanctions regime on Russia. As discussed earlier, the largest element of Orbán's relationship with Russia is in the energy sector, where Hungary seeks to become a key pipeline terminus and transit country, which would ensure a constant flow of transit revenues and politically controlled rents to grease the wheels of what Bálint Magyar calls the "post-communist mafia state" in Hungary.[32] But significantly, Russia also has coordinated policy with Hungary in Ukraine, where Hungary has a large minority population. Orbán used the Ukraine crisis to advance Hungary's own irredentist claims on a portion of Western Ukraine and support separatist Hungarian organizations, most likely with Russian support.

After campaigning to secure a Hungarian veto of EU sanctions on Russia, Russia realized that Hungary has a limited ability to openly defy the EU. It is a smaller, poorer EU member state that needs to remain in good standing in order to ensure the inflow of EU loans and structural funds, and to operate without discrimination within EU institutions. While Prime Minister Orbán has frequently spoken out against sanctions on Russia, vetoing important legislation in a transparent effort to help Russia could seriously jeopardize Hungary's standing within the EU. Therefore, Russia has tolerated and accepted the fact that weaker EU states like Hungary cannot veto Russia sanctions. Russia's response has been to cooperate with Hungary in more covert ways, for instance using its position within the EU to gain information about EU activities, or to develop contacts with other countries and politicians. Russia is taking a long-term approach, developing its assets and relationships and building, over time, opposition to EU and NATO membership. A good part of Hungary's help to Russia is covert, providing a home within the EU for Russian spies.

In 2017, a former Hungarian counterintelligence agent, Ferenc Katrein, gave a press interview in which he alleged that the Orbán government in Hungary was facilitating Russian intelligence operations against the EU. He claimed that the Orbán government first sought to obstruct Hungary's own counterintelligence operations against Russia by reassigning experienced agents and turning a blind eye to individuals suspected of espionage activities in Russian "state-owned or state-backed companies, airlines, travel agencies, cultural centers, educational institutions, and state-owned media." The former agent further accused the Hungarian government of not sharing information about Russian intelligence threats and support for far-right organizations with its NATO allies. He alleged that a "bond" program that allowed foreigners to buy Hungarian citizenship for a few hundred thousand dollars without proper background checks had enabled Russia and China to plant long-term illegal agents in the EU, with EU citizenship. Katrein stated unequivocally that Russia was fighting a secret intelligence war against the European Union that constituted a major threat, for instance "aggravating the migration crisis" by blowing up anti-immigrant sentiment to undermine EU leaders.[33] He described a campaign consisting of gathering information, deploying agents of influence, and spreading disinformation designed to harm the EU and popularize Russian narratives.

Hungary is perhaps the best-known example of an EU government's cooperation with the Russian government and intelligence services, but it is not alone. Some have claimed that the Czech prime minister, Andrej Babiš, has Russian business ties and point out that he frequently mouths a Russian foreign policy line, speaking out in favor of Russia's annexation of Crimea and against EU sanctions.[34]

Recruitment of political allies goes in tandem with efforts by the Russian security services to exert influence over state decisions. In its 2015 annual report, the Czech Security Information Service reported that "in 2015, Russian activities focused on the information war regarding the Ukrainian and Syrian conflicts and on political, scientific, technical and economic espionage." In its information war, Russia focused on "covert infiltration of Czech media and the Internet, massive production of Russian propaganda and disinformation controlled by the state," and "attempts to disrupt Czech-Polish relations, disinformation and alarming rumors defaming the US and NATO, [and] disinformation creating a virtual threat of a war with Russia." Russia also focused on "maintaining and strengthening Russian positions and outlooks in Czech power engineering" and other economic, scientific, and technological espionage.[35]

MEDIA INFLUENCE

Except in the Baltic republics of Estonia and Latvia, where there is a sizable Russian-speaking population, Russia cannot rely on Russian-language media to distribute its political messages in Central and Eastern Europe. People tend to receive their news from sources in their own local language. This has created stronger incentives for Russia to distribute its propaganda through far-right websites and news organizations linked with sympathetic oligarchs.

Russia has sought to undo the high public confidence in the EU in Central and Eastern Europe by popularizing its own anti-EU, anti-NATO, and anti-US narratives. The objective is to turn CEE populations away from the EU and NATO and prepare the way for these countries eventually to leave NATO. Russian propaganda often suggests that the United States is the puppeteer behind NATO and controls European politics without the assent of Europeans. It emphasizes the voices of Europeans who oppose sanctions against Russia, pointing out the economic costs of sanctions and speaking out against policies supposedly imposed on Europe by the United States. Russia argues that the sanctions are both unjustified and unlawful. Russian propaganda in Central and Eastern Europe also espouses pan-Slavism as a connection between Slavic nations of Central and Eastern Europe and Russia. One Slovak outlet quoted the chairman of the Russian State Duma, Vyacheslav Volodin, stating, "The West genetically despises Russia and basically all Slavic nations," raising images of Nazi race rhetoric to defame the West. Russian propaganda has also tried to convince Central Europeans that the United States is conspiring to sell

Europe expensive American gas, rather than cheap Russian gas. Another common theme has been to discredit Ukraine as much as possible, portraying it as aggressive, full of Nazis (when in fact Russia is a primary sponsor of the Far Right in Europe), and chaotic, unable to govern itself. These messages are spread from multiple sources, including extremist new sites, but also by mainstream politicians allied with Russia.[36]

Beyond spreading its propaganda narratives, Russia also promotes straight disinformation, for instance when one far-right Hungarian website spread the story that Hungary was exporting tanks to Ukraine during the Ukraine conflict. Most likely launched to make people believe that NATO was arming Ukraine and putting Hungary at risk, it proved not to be true, though it was picked up by mainstream news sites in the West during the height of the Ukraine crisis.

In the Baltic republics, a substantial Russian-speaking population gets much of its news directly from Russian sources, making it vulnerable to the alternative worldview promoted by the Kremlin, with its disinformation, falsification, and tight state control over the daily news narrative.

These narratives appeal also to a section of Central and East Europeans who, like their counterparts in the lands in between, do not want an either-or choice of Russia versus EU. With substantial historical ties with both East and West, there is popular support for good relations with both sides. In Hungary, for instance, in 2017, a majority of voters polled supported NATO membership for Hungary, but Vladimir Putin was more popular than Western leaders such as Angela Merkel. Nearly half of Czech respondents to a survey in 2016 believed that, notwithstanding strong support for Western institutions, Czechia should be somewhere in between West and East.[37] Many Central Europeans clearly see their countries as a bridge between East and West and thus have some sympathy for Russian narratives.

MILITARY INTERVENTIONS
AND THREATS

While many Russian influence techniques are designed to escape notice and not provoke the EU or NATO to view Russian intervention as a military threat requiring a response, Russia does threaten EU member states militarily. Russia has launched military interventions in countries that border on the EU (such as Ukraine and Moldova) and, through military exercises, penetrations of member state airspace, cyberattacks, and other means, also threatens EU member states, with a particular emphasis on the Baltic republics of Estonia, Latvia, and Lithuania.

The Baltic republics were formerly incorporated into the Soviet Union from 1940 to 1991, are geographically vulnerable, and have the greatest fear of Russian intervention. Their large Russian-speaking populations give Russia a potential excuse for intervention, particularly in Estonia and Latvia, where the Russian-speaking population reaches 25 and 35 percent respectively. Due to being part of the Soviet Union, the Baltic States' infrastructure is even more connected to Russia than that of other CEE member states of the EU. Estonia was subject to a Russian cyberwarfare attack in 2009 that shut down a number of government services, and an abduction in 2014 of one of its border guards, who was seized in Estonian territory and brought to Russia, where he was imprisoned. Russia has also confronted the Baltic republics over World War II memory, protesting the move of a statue commemorating the Soviet "liberation" of Estonia from the Nazi regime, which resulted in Estonia's incorporation into the USSR, an event that is not exactly remembered fondly in Estonia. Russian military exercises have regularly targeted the Baltic States by practicing a beach landing in the Baltic and placing missiles in Russia's Baltic enclave of Kaliningrad. Russia has also illegally penetrated Baltic airspace many times since the Ukraine crisis. Russian incursions into NATO airspace and dangerous overflights of NATO ships and airplanes have occurred at a rate of forty to fifty per year since 2014.[38]

Some speculate whether Russia might someday seek to invade the Baltic States, for instance the Russian-speaking enclave of Narva in Estonia. While the Baltic States are vulnerable, their status as NATO states makes it likely that an invasion would provoke a unified response, a major deterrent. While Russia often seeks more covert and deniable forms of influence, the threat of military intervention is keenly felt in CEE states that, while part of the EU, border on Russia or Belarus. Russian military threats also concern Poland, the largest CEE member state. One Russian exercise in 2009 simulated a tactical nuclear strike on Warsaw and subsequent invasion.[39]

POLARIZATION AND POWER BROKERS

Russia's hybrid war on CEE states that are already members of the European Union has a number of objectives. Russia seeks to sow conflict within the EU itself, end the sanctions regime, and produce a more pro-Russian EU while diminishing US influence. As a result, we can observe in Central and Eastern Europe some of the same political pathologies as in the lands in between. These include increasing polarization of political parties, increasing difficulty in forming centrist alliances, growing anti-EU and anti-NATO sentiment, growing influence of Russian narratives in political discourse, as well as campaigns of disinformation.

While Central and Eastern Europe previously enjoyed a very strong, cross-party consensus on European Union integration, this appears to be breaking down as a growing number of political leaders and parties advocate Euroskeptic and even pro-Russian positions. Extremist parties are emboldened and winning a growing number of seats in parliament. At the same time, we can also observe power brokers emerging who seek rewards from both the EU and Russia. These power brokers change positions over time, always seeking maximum advantage. They are far from ideological. One year, they may issue their country into NATO. Another year, they may acclaim the annexation of Crimea or seal a massive energy deal with Russia, most likely replete with massive kickbacks. While many regard these power brokers, such as Zeman or Orbán, as Russian agents, they likely do not wish to join the Russian empire, but rather to maximize their own political power and resources. They do not wish to break with the EU, but rather to continue to profit from the EU and Russia at the same time. Not all countries in Central and Eastern Europe have such power brokers at the helm. But they are becoming increasingly common in countries that everyone assumed had joined the Western world once and for all when they signed up for NATO and the EU in the 1990s and 2000s.

CONCLUSIONS

Russia has launched a comprehensive campaign to influence CEE member state governments within the EU. Its intent is clear—to destroy the EU from within by destabilizing and controlling CEE governments. CEE governments are, from the Russian perspective, the soft underbelly of the EU, since democracy and rule of law have weaker traditions there and Russia has stronger historical ties to these countries than to other EU states. Since CEE countries made their "civilization choice" and are now EU members, Russia faces considerable headwinds when trying to bring them back. Support for EU and NATO membership remains strong throughout Central and Eastern Europe, and EU institutions have mobilized to fight back to a much greater degree than in the lands in between. Yet, despite these difficulties, Russia continues to try to tear these countries away from the EU, realizing this might be a long game. Russia seeks to bribe mainstream politicians and to fund radical extremists who oppose the EU and voice controversial Russian foreign policy positions while toeing the line on Russian energy projects. It has targeted the information space by recruiting a wide range of outlets for its state propaganda and seizing on controversial issues such as migration. Where possible, Russia uses energy blackmail, cyberattacks, and the threat of military intervention to scare people into cooperation with Russia. Russian covert activities in the CEE new member states has reached or exceeded Cold War levels in order to develop various levers of influence—over energy businesses, fringe political parties, governing parties, criminal networks, and intelligence services.[40] Russia's campaign against the EU has contributed to a polarization of the political scene as well as to the rise of power brokers like Viktor Orbán in Hungary who seek rents from Russia in addition to the benefits of EU membership.

However, these strategies have their limits. As Russia learned when encouraging its Trojan horses to dismantle EU sanctions policy, CEE member states simply do not have the power to undermine strategic decisions of the EU taken by the EU Big Three: Britain, France, and Germany. For this reason, Russia has intensified its efforts to exert a strong influence on the politics of core member states of the European Union—and the United States.

CORE EUROPE AND

THE UNITED STATES

WHEN I BEGAN WORKING ON THIS book, I was under the impression that the types of Russian influence campaigns I was describing would only be possible in the weak and vulnerable countries between the EU and Russia or in new member states of the EU that had been part of the Soviet empire, where Russia had stronger links and greater leverage.[1] Despite researching and teaching about these issues for years, it never occurred to me that Russia would bring its hybrid war to the Western countries. Many analysts ignored the possibility that the lands in between were only training grounds for more ambitious Russian targets. The US presidential election of 2016 shattered this sense of invulnerability to Russia's covert destabilization. As policymakers and analysts, we should have been paying far more attention to what was going on in the lands in between and drawing the right lessons.

Now that the United States, Britain, France, Germany, and other Western countries face regular electoral attacks from Russia, threat perceptions have radically changed, and countries openly debate how to respond. While the tenor of this debate is often anxious, this discussion is part of a vigorous response to an unexpected challenge that may eventually enable the West to fight back with strong public support. Public debate on these issues is vital. It is hard for democracies to fight back against hybrid war techniques when people have underestimated the threat for so long and continue to do so. Waging a conflict against subversion inevitably entails sacrifices and, in a democracy, citizens need to have understanding and input into decisions on priorities and trade-offs. Public support is crucial to success in countering propaganda and election disruption.

With core Europe and the United States facing the same types of attacks that the lands in between have suffered for more than a decade, I will argue that this struggle has affected our politics in much the same way. We are increasingly experiencing the same politics of polarization and power brokers as the lands in between. These countries should no longer be perceived as exotic,[2] but rather as providing a vital—and unheeded—early warning of the challenges the West is now facing. Many aspects of the West's current politics could be better understood if we paid more attention to the lands in between.

In this chapter, I will spell out the threat posed by Russian covert influence in Western democracies while also demonstrating the resources and strategies by which the West is fighting back. While it is unfortunately true that the Western countries were initially surprised by and unprepared for a covert Russian onslaught, core Europe and the United States have many tools that can and will be deployed, including economic sanctions, energy diversification policies, and financial regulations against money laundering. The battle for the soul of the West is on and, while Russia has scored some impressive victories, it has also awakened determined opposition.

A COVERT CAMPAIGN

While Russian influence in core Europe and the United States is similar to what has been described in Central and Eastern

Europe and the lands in between, Russia lacks some forms of leverage over the more distant and powerful Western countries. For instance, Western countries are far less susceptible to gas and energy blackmail, as they are not contiguous with Russia or as reliant on Russian pipelines for gas imports in the winter. As a consequence, Russia has less ability to use gas deliveries as an instrument of geopolitics in the Western countries. Russia has had to work hard to build up the type of intelligence assets in Western countries that it has in the former Warsaw Pact nations or the former Soviet Union. It cannot rely on preexisting networks of cooperation to the same degree. Russia therefore has less ability to organize supportive paramilitary organizations in the West, though Russian fight clubs are present in Germany and the United States.[3] Russian businesses own a smaller proportion of the economy in developed Western countries and have less opportunity for economic leverage, though Russian ownership of substantial stakes in Facebook and Twitter has raised concerns.[4] As a result, the main avenues of Russian influence in core Europe and the United States have been via hearts and minds—distributing Russian narratives through fringe and mass media, spreading disinformation, mobilizing agents of influence, and supporting extremist, anti-EU political parties, leaders, and movements, such as France's National Front, Germany's Alliance for Germany, the Brexit campaign, and, of course, the presidential campaign of Donald Trump. The ultimate goal is to break up the Western alliance and its institutions. As Tim Snyder put it, "To support the [National Front] was to attack the European Union."[5]

In disbursing its media messages to the West, Russia has relied on foreign-language broadcast services, especially Russia Today (RT) and Sputnik. While this may not be clear to its viewers, both are Kremlin-controlled operations that put out news and disinformation carefully tailored by Russian intelligence services. Russia Today is also a conduit for Russian state payments to Western analysts and politicians who take a pro-Russian line. Former UK Independence Party leader and Brexit campaigner Nigel Farage, for instance, was a paid commentator for Russia Today. He has refused to disclose how much he was paid. Wikileaks head Julian Assange had a show on Russia Today and was, as a result, a paid employee of the Russian government. In countries where it operates, Russia Today has close connections to and amplifies the views of fringe politicians, normally on the far right, but also on the far left. Western politicians who appear regularly on Russia Today develop and articulate anti-EU positions, whether or not they held them before, and support controversial Russian foreign policies such as the annexation of Crimea. France's Prorussie television, a branch of Russia's Voice of Russia,[6] was closely connected to Marine Le Pen's National Front and frequently included National Front politicians in its news segment, making up for their infrequent appearances in mainstream news media.[7] In the United States, Russia Today has given airtime to the Libertarian and Green Parties, as well as other fringe politicians. During the 2016 US presidential election campaign, both Green Party candidate Jill Stein and Libertarian Party candidate Gary Johnson opposed US support for Ukraine and favored Brexit.[8] In sum, Russia Today seeks to mainstream fringe and extremist views that are anti-EU and anti-NATO or that will toe the Russian line on controversial foreign policy issues and polarize Western politics.

Whereas Russia Today looks and feels a lot like CNN in its production values, Russia's other foreign-language state media network, Sputnik, is more of a down-market conspiracy tabloid. It is at Sputnik radio that the Kremlin publishes sensational, whole-cloth fabrications, similar to what one finds in much of the Russian-language state-controlled media. Andrew Feinberg, a journalist who worked as Sputnik's White House correspondent before he quit, writes that "Sputnik's mission wasn't really to report the news as much as it was to push a narrative that would either sow doubts about situations that weren't flattering to Russia or its allies, or hurt the reputation of the United States and its allies."[9] For instance, Sputnik lead stories have included reports that the United States and UK sent chemical weapons to terrorists in Syria, according to the Syrian government. The rest of the news consists of mostly unfavorable stories about disasters and problems that occur in the United States or Europe, with heavy coverage of riots and floods. RT comments pages also provide a venue for far-right extremists. Andrew Feinberg reports that he was fired from Sputnik after refusing to promote the Seth Rich conspiracy theory at a time when Fox News had already repudiated the story. Seth Rich was a US campaign worker killed in a robbery; Fox News alleged that he was killed by Hillary Clinton in a grand conspiracy that was revealed as a hoax.

There has been a vigorous debate over the visibility and impact of these foreign-language propaganda networks. Some accounts suggest that RT's reach is rather limited, with 8 million viewers per week in the United States, for instance, and 70 million worldwide. However, others suggest that their broadcasts are amplified by a strong social media presence and their stories sometimes get picked up by other media outlets, especially those of the far-right and extremist media in countries worldwide.[10] In essence, these pseudo-news stations have become Kremlin tools for directing coverage on extremist websites worldwide. With them, the Kremlin can influence the news around the world, at least to some extent.[11] In addition, these networks create an opportunity for Russia to recruit and pay agents of influence, including Western politicians.

As part of the Russian media's broader purpose of spreading alternative narratives and propaganda messages, it also purveys politically targeted disinformation, most likely cooked up by Russian intelligence agencies to disrupt and polarize Western polities. One of the most prominent attacks was the "Lisa" case in Germany. At the height of the European refugee crisis in January 2016,[12] when the German government was facing public criticism for its lenient approach to admitting migrants, reports originating in Russia alleged that a group of migrants had kidnapped and gang-raped a German teenager of Russian origin. These reports were broadcast via social media to the Russian-speaking community in Germany, made up primarily of ethnic Germans who lived throughout the Soviet Union and left after 1991. Street protests, possibly organized by Russian intelligence operatives, then broke out in Germany; mainstream German media began to cover the story. However, a police investigation quickly discovered that "Lisa" had not been kidnapped or raped. Instead, she had run away from home for a few days to stay with a German boyfriend of Turkish origin. Yet even after German police announced the results of their investigation, Russian government officials, including Foreign Minister Sergei Lavrov, continued to insist that Germany strengthen its position on minorities and to allege that Russians were at risk in Germany. This latter point was highly confrontational, as Russia had excused its intervention in Ukraine and its designs on "Novorossiya" as an attempt to protect Russians abroad. Russia's creation, from whole cloth, of the "Lisa" case served to heighten tensions in Germany at the peak of the refugee crisis, a difficult time for Chancellor Angela Merkel. It was easy to see why Russian intelligence focused on Merkel: she was the linchpin behind European Union sanctions against Russia. It was Merkel who decided that Putin was "on another planet" as far as his intervention in Ukraine was concerned and moved Germany from supporting a "modernization partnership" with Russia to advocating a tough EU sanctions regime. The "Lisa" case was clearly a Russian intelligence operation pursued in part through media disinformation to attack a Western politician supportive of Russia sanctions.

Germany has not been the only target. Similar cases of disinformation have popped up in multiple Western countries. In August 2017, a fake *Guardian* (UK) news article appeared on a website that had an address and look similar to that of the official *Guardian* page. It was clearly written by a nonnative and made a number of errors characteristic of a literal translation of Russian. The fake article purported to quote former British MI6 head Sir John Scarlett as admitting that British and American intelligence agencies had organized Georgia's Rose Revolution in 2003 as part of a broader, but failed, effort to cause Russia to disintegrate. This clearly served to bolster Russian propaganda messages at home, as articles citing this fake *Guardian* article were distributed widely in Russia. It fit with a number of Russian propaganda narratives. The Russian government constantly tries to frighten Russians into believing that the West is out to get Russia, that domestic prodemocracy protests originate in and are paid for by the West, and that the West is planning a color revolution in Russia to undermine the Putin regime. In trying to show prodemocracy movements to be unpatriotic, it seeks to head off an existential threat to the Putin regime that it perceives from the West's support for democratization.

In a more bizarre and seemingly inexplicable instance of Russian disinformation, on September 11, 2014, Russian intelligence organized a social media campaign to spread rumors of what turned out to be a fake explosion at a chemical plant in Louisiana. Russian Twitter bots distributed fake news stories of an explosion at the Columbian Chemicals plant in Centerville, Louisiana, accompanied by a fake YouTube video purporting to show a man watching a TV news report stating that ISIS had claimed responsibility. People in the area received texts stating, "Toxic fume hazard warning in this area until 1:30 PM." According to the *New York Times*, "Dozens of journalists, media outlets and politicians, from Louisiana to New York City, found their Twitter accounts inundated with messages about the disaster." An investigative report found that this cyber-attack and others—including reports of an Ebola outbreak in Atlanta—were ginned up by a "troll factory" in St. Petersburg, Russia, where hundreds of paid trolls regularly used social media to conduct information warfare against the United States. This may have been a precursor to Russian intervention in the 2016 presidential election, or an exercise that allowed Russian intelligence to hone their techniques in destabilizing polities, sowing confusion, and spreading fake information, particularly during a crisis.[13]

A core mission of Russia Today and other Russian media is to foster anti-Western conspiracy theories, for instance that the 9/11 attacks were an "inside job."[14] Russia does this to undermine faith in government in the West and to turn as many of its viewers as possible against the EU, NATO, and the Western international system. It seeks to achieve this goal in foreign countries and to provide "a televisual home for disaffected viewers in the west." Any possible source of disaffection is encouraged. Russia Today, for instance, initially built its reputation by covering the Occupy Wall Street protests. Tearing down the West also serves to build up Russia. As one *New Statesman* journalist in the UK concluded, the Russian government "funds RT to persuade everyone else that their own countries are no better" than Russia.[15] Russia hopes that by doing so, people will regard Russia as a normal country, not a deeply defective authoritarian state. It is not clear that this campaign is working, however, as public opinion polls show Russia to be deeply unpopular in the world, as its tactics become known.[16]

HACKING ELECTIONS

Awareness of Russia's tactics has grown exponentially since the US presidential elections of 2016, when the world learned of Russia's expertise in hacking and influencing elections by electronic means. Russia's cyberwar on democratic elections has been going on at least since 2004, when Russia hacked the Central Election Commission of Ukraine to produce a fake victory for candidate Viktor Yanukovich.[17] While Russia did not, in the end, seek to falsify the election results directly in the United States in 2016, it did infiltrate voter systems in a majority of US states, giving it the capability to do so.[18] Instead, Russia concentrated on paying for and equipping Twitter bots with the ability to quickly disseminate fanciful fake news reports originating from Russian or conservative media, as well as using its intelligence services to hack and disseminate opponents' emails at maximally embarrassing times. These tactics were deployed in the US presidential campaign in 2016 and in other Western countries.

For instance in the French presidential election of 2017, Russia openly supported far-right candidate Marine Le Pen. Le Pen won the largest share of votes in the first round of the election, only to fall to challenger Emmanuel Macron by a wide margin in the second round. Nonetheless, Russia had high hopes for Marine Le Pen. Russian banks lent her party 9 million euros for the presidential campaign,[19] and, in exchange, Marine Le Pen made a high-profile visit to the Kremlin during the height of the election campaign. She repeatedly emphasized her support for key Russia foreign policy goals, such as the annexation of Crimea. Le Pen had previously visited Russia in 2014 and 2015, even taking a side trip to Crimea. She has long supported replacing the EU with a nationalist great-power alliance including France and Russia.[20] Le Pen was also a prominent supporter of Donald Trump. and her overtures were rewarded when many of the same Twitter bots that supported Trump in the United States came to life again to support Le Pen in the 2017 French election.[21] As in the United States, during the 2017 presidential election campaign in France, Russian hackers stole

Le Pen opponent Emmanuel Macron's emails and dumped them on Wikileaks. Wikileaks has cooperated closely with Russian intelligence agencies in recent years, and Wikileaks founder Julian Assange has been an employee of the Russian state, a paid TV host on Russia Today.[22] During the election campaign and after, victorious candidate Emmanuel Macron denounced Russia Today and Sputnik as Russian propaganda channels whose "agents of influence" spread "falsehoods" about him. He made headlines when he refused to accredit RT and Sputnik "journalists" to his presidential campaign and when he denounced their activity after the election at a press conference with Vladimir Putin.[23] Even though Macron's emails were dumped a day before the final round of the election on Wikileaks, they had little impact since they revealed no serious scandals. Macron, it seems, was clean.

Another potentially damaging Russian hacking attack took place in Germany in May 2015 in the German Bundestag, as its parliament is called. The Russian hacker group "Fancy Bear," associated with Russian military intelligence, successfully phished and broke into the email accounts of several German parliamentarians using fake look-alike websites, eventually taking over five of six administrator accounts of the Bundestag. Russian hackers then copied whole computers and roamed at will throughout the German parliament's systems until the hack was discovered some two weeks later. It turned out that the German parliamentary system was far less well guarded than that of the executive branch, which had protection in place to prevent such an attack. It remains unclear what files the hackers stole, but the German intelligence service believed that the most damaging information would be leaked during the 2017 parliamentary election campaign, when the ruling Christian Democrats and Chancellor Angela Merkel, who took a tough line on Russia sanctions, were up for re-election. However, while Russia supported the far-right Alliance for

Germany party, which nearly tripled its percentage of the vote from 4.7 to 12.6 to become Germany's third largest party, in the end Russia abstained from dumping stolen information against the Christian Democrats, perhaps because of the negative publicity from previous attacks or threats of a proactive defense by German intelligence.[24]

The November 2016 presidential election in the United States and subsequent investigations shone a light on Russian electoral hacking. Candidate Hillary Clinton called Donald Trump Putin's "puppet" during a televised debate on October 19, 2016.[25] On July 27, Donald Trump had invited the Russian government to release Hillary Clinton's emails in a talk broadcast on national TV. He said, "Russia, if you're listening, I hope you're able to find the 30,000 emails that are missing. . . . I think you will probably be rewarded mightily by our press."[26] When hacked Democratic emails were dumped on Wikileaks, it was presumed that Russia had played a role, and the hacked emails received extensive media coverage. In addition, Russian trolls had a strong presence on US social media, attacking commentators they disliked and promoting fake news, often created by Russian media and broadcast to the world via US fringe websites and conservative and far-right media. Revelations after the election that the Trump campaign may have coordinated some aspects of this campaign with Russian intelligence services led to FBI and congressional investigations. President Trump then fired FBI director James Comey and the Justice Department appointed Special Counsel Robert Mueller to investigate further. It was alleged that key Trump advisers, including Paul Manafort, Trump's campaign chairman, met to arrange Russian assistance to the campaign in exchange for promises to drop US sanctions. In this manner, the world became fully aware of Russian attempts to influence the US presidential elections and Russia's modus operandi in countries around the world, including in Europe.[27]

Russia has also sought to influence elections through more standard means, such as campaign contributions. For instance,[28] a number of reports have suggested that Russia had a hand in financing the Brexit campaign, which did significant damage to the EU, removing a key military and economic power from the EU and plunging it into political and economic crisis. Nigel Farage, the UKIP leader who was the most visible Brexit campaigner, has long been a paid commentator for Russia Today, earning a paycheck from the Russian government.[29] At a time when few British outlets carried his interviews, Russia Today gave him valuable airtime. At the same time, Farage began mouthing Kremlin talking points on foreign policy, notably supporting the Crimea annexation and also making positive statements about the strong leadership of President Putin. Apparently, this media cooperation flourished into something greater. One of the key funders of the Brexit campaign, Arron Banks, allegedly has business connections with Russia and may have channeled Russian funds to the Brexit campaign.[30] UK political finance laws ban foreign entities from donating to political campaigns, but allow UK companies to do so. Therefore, Russian entities seeking to donate to the Brexit campaign may have used proxy companies, including those related to Arron Banks.[31] Another top aide of Nigel Farage, George Cottrell, was arrested in an FBI sting operation in Chicago in 2017 and convicted by a US court of money laundering.[32] Given that Brexit financier Arron Banks accompanied Farage when he became the first foreign official to meet with Donald Trump after his election, questions have been raised whether Farage and his associates had a role in financing the Trump election campaign, which has been dogged with allegations of collusion with Russian intelligence services. Trolls from Russia's infamous Internet Research Agency tweeted on behalf of Brexit, creating a large portion of the Brexit discussion on Twitter. "Britons who considered their choices had no idea at the time that they were reading material disseminated by bots, nor that the bots were part of a Russian foreign policy to weaken their country."[33]

SUPPORT FOR THE EXTREMES

In order to further polarize politics in core Europe and the United States and render democratic political systems dysfunctional, Russia has supported a wide variety of extremist parties and paramilitary organizations on the far right, but also on the far left. Russia has supported separatist groups in Western countries, extremist paramilitaries, and fight clubs, in addition to using its intelligence agencies to develop political and business networks with a pro-Russian emphasis. This mirrors operations in Central and Eastern Europe and the lands in between.

Key to this effort is Russia's material support for far-right parties and movements in Europe and the United States. In addition to the case of the French National Front mentioned earlier, Russia has supported Jobbik in Hungary, a neofascist movement. One of Jobbik's European parliamentarians has been accused of channeling Russian funds to the party and being a Russian agent.[34] Russia has funded Golden Dawn in Greece, a neofascist party, and Ataka in Bulgaria. Ataka, a small anti-EU party, joined the pro-EU coalition government in Bulgaria in 2017.[35] During the 2017 elections in Germany, Russian social media supported the Alliance for Germany, the first far-right party to win election to the German parliament in the postwar era. Austria's far-right Freedom Party openly concluded a partnership agreement with Putin's United Russia Party in 2016.[36] Russia's support for the Far Right in Europe is designed to draw voters away from mainstream parties, undermine political support for the EU, win a voice for Russian foreign policy views in European parliaments, distribute Russian propaganda, and sow dissent, causing or exacerbating crises.[37] To the extent that extremist parties win seats in parliament, mainstream parties face greater difficulties forming governments.

In addition, Russia has gone further, establishing pro-Russia paramilitary organizations in Western states. A Germany-based researcher found that the Russian military intelligence (GRU) service had organized sixty-three "systema" fight clubs across the EU and North America, teaching Russian hand-to-hand combat methods. The founders of these clubs were all GRU or FSB (the Russian federal security service) agents. He alleged that these clubs were being used to recruit agents in sleeper cells that could be used to stage violent provocations. An Estonian intelligence agent pointed out that Russia has gone beyond media influence operations to organize protests, noting that the International Convention of German-Russians organized a protest of some seven hundred people in front of German chancellor Angela Merkel's office, coordinated with the "Lisa" case disinformation.[38] Relatedly, Mark Galeotti, an American expert on Russian intelligence operations, issued a report alleging that the "highly criminalized" Russian state was occasionally using Russian crime organizations to carry out intelligence work throughout Western nations. He advised Western states to crack down on Russian criminal networks and view them as instruments of the Russian state, noting that prominent Russian underworld financier Simon Mogilevich continues to live and work openly in Russia.[39] Timothy Snyder writes that "Russia's support of the NRA resembled its support of right-wing paramilitaries in Hungary, Slovakia, and the Czech Republic," noting that the NRA complained that the United States took too soft a line on Russia through 2015, until it accepted Russian financial support.[40]

Russia has also frequently supported secessionist movements in Western states, in order to create political crises and weaken democratic polities through internal dissent. In the United States, the California secession movement, launched during the Trump election campaign in an effort to sow discord in America by detaching a pro-Hillary state, has well-documented ties to Russia. The founder of California Yes, Louis Marinelli, is a right-wing activist (though the movement is avowedly leftist) who is based in Yekaterinburg, Russia, has a Russian wife, and opened a Russian "embassy" for his organization with Russian financing. He has spent more time living in Russia than California.[41] Shortly after the election, Marinelli closed down California Yes and returned to Russia.[42] He admitted to receiving office space and travel expenses from a far-right Russian group.[43] Russian support for "Calexit" should give one pause to consider what Russia's attitude was to Brexit from the European Union. In 2018, the head of the German intelligence service BfV (Bundesamt für Verfassungsschutz) stated that it was "very plausible" that Russia had carried out a disinformation campaign in Spain in 2017 to encourage voters to support Catalan independence.[44]

LEVERAGING BUSINESS TIES

In addition, Russia has financed and built networks of ties with mainstream political parties in Europe, such as the French Republicans, the British Conservative Party, and the German Social Democrats and the Left (Die Linke). In several European countries, Russia has worked through associations designed to support Russo-German cooperation, using these as a platform for developing relations with Russia-friendly corporate leaders and politicians. In Germany, these include the German-Russian Forum and the Petersburg Dialog, funded mainly by the German foreign ministry. Russia uses these organizations to develop supporters at the top level of German industry, people who have strong business ties with Russia and can influence German and EU policy against sanctions and in favor of continued engagement. "While post-Soviet Russia was weak, these institutions were mostly seen as a way of transferring western values east. But now, their critics view them as channels of Russian influence into Germany."[45]

In a 2017 Atlantic Council report, Steffan Meister showed that the Eastern Committee of Germany's powerful business lobby "continues to try to influence decision makers to alter their position on Russia," organizing a trip to Moscow in 2016 "to give representatives of leading German companies the opportunity to meet with Putin and hear arguments for the improvement of relations through a common economic space and the lifting of sanctions." In France, where the far-left, far-right, and center-right Republicans all support closer relations with Russia, the business community has led the way. Analyst Marilyn Laruelle writes that "many chief executive officers (CEOs) of these big industrial groups have close connections to the Kremlin's inner circle and have been acting as intermediaries of Russian interests and worldviews for the Republicans." French businesses have developed close ties in "the defense industry (Thales, Dassault, Alstom), the energy sector (Total, Areva, Gaz de France), the food and luxury industry (Danone, Leroy-Merlin, Auchan, Yves Rocher, Bonduelle), the transport industry (Vinci, Renault), and the banking system (Société Générale)."[46] Laruelle argues that, at least for the center right, France's alignment with Moscow should be understood in the Gaullist tradition of balancing between the United States and Russia. Likewise, the German Social Democrats have long supported an "Ostpolitik" of rapprochement with Russia. In the United States, Russian intelligence has tried to develop support among the think tank community in Washington, DC, recruiting individuals and institutions to support a Russian foreign policy line, as well as cultivating support among business leaders.

As a result of these ties, European countries always seem to be one election away from electing a pro-Russian government that would significantly alter EU positions toward Russia, starting with the sanctions regime. Russia has become a fundamental issue, with French president Emmanuel Macron taking a tough stance during his successful bid for the presidency in 2016, accusing Russia of undermining his campaign through its state propaganda stations and speaking out against the pro-Russia stances of the far-right National Front, far-left candidate Jean-Luc Melenchon, and mainstream Republicans. In the 2017 German elections, Chancellor Angela Merkel's Christian Democratic Union was weakened by the Russian-supported Alternative for Germany, a far-right party with strong sympathies with the authoritarian Russian president and strong support among German's Russian-speaking minority.[47] Interestingly, politicians critical of Russia and supportive of the sanctions regime have won elections in France and Germany in recent years. However, it is uncertain whether this will continue to be the case indefinitely. At some point, Russia's campaign of influence and alignment may come to fruition through the election of a government in a major European country that will have the power to reverse the sanctions regime. The electoral success of the Five-Star Movement in Italy, whose leader, Beppe Grillo, once a critic of authoritarian Russia, has become a vocal supporter of Putin's policies, could be a precursor of such changes.[48] The entry of the Austrian Freedom Party into government after October 2017 elections in which it won 26 percent of the vote may also be a sign of things to come.

MILITARY THREATS

Russia's interventions include not only support for mainstream and fringe political parties and movements and the dissemination of Kremlin propaganda and disinformation, but the threat of military force against Western countries. Starting in 2010, Russia declared the Western countries to be the primary source of "military dangers" in its official military security doctrine, in a move that puzzled EU countries that had been trying to develop a partnership with Russia. Russia also increased unauthorized overflights of NATO airspace, particularly in the Baltic States. Reports count some thirty-nine unauthorized overflights in 2014 and 50 in 2015.[49] Russia has also attempted overflights of US and Canadian and British airspace, timed to political events. For instance, Russia flew close to Canadian airspace during the visit of Ukrainian president Petro Poroshenko in 2014, sent bombers close to American airspace in 2015, and simulated an attack on Denmark in 2014.[50] In 2014, a Russian submarine was sighted in Swedish waters.[51] Russian officials have also reminded their Western counterparts of the possibility of nuclear war, threatening to aim nuclear weapons at Danish ships should the country join NATO's missile defense shield and to retaliate with nuclear force over an attack on Crimea or Kaliningrad, Russia's Baltic territory.[52] Russian military jets were intercepted 110 times in 2016 by NATO jets for violating NATO airspace.[53] Even this brief summary suggests that Russia couples its influence campaign in Europe with provocative military measures and rhetoric designed in ensure that Western countries fear Russia.

IMPACT

While the nature and extent of Russian influence in core Europe and the United States has become clear in recent years, what effect has it had on politics in these countries? Some have argued that the effects are sometimes the opposite of what is expected. For instance, in Ukraine, Russia's annexation of Crimea created a pro-EU consensus in the country. Thomas Risse and Nelli Babayan argue that in some cases, "efforts by illiberal regimes [to oppose democracy] have the counterintuitive effect of fostering democracy by strengthening democratic elites and civil society."[54] I argue that the main effects of Russia's hybrid war on core Europe and the United States have been similar to those in the lands in between. They have helped to create a new politics of polarization and power brokers.

As in lands in between, Russian intervention has become a key issue in democratic elections in the West. A discourse about "civilization choice" is growing in the West. In 2018, President Macron spoke of a "European civil war" between forces of liberal democracy and authoritarian nationalism. "We are seeing authoritarianism all around us. . . . In these times European democracy is our best chance. . . . I don't want to be part of a generation of sleepwalkers, a generation that has forgotten its past. . . . I will not give in to any kind of fixation on authoritarianism. . . . I want to belong to a generation that will defend European sovereignty because we fought to attain it."[55] Echoing these sentiments, outgoing US National Security Council director H. R. McMaster gave a parting warning about Russia in 2018 when he said that the West is "engaged in a fundamental contest between our free and open societies and closed and repressive systems," and that "revisionist and repressive powers are attempting to undermine our values, our institutions, and our way of life." He also claimed that the United States had failed to be tough enough in addressing these challenges.[56] What are these statements if not an articulation of a civilizational choice facing Western democracies?—as the lands in between faced years before.

Indeed, Western politics at each election seems to be posed with a choice between authoritarianism and democracy, between free markets and crony capitalism, between the quest for truth and reliance on propaganda. US president Barack Obama told the UN General Assembly in 2016 that the world faces a stark and urgent choice between democracy and the lure of populist demagogues, xenophobia, and division.[57] In most Western countries, political parties now divide sharply along these lines, with distinct views on both sides of whether the West should continue to support the liberal international system or a new system based on great-power politics, allegiance to prominent power brokers, and nationalism.

Russian support for extremist parties in the West also has led to a polarization of the political system, as in the lands in between. Germany is one example. Mainstream parties are losing support while Russia-supported far-left and far-right parties rise. This weakens the pro-EU center of the political spectrum and enhances the power of the anti-EU parties, which seek to do away with the key institutions of the liberal international order, democratic checks and balances, NATO, and the European Union. Italy provides another example. The success of the Five Star Movement and Liga in the 2018 parliamentary elections made it difficult to form a coalition government because mainstream parties were sidelined and extremist parties had trouble agreeing with one another's extreme positions on issues such as how to behave within the EU. Polarization makes coalition politics and government formation harder and threatens the stability and democratic character of Western countries.

A third manner in which politics in the West mirrors the lands in between is that Russian intervention has elevated oligarchs and power brokers who seek to profit both from Russia and the West, taking rents from both sides.

A key example is President Donald Trump. Trump rose to power in part by mobilizing resources gained from the Russian government, which has a vendetta against the West. Trump properties have relied heavily on Russian money, often purchased through shell companies.[58] A *New Republic* article called Trump at least "a convenient patsy for Russian oligarchs and mobsters," implying that he may have had direct knowledge that condos in his buildings were being used to launder money from Russian mafia figures.[59] Trump's presidential campaign benefited from substantial Russia support, including the purchase of Facebook ads. In exchange, he has campaigned for an end to sanctions, tried to get Russia reinstated to the G7, and sought to develop business opportunities in Moscow. These efforts should be seen as an attempt to cooperate with Russia for mutual economic benefit, with corrupt rents accruing to the ruling family, a familiar pattern that Russia cultivated, for instance, with Silvio Berlusconi of Italy and many business leaders in Europe. Were Trump not constrained by Congress, which has acted to prevent him from removing sanctions, he would most likely pursue this role as a broker between Russian and US business interests, with his family as the key beneficiaries.

As a result, politics in core Europe and the United States now reflects the pathologies of politics in the lands in between. Increasingly, all countries in Europe and North America occupy a zone of insecurity between a resurgent Russia and an embattled West. All developed Western countries face a "civilization choice" between a liberal international order fraying at the edges and a brave new world of xenophobic nationalism and great-power order, between free markets and rule of law or crony capitalism and oligarchic rule. Elections have become referenda on authoritarian nationalism and Russian influence. Political parties are shifting and polarizing along these lines. And in all Western countries, power brokers are emerging to take advantage of the business opportunities presented by this new politics of polarization and civilizational choice. The intensity of this conflict remains far higher in the lands in between, where these issues are hotter due to shooting wars, occupations, and provocations by Russia. But the reality of governance under hybrid war is here. In the lands in between, we can see the future of Western politics, a dystopia of division.

FIGHTING BACK

Nonetheless, Western countries, after failing to react and then being blindsided by Russia's assault on their institutions, have begun to fight back. As discussed in chapter two, the United States, EU, and other Western countries voted to impose damaging economic sanctions on Russia after 2014, sanctions Russia is desperate to remove. Intelligence services and law enforcement agencies have begun to investigate and monitor Russian subversion of elections and the information space. The EU launched a counterpropaganda agency to debunk Russian propaganda and fake news. President Macron, after his election, called the Russian president out directly, in person, for attacking him through Russia's propaganda networks and hacking operations. Public opinion polling shows a sharp drop in support for Russia and a big upswing for the EU after the Brexit vote, indicating a resilience of Western international institutions. So, despite the tough challenges previously discussed, there have been responses. But will this be enough? Or is it too little too late? The following chapter will ask what more is to be done. While there is much reason to despair, the good news is that Russia's strategy of division thrives by encouraging inaction in the West. With even modest action, the West can confront these challenges effectively.

THE NEW POLITICS

OF HYBRID WAR

AT ITS HEART, THE STRUGGLE between Russia and the West is a struggle for Europe. On the one hand, the Western powers wish to pursue the project of a European Union Europe: a vision of democratically governed nation-states coming together in a union that renders conflict unthinkable and promotes prosperity through free trade and common regulation. On the other hand, a revisionist Russia wants to create a great-power Europe: a Europe in which Russia and other European powers are accorded rightful spheres of influence and meet periodically to resolve European issues through summit negotiations. Such a great-power Europe would provide Russia with renewed influence in its "near abroad," and give Russia a seat at the table that it feels it has been lacking in European affairs. The problem is that these visions are fundamentally incompatible. Historian Tim Snyder calls this a "difference between a Europe of empire and a Europe of integration."[1] As a result of these two competing projects, European affairs are characterized by a new confrontation between Russia and the West that some have compared to the Cold War.[2] But this is not like the Cold War.

In the Cold War, an agreement was reached at Yalta in 1945 on spheres of influence: one system on one side of the Iron Curtain and another system on the other. Each side threatened the other with nuclear weapons, but mutual assured destruction kept both sides in check and peace was maintained in Europe, though proxy wars were fought elsewhere. The current conflict does not respect borders. It is about the governance of the West as a whole and the lands in between. The West is not content to allow Russia to dominate its former Soviet neighbors, since the West wishes to export its vision of European peace. The West believes that the former Soviet countries' choice of alliance is a fundamental sovereign right. Meanwhile, Russia wants to dismantle the EU, which it regards as a geopolitical competitor, and undermine liberal democratic institutions at the national and international levels. Though fought largely through covert and indirect methods, and with limited use of force, this conflict threatens everyone on both sides of an emerging divide in Europe. It could be described, in former US ambassador to Russia Michael McFaul's words, as a move from "Cold War to Hot Peace."[3]

There are many theories of why this conflict has occurred. Some blame the West for the expansion of NATO and the enlargement of the EU, which frightened Russia into a hostile reaction.[4] Some say the United States and Europe humiliated Russia by treating it like a defeated power and expanding Western institutions after 1989 rather than developing new institutions that would include Russia in a new European security structure.[5] Others point to Russia's failure to accept its own postimperial situation after the collapse of the Soviet Union.[6] After Gorbachev declared an end to the Soviet empire, Russia and other successor states were plunged into a deep political, economic, and identity crisis. A few states, notably the Baltic States, managed to integrate successfully into EU Europe, but the rest failed, suffering massive damage to their economies and to their pride. Russia's revisionist hostility is a reaction to this internal crisis, a time of troubles, expressed in a time-honored tradition of imperial aggression. Others point to the incompatible geopolitical cultures of Russia and the West.[7]

While there are many theories of why this conflict has occurred, the proximate cause is easy to identify. It began with the ascension of Vladimir Putin to the presidency of Russia in 1999–2000. Hand-picked for the presidency by President Boris Yeltsin in 1999, Putin rejected Yeltsin's pro-Western foreign policies in favor of restoration of Soviet pride and tsarist nationalism.

At that time, in 2000, the first year of the new millennium, I happened to be working at the Moscow State University's Faculty of Public Administration, administering a technical assistance program for the US Department of State and teaching a course called Public Administration and Democracy. Moscow State University, Russia's greatest university, like other universities, had fallen to great depths during the 1990s. Professors had to work three or four jobs to make ends meet and had little time for research, the buildings were falling apart, and corruption had taken hold. To counter this, Putin began to plow money back into the universities and scientific research institutes that had been the pride of the Soviet era. One of the first projects undertaken at Moscow State University was to sandblast the outside of the landmark university building and burnish the symbols of Soviet pride, cleaning the massive crests of the CCCP on the four sides of the great tower and polishing the red star at its apex.[8] Putin sought to restore Russian pride in the Soviet legacy, even adopting the Soviet anthem as the new Russian anthem, but with new words.

Vladimir Putin called the collapse of the Soviet Union the greatest geopolitical catastrophe of the twentieth century.[9] In one of the defining moments of his career, he defended the KGB headquarters in East Germany from the type of sacking that befell the East German Stasi building. Upon coming to power in Russia as the successor to Yeltsin, he developed a popular but self-serving narrative about Russia and the West. He argued that the 1990s were a disastrous decade for Russia—and that the

West was largely to blame. Trying to impose Western capitalism and democratic governance led Russia to terrible results: a social and economic catastrophe of unimaginable proportions. Russia's economy declined to less than half its 1989 level of production.[10] Death rates skyrocketed by 50 percent, with male life expectancy falling by nearly ten years from sixty-six to fifty-seven, a collapse unprecedented in peacetime in any country of the world.[11] The 1990s were a bizarre time in Russia, with promises of prosperity and Western governance linked with an obvious growth of mafia activity, human trafficking, prostitution, and collapse of social institutions. Any country would be embarrassed and angry after what Russia endured in the 1990s.

While Western economists can be accused of being overly optimistic that neoliberal economic reforms would create a capitalist utopia in Russia, the West did not create the Communist system. Western politicians did not create the mass corruption, failed leadership, and lack of public sentiment that fueled terrible abuses of public trust. The West was not responsible for cutting Russians off from the rest of the world, resulting in limited understanding of how the world worked. Russian economists played a key role in designing and implementing programs such as voucher privatization. Russian businessmen and the Russian government developed the infamous "loans for shares" scheme that enabled President Yeltsin to win another term in office in exchange for transferring leading enterprises into the hands of oligarchs. Other transition countries, with similar Western-oriented economic programs, fared far better. Russia was, to a large extent, the author of its own fate.

Nonetheless, it was Putin's genius to turn Russia's anger and frustration over the transitions of the 1990s against the West. Putin offered Russians an opportunity to blame all their troubles on the West. And it was wildly popular. Blaming the West for Russia's failure to thrive in democratic governance or

market economics has become a core part of Kremlin propaganda and the worldview of the better part of the Russian population. As a corollary to this, Putin pined for a soft recreation
of the Soviet Union (or the tsarist empire). It seems that, from
the beginning of his rule, he sought to revive the Soviet system,
using many old techniques, values, approaches, and even per-
sonnel, with some updates derived from Russia's nationalist
and tsarist legacy.

GREAT-POWER VERSUS EU EUROPE

Russia's hybrid war on the West arises from its aspirations to
be a great power, and many have remarked on the fact that
Putin's geopolitical vision is reminiscent of the nineteenth century.[12] Yet few have spelled out what this means.[13] To get a little
into the history here, it appears that Putin's view of Russia's
relations with the West are modeled on the world of post-
Napoleonic Europe, in which the emissaries of the Russian
tsar sat together with those of the German and Austrian em-
perors and the French and British kings to arrange European
affairs in a series of "congresses," or meetings, to solve the
international crises of the day. Putin seems to aspire to be a
modern Metternich, the Austrian count and foreign minister
who created the Congress of Vienna and what later evolved
into the "Concert of Europe," or the "Congress system," which
kept the peace in Europe from 1815 to 1848. The reason is
simple. Whereas Russia will never be a core member of the
Western institutions and in particular the European Union—
it is not democratic and cannot tolerate either the legal culture
or the pooling of sovereignty required by the EU—it can be
a key player, if not first among equals, of a new great-power
Europe that fits its nationalist vision.

Russia's ideal is for the EU not to exist, or to be down-graded, and for the great powers of the European continent to manage affairs among themselves: Russia, Germany, France, and the UK, as independent nations. This is why Putin prefers the "Normandy format" as a mechanism to resolve the Ukraine conflict. He prefers to sit with the German chancellor and the French president rather than with representatives of the European Union as a whole. This is why Russian president Dmitry Medvedev in 2008 proposed a new security architecture for Europe, based on "indivisible security" for all countries in Europe, regardless of their bloc affiliations. The proposal was not to set up a new institution, but rather to declare respect for the rights and interests of all European states—indeed all states involved in European security—and agree to convene meetings when necessary to prevent conflict. Western leaders dismissed Medvedev's proposals as "vague, with uncertainty over whether the Russian president wanted to create a new institution or simply strengthen Moscow's means to oppose European security developments that it did not like."[14] In retrospect, one can see these proposals as being modeled on congress Europe, an arrangement in which the Christian great powers of the day—Russia, Prussia, Austria, France, and Britain—met periodically to address security challenges as they arose. They divided responsibilities and spheres of influence among themselves and prevented a major war for thirty years. In essence, this is what Medvedev proposed—a return to great-power concert, rather than the institutional structure and legal requirements of EU membership or the permanent alliance of NATO. In theory, every European country would have a voice. In reality, the great powers would decide. Sergei Karaganov, a senior Russian government strategist, spoke of the "idea of forming a club of great powers, which would be able, on a par with the UN, to make the world at least a little more manageable."[15]

The fundamental problem with Russia's vision of a great-power Europe is that most EU Europeans see it as a throwback to a nineteenth-century vision of international relations that catastrophically failed. While congress Europe kept the peace for thirty years, the structure collapsed after the democratic revolutions of 1848, and then, decisively, in World War I, when the complex balance of alliances between large and small powers in Europe imploded in the "war to end all wars." For most Europeans, great-power politics is and should be a thing of the past. By contrast, the Europe of NATO and the European Union has kept the peace in Europe for seventy years and still shows no signs of failing. Indeed, Western institutions were given new life after the end of the Cold War when a dozen or more countries of Eastern Europe, former satellites of the Soviet Union, clamored to enter the European Union and NATO. Eleven new member states were admitted to the EU in the 2000s, after having been previously admitted to NATO. An enlarged Europe confidently believed in the ability of its institutional structures to forge peace through economic integration, democratic governance, respect for internationally recognized borders, and minority rights.

With Russia proposing what it sees as a legitimate security arrangement and the West meeting it with a blank stare, Russia has sought to oppose EU Europe's efforts to expand its zone of influence by imposing its vision of world politics on the West. Russia has opposed the EU's efforts to integrate the lands in between and begun its own campaign to shape Europe and North America in its own image. Realizing that confronting the West directly through military tactics would fail, Russia launched a hybrid war on the West. It combined a political war on Western institutions with traditional wars and frozen conflicts in its near abroad. In this way, Russia sought to establish a sphere of influence in Europe, stem the advance of EU Europe, and disable its enemies from reacting forcefully.

NEW POLITICS OF POLARIZATION AND POWER BROKERS

Russia's hybrid war on the West has created serious problems for Western democracies. Russia's support for far-right and far-left parties has exacerbated political polarization. Of course, Russia did not create political extremism in the West, but by funding it and supporting it with media messaging, Russia has enhanced its challenges to mainstream politics. Growing extremism has made it more difficult for mainstream parties to form governments. Russia has planted divisive messages at the core of Western politics, aggravating the immigration crisis through its disinformation, as in the "Lisa" case, and feeding a wide range of divisions between races, ethnicities, and regions. In the small, vulnerable countries in between Russia and the EU, there is talk of "civilizational choice" between two worlds—one Eastern and autocratic and another Western and democratic. They have been living with this for some time.

While some mock the notion of civilizational choice, seeing it as a reflection of Samuel Huntington's controversial work on the "clash of civilizations,"[16] similar language has become increasingly evident in the new member states of the European Union and the West itself. President Macron of France has pointed to an emerging "European civil war" between the forces of liberal democracy and authoritarian nationalism. Each Western election in this hybrid war era has become a referendum on the future of democracy, as authoritarian nationalists compete for power on xenophobic nationalist and pro-Russian platforms. The fundamental institutions that structure European politics and security—the European Union and NATO—are under constant attack. As Timothy Snyder writes, we cannot take for granted the Western democratic institutions and, instead, must fight to preserve them again and again.[17] The experience of Hungary reminds us that Western democratic institutions remain fragile. They can break down and a new civilization could be born at any time.

Perception that countries face a civilizational choice heightens the stakes in politics and contributes to polarization. Political parties divide sharply into those that support the liberal international order and those that do not. The choice is stark. A party like the National Front wants to take France out of the European Union, while Macron sees France as a leader of EU Europe. This helps to explain why, even when the National Front candidate wins enough votes to enter the second round of the French presidential election, as Marine Le Pen did in 2017, voters on the right and the left combine to defeat the National Front. One can say that the most important aspect of politics is not right or left, but whether France stays in the European Union and remains a democracy and an open society.

Paradoxically though, many of the big winners in this polarized political context are power brokers who find a way to profit from both sides of this emerging civilizational divide. This requires enormous craftiness and high risk. Some might judge the task to be impossible. Liberal democrats and nationalist authoritarians are far apart from an ideological standpoint. Yet politicians who care about the here and now rather than ideologies have found ways to benefit from the politics of civilizational choice by mobilizing the resources of both sides.

For instance, Russia offers big rewards to politicians who cooperate, including preferential oil deals, real estate deals, media support, and funding for political campaigns. In the 2016 US presidential election, Russia sought a direct line into the Trump and Stein campaigns in order to defeat Hillary Clinton. Candidates proved happy to accept the material support Russia offered. Russian social media manipulation and hack and release attacks of sensitive information played an important role in the campaign.

At the same time, politicians who have been "bought" by Russia also seek material benefits from their relations with or continued membership in the West. Prime Minister Viktor Orbán, for instance, does not seek to depart from the European Union and join the Eurasian Economic Union. He wishes to enrich himself, his party, and his country with structural funds from the European Union at the same time as he turns Hungary into a hub for Russian gas exports to Europe and wins Russian financing for a nuclear power station. The point is to win from both sides. And strangely, in a polarized political environment, this is more possible than one might expect. Each side is so afraid of the inroads made by the other side, they are willing to pay more for the allegiance of an ally or potential ally in danger of developing ties with their rival. Small states understand these dynamics very well. Czechia celebrates the ability to take advantage of both sides in a conflict through a mythical literary hero: the Good Soldier Schweik. In Jaroslav Hašek's famous book, the seemingly dim-witted Schweik kowtows to the great powers of the day, joins the Austro-Hungarian army, hilariously mocks all commands, and, when the opportunity arises, defects to the Russian side to save his skin.[18]

Neither side wishes to lose allies to the other. Therefore both Russia and the West are willing to offer concessions when it seems possible that a country or its political leaders will switch to the other side. Politicians beyond ideology, concerned primarily with their own material interests, see only benefits in cooperating with both geopolitical rivals. It is not surprising to see leaders of small, vulnerable nations playing this game; this has been characteristic of the behavior of small states from time immemorial. Accommodating great powers has always been a necessity for states unable to anger powerful neighbors. It is more surprising to see this politics of polarization and power brokers take shape in large, successful states that are members of the European Union or core Western countries. Yet politics in the West today increasingly mirrors the contradictions of politics in the lands in between. Today, we are all vulnerable.

WHAT IS TO BE DONE?

The West is not defenseless. There are a number of steps that countries can take to reduce the threat of hybrid war. These include combating money laundering, responding to disinformation, and responding more aggressively to cyberattacks. The problem is that Western leaders have been blind to this threat for so long and, in many cases, remain unwilling to recognize it. We have been disabled from within. The good news is that the outlines of an effective response have become clear and remain within reach.

The most effective response to Russia's hybrid war would be to limit Russia's ability to use Western countries for money laundering. This has become a major issue in the UK recently in the conservative government's response to the Skripal attack, in which a former Russian agent and his daughter were subject to an attempted assassination in Salisbury using nerve agent. Russian oligarchs and government figures use London as a safe space to park their money. They transfer ill-gotten gains to bank accounts and funds based in London, buy expensive real estate, and send their kids to school in the UK. The same is true for other European capitals, but London is, by far, the first choice. The British government has begun to take actions, scrutinizing the sources of the money that Russian oligarchs have used to win UK "investor" visas.[19] In 2018, it refused to allow Roman Abramovich, the owner of the Chelsea football club, back into the country until it investigated his financial dealings. However, Britain and other Western countries overall have struggled with requiring greater transparency in financial transactions, such as banning shell companies from buying

real estate, or requiring companies to disclose their benefi-
cial owners. Until the West requires transparency in financial
transactions, foreign money laundering will continue to enable
foreign money to enter Western politics. Many experts agree
that tougher financial regulations are the first place to start. But
politically, this has proven difficult, as "UK governments have
shied away from hitting the moneyed Kremlin-linked interests
that, by an extraordinary coincidence, enrich a well-connected
stratum of UK-based bankers, accountants, solicitors, and estate agents."[20] However, political support is building in the UK
for taking a harder stance. In 2018, a British parliamentary
report titled "Moscow's Gold" concluded that "measures to
combat money laundering should therefore form a central aspect of Government strategy towards hostile regimes, including
that of President Putin."[21]

The West can also do more to confront Russian disinformation, propaganda, and information warfare. This is difficult in democratic societies where free flow of information is
a core principle. Most Western countries would face difficulties
banning Russian news sources like Russia Today or Sputnik,
though French president Emmanuel Macron did call them out
as "propaganda" outlets during his election campaign in 2017
and barred them from joining the regular press pool.[22] Baltic
states that have borne the brunt of this information warfare for
years have bolstered their own public information campaigns
in response. They have sought to inform the entire population
that they are subject to Russian disinformation campaigns and
to "emphasize media literacy and critical-thinking skills" in el-
ementary schools to "inoculate future citizens against misin-
formation."[23] Facebook has enacted a policy that political and
policy ads in the United States must now identify their source
in an effort to address the problem of Russian-funded disinformation spread in the 2016 US presidential election. In 2018,

Facebook began requiring that political advertisers verify their identity by producing government ID and disclosing their addresses.[24]

There are many more potential responses, including making it more difficult for anyone to hack into and disable public infrastructure, enabling critical infrastructure systems to get back online as quickly as possible after an attack, and enabling cyber defenders to wipe out attacking computer systems. Australia recently passed an important law aimed at safeguarding democratic elections from foreign interference.[25] The real problem is not that the West lacks defenses, but rather that Russia's hybrid war has succeeded in delaying and disabling these responses by sowing confusion in the West about the nature of Russia's hybrid war and paying off supporters to prevent a substantial Western response. If Western countries were to respond forcefully, there is much that can be done to blunt the impact of Russia's hybrid war.

Yet it is fair to assume that Russia's hybrid war on the West will be a feature of our politics for a long time to come. Relations between Russia and the West will not substantially improve without a change in government in Moscow. As a House of Lords report on EU-Russia relations noted, "The EU and Member States face a strategic question of whether Europe can be secure and prosperous if Russia continues to be governed as it is today."[26] Russia continues to believe that interfering with Western elections to promote pro-Russian politicians is a solution to its problem. Its campaign continues even though its obvious attempts to interfere with other countries' elections have produced a massive backlash against Russia in the West. The current regime in Moscow is committed to policies that are unacceptable to Western governments. Meanwhile the EU and NATO continue to insist that independent states bordering Russia have the right to join whatever economic and security organizations they choose and Russia does not have a legitimate right to veto membership for its neighbors in Western organizations. Russia cannot change the European Union's current strategy of integration. The most important question in EU-Russian relations today, then, is which will outlast the other: President Putin or the EU and NATO?

In this context, the EU and NATO have little choice but to confront Russia on issues where they strenuously disagree, while finding opportunities for engagement on other issues, such as counterterrorism and student exchange. As David Kramer put it, "Nobody wants war with Putin's regime, but calling for a strong stand against his egregious behavior is not tantamount to launching World War III. . . . [it] is not only necessary but also the right, moral thing to do."[27] Western institutions must develop techniques of opposing Russia's attempts to co-opt its business and political classes, as well as its information offensive, cyberwarfare, and other forms of hybrid war, in the hopes of enduring Russia's assault on the West's core institutions. And wait for a change of government in Moscow.

If engagement can occur under such circumstances, that would be desirable.[28] However, as chair of an academic department engaged in various cooperation projects with Russia, I observe steady deterioration. One of the universities we cooperate with, European University of St. Petersburg, was denied a license to teach in Russia in 2018 for political reasons and effectively shut down as a teaching institution, before being suddenly reinstated. Increasingly, we see US students choosing to study the Russian language outside of Russia, in part because of security concerns, but also because of the high cost of visas. Students who in past years would have studied in Russia now attend programs in the Baltic States or Central Asia. Engagement is becoming more difficult as the Russian regime further represses civil society.

AFTER PUTIN?

Some question whether Russian foreign policy will change after Putin and suggest that Russia's foreign policy could remain anti-Western or become more nationalistic still.[29] However, change is to be expected. Over the last century, every Russian leader has taken a different foreign policy approach, reflecting individual preferences. Gorbachev, Yeltsin, and Putin have had incomparable foreign policies, with the first two highly pro-Western and the latter anti-Western and aggressive. Soviet leaders also took very different foreign policy approaches. Think of the transition from Stalin to Khrushchev. As a result of the important role that individual leaders take in setting Russian foreign policy, it is very likely that any future president of Russia will take a different approach toward the West, changing from the hyper-aggressive stance of President Putin. This change is likely to lead toward moderation, since it is hard to imagine a Russian president embracing a more aggressive and warlike stance than what we have today.

Keep in mind too that Russia's political system suffers from fundamental weakness. There is no succession strategy. Russia today is a personalistic dictatorship. That means that when political change comes, it could lead to catastrophic instability. The Soviet regime had a system of leadership transition that, while not perfect, worked reasonably well. In the event of the death of a leader, the Politburo would choose a new leader from among its ranks. There were controversies and disagreements, but there was a clear and widely accepted process that determined who got to choose the new leader and how. In Putin's dictatorship, there is just Putin. No strategy, no policy on succession. Putin came to power because the previous president resigned early and appointed him to the office prior to an election, on the theory that people would vote for the incumbent. Will Putin follow the same strategy? Will he avoid leaving office at all costs, ultimately dying in office as his Soviet forebears did, or be ousted in a palace coup? President Putin is paranoid about the United States sponsoring a color revolution in Russia for a reason: he worries that he could be turned out in a wave of popular protest. Russia's political system is fundamentally unstable. While its centralization is a strength, it creates the ever present possibility of a descent into chaos, as Russia experienced in the 1990s.[30]

Which will go first, Putin or the EU and NATO? It is very possible that Russia's attempts to undermine Western institutions will succeed. With a wave of populist politics rising, coinciding with growing concerns about immigration, pro-Russia populists have scored significant victories in EU Europe. The most important has been Brexit, a major blow to the EU, the campaign for which may have been financed primarily by Russia. The victory of pro-Russia populists in Italy is another blow. It remains conceivable that the EU will break apart or, at least, radically change its policy on Russia. At the same time, some of the recent misfortunes of the EU, such as Brexit and the clash with Russia, have induced more unity in the EU. Public opinion polls show that, after Brexit, voters in other EU countries felt greater allegiance to the EU. In many countries, support for remaining in the EU has increased by 10–20 percent.[31] Similarly, EU member states have achieved a remarkable foreign policy unity on the issue of Russia, notwithstanding frequent critiques of the sanctions from Trojan horse governments within the EU.[32]

For the West, the key strategy must be to survive to play another day and deal with a different Russian government in ten, twenty, or thirty years. This will require the West to respond forcefully to Russian covert operations and cyberwarfare while avoiding a major military confrontation. The West will need to continue and even deepen economic sanctions, improve cyber defenses, bolster alliances, protect elections, and maintain open channels to the regime that would enable it to reach solutions if so desired. Most of all, it will require protecting the core institutions of the West. And waiting.

It does not make sense to actively pursue regime change in Russia. No regime that comes to power with Western assistance will be legitimate in Russia. It has been a mistake, in the past, for the United States to support particular candidates in Russian elections, as the United States did in Russia in 1996, supporting an extremely unpopular and incompetent Boris Yeltsin in a campaign against the Communist candidate Gennady Zyuganov.[33] It would arguably have been better to let the cards fall where they may in 1996 than to deal with the situation we face today. Russians need to make their own choices, their own mistakes, and to learn from them. The West should make its messages heard in Russia in defense of liberal values, in opposition to Russian aggression, in defiance of Putin's campaign against the EU, but it should not seek to influence democratic elections or the course of any palace coup. Russia will choose another leader, at another time.

Until that point, however, it must be recognized that confidence-building measures are unlikely to succeed. Since 2007, Russia has seen the West as a strategic danger. No amount of small confidence-building measures will cause the Putin regime to abandon that decision. The Obama-era reset—and the short Trump-era reset—accomplished little and has little prospect of success given the mindset of the Putin administration. The West needs to dig in and maintain a firm defense against Russian subversion. As the British House of Lords concluded in 2015, that starts with analysis. The West failed to notice Russia's hard opposition to the West for at least four years and stumbled into the current conflict. In part, this blindness results from a lack of qualified Russia analysts. For years, Western governments and academics regarded Russia as a country that could be ignored. Its compliance with Western rules and its second-class citizenship in Europe and the West, they believed, could be taken for granted. Western leaders still misunderstand Russian intentions and fail to recognize how determined the regime in Moscow is to undermine the West. In part, Russia's use of covert methods to achieve plausible deniability has worked. Better analysis is needed. Elites and the general public need to understand the high stakes in this conflict.

LOOKING IN THE MIRROR

But ultimately, the current struggle for Europe will not be won in Russia, but in the West itself. In the current marketplace of ideas, the West needs to work on bettering its own socioeconomic model and addressing some of the underlying reasons for discontent that Russia exploits. The rise of populism in the West is fueled by two sources. The first is a xenophobic anger at the others who, through trade or migration, are claimed to be "stealing our jobs" and changing our way of life. Second is the legacy of thirty years of neoliberal economic policy, which has reduced safety nets to a minimum, destroyed the consensus on full employment as an aim of policy, and made workers more vulnerable to a range of risks. Europe and the United States need to develop new policies to address problems in both of these areas, at the level of values and economic policy.

While populist parties portray nationalism as the answer to both problems, liberals need to address the challenge in the realm of economic policy. Economic policy is fundamental because, if workers felt more secure, they would be less likely to buy into xenophobia. What is needed is a revision of many of the neoliberal policies that the West has embraced for thirty years and greater emphasis on social protection and labor force activation, with the creation of works programs, a return of full employment as a key policy target, more job training, more day care, and more support for continuing education. Government needs to take a more active role in making sure the economy works for everyone; this is a key part of the populist challenge. In Europe, populist governments are clawing control back from foreign banks, initiating social welfare programs that guarantee a minimum income to various categories of people like young children and pensioners, while building domestic industries and a domestic capital class. In short, populists have stolen a good part of the old social democratic agenda. The EU, by contrast, has embraced austerity. This has been poisonous for European politics.[34]

In addition, Western societies have to rearticulate the values of political liberalism, equality before the law, protection of minorities, and the benefits of democracy, all values that are under attack. It may be a long struggle, but the West needs to put up a vigorous defense in the face of an onslaught from domestic populists and foreign spoilers. This war can be fought in the marketplace of ideas, as well as in economic policy. Ultimately, the West is challenged to demonstrate the superiority of its international system, its economic model, and its values.

Fighting this battle and maintaining a firm line on Russia, however, does not require that all relations with Russia should stop. It means recognizing that we cannot expect a change in the Kremlin's fundamental opposition to the West. Nonetheless, as usual, there can be areas of cooperation with Russia on shared foreign policy objectives, such as antiterrorism. People-to-people connections with Russia remain important to increasing understanding and setting the basis for future cooperation. Exchange programs, travel, and study abroad are worthwhile, since Russia eventually will change and it is primarily the highly centralized government that is responsible for current policies, not the people.[35] Russians love Europe and the West, where they vacation, and live, and work. Russian elites park their money in the West because they see it as safer than Russia, buy expensive European real estate because they like to spend their time in Europe, and send their children to school in Europe because they see it as an investment in the future. They wish to have expedited Schengen visas or, better yet, visa-free travel. Europe's attraction for Russia, as in the lands in between, is real and powerful. However, one cannot expect people-to-people measures to add up to a change in the Kremlin's policy of undermining the EU and the Western alliance. Policies of engagement have a long-term impact in building a European future after Putin.

Prior to a fundamental change in the Kremlin, most likely a leadership change, the future of EU-Russia relations will be marked by sanctions, continuing difficulty in managing relations with the lands in between, differences of opinion, frozen conflicts, and counterespionage. The West will defend its institutions that have worked for decades to ensure peace in Europe. Alternatively, Putin-friendly oligarchs will come to power and enrich themselves by participating in Russian business networks and corrupt special deals. Russia will stick with its anti-Western orientation and subversion. While economic sanctions surely hurt the West, they hurt Russia more. Eventually, we know not when, a government will come to power in Moscow that seeks to close this divide—at least a bit—and work toward greater peace and cooperation on the continent.

CAUGHT IN BETWEEN?

Until that time, Europe faces renewed tensions in its eastern borderlands. The lands in between remain burdened with the politics of civilizational choice. Many would prefer an independent existence in the world and chafe at being forced to choose between Russia and the EU. As one Opposition Bloc politician told me recently in Kiev when I asked to interview her for a book about the lands in between, "your title made me sad." Ukraine, she said, wanted to be its own independent country. Ideally, the lands in between would achieve a happy coexistence with both the European Union and Russia, charting an authentic pathway toward national development. Yet for now, this option is not on the table.

Instead, as with Ukraine in 2013, the lands in between face a stark choice of trying to leave the Russian empire behind and fighting for their independence or being reincorporated into Soviet Union 2.0. If they choose independence, they must follow the dictates of the European Union, engaging in a thorough transformation of their economies and governance to make them compatible with the rest of the continent. It is understandable that this appears to be a civilizational choice and both choices require them to surrender something important, if not essential.

It is no wonder that politics in the lands in between have become deeply polarized. Some groups in society advocate a beautiful future within the EU, one that may not be fully attainable due to Russia's opposition and downplaying the difficulties of economic transformation. Others believe everything will be simpler with Russia, with fewer demands, fewer transformations, but a constrained future with limited relations with the great economic engine of Europe and a fundamental loss of sovereignty. Given this deep polarization, these countries have fallen prey to their own oligarchs and power brokers, who eschew idealistic futures to concentrate on material gains in the present. What they have learned is that it is possible to profit from the dreams and aspirations of both sides. If the EU wants legislation and is willing to pay for development programs, they can pocket part of the money while pretending to pass laws. If Russia wants to broadcast its propaganda and subvert EU trade through smuggling, they can pocket a share while resisting Russian buyouts. The result is a tense and fearful politics dominated by power brokers seeking to profit in the moment and change sides when necessary in the future.

What I have learned from researching this book, from conducting interviews throughout the former Soviet space and Central and Eastern Europe over the course of almost ten years, is that the politics of the lands in between presages our own. While the West blithely ignored Russian influence for years, pretending that President Dmitry Medvedev represented a liberal Russian future, the same deep conflict was growing first in the new member states of the EU and, finally, in core Europe and the United States itself. Today, we too find ourselves vulnerable to false news stories spread by dubious social media accounts. We too find ourselves on the brink of civil war due to an extreme polarization of politics fostered by the rise of far-right parties. We too face a civilizational choice between whether we prefer to live in the liberal international order or subvert it in the name of nationalistic, great-power politics. We too find ourselves in the midst of a war between two conceptions of the international order—one Western and democratic, another Eastern and autocratic, one that adheres to a law-bound economy and another based on crony capitalist links between top leaders. We too find ourselves governed by oligarchs who find these debates about values amusing and prefer to enrich themselves while maneuvering between both sides.

In this battle to the finish, the stakes are very high indeed, "too high for both sides to back down," in the words of one analyst.[36] The challenge of our age is to fight this hybrid conflict while bolstering a liberal democratic civilization that is increasingly under threat.

We too are the lands in between.

NOTES

Chapter 1

1. "Plahotniuc Meets European Socialists and Democrats in Brussels," Crime Moldova, June 21, 2017, accessed February 19, 2018, at https://en.crimemoldova.com/news/politics/plahotniuc-meets-european-socialists-and-democrats-in-brussels/.
2. Josh Wilson, "Plahotniuc: For Stability or Authoritarianism," Geohistory, January 23, 2018, accessed May 3, 2018, at http://geohistory.today/moldovan-politics-vladimir-plahotniuc/.
3. "Offshoreplaha: How Plahotniuc Built His Empire," Crime Moldova, October 4, 2016, accessed May 3, 2018, at https://en.crimemoldova.com/news/investigation/offshoreplaha-how-plahotniuc-built-his-empire/.
4. Andrew Higgins, "Moldova Is Rattled as Washington Welcomes a Feared Tycoon," *New York Times*, June 3, 2016, accessed May 3, 2018, at https://www.nytimes.com/2016/06/04/world/europe/moldova-vlad-plahotniuc.html; Kamil Całus, "Moldova: From Oligarchic Pluralism to Plahotniuc's Hegemony," April 11, 2016, OSW, accessed May 3, 2018, at https://www.osw.waw.pl/en/publikacje/osw-commentary/2016-04-11/moldova-oligarchic-pluralism-to-plahotniucs-hegemony.

5. Mihai Popșoi, "Deconstructing Vlad Plahotniuc's Article in the Wall Street Journal," *Moldovan Politics*, January 24, 2018, accessed May 3, 2018, at https://moldovanpolitics.com/2018/01/24/deconcstructing-vlad-plahontiucs-article-in-the-wall-street-journal/.

6. Cristi Vlas, "MEP: Brussels Starts to See Vlad Plahotniuc as Part of the Solution, Not the Problem," May 7, 2016, Moldova.org, accessed February 19, 2018, at http://www.moldova.org/en/mep-bruxelles-starts-see-vlad-plahotniuc-part-solution-not-problem/.

7. Cristi Vlas, "President Timofti Rejected Vlad Plahotniuc as Candidate PM of Moldova," January 13, 2016, Moldova.org, accessed February 19, 2018, at http://www.moldova.org/en/president-timofti-rejected-vlad-plahotniuc-candidate-pm-moldova/.

8. Anna Maria Touma, "Moldovan President Ridiculed after Putin Joke," *Balkan Insight*, June 6, 2017, accessed February 21, 2018, at http://www.balkaninsight.com/en/article/moldovan-president-ridiculed-after-putin-joke-06-05-2017.

9. Kamil Całus, "Moldova's Odd Couple: Plahotniuc and Dodon," *New Eastern Europe*, June 1, 2017, accessed February 28, 2018, at http://neweasterneurope.eu/2017/06/01/moldova-s-odd-couple-plahotniuc-and-dodon/.

10. Popșoi, "Deconstructing Vlad Plahotniuc's Article."

11. Timothy Frye, "The Perils of Polarization: Economic Performance in the Postcommunist World," *World Politics* 54, no. 3 (2002): 308–37, analyzes polarization between former Communist and anti-Communist parties, rather than pro-Russian and pro-EU.

Chapter 2

1. "An Open Letter to the Obama Administration from Central and Eastern Europe," July 16, 2009, Radio Free Europe / Radio Liberty, accessed May 3, 2018, at https://www.rferl.org/a/An_Open_Letter_To_The_Obama_Administration_From_Central_And_Eastern_Europe/1778449.html.

2. David J. Kramer, *Back to Containment: Dealing with Putin's Regime* (Washington, DC: McCain Institute, 2017); Angela Stent,

The Limits of Partnership: U.S.-Russian Relations in the Twentieth Century (Princeton, NJ: Princeton University Press, 2015). Stent shows on p. 163 that President George W. Bush and his secretary of state, Condoleezza Rice, also believed that Medvedev could turn Russia in a liberal direction.

3. Katie Sanders, "Romney: Obama Stopped Missile Defense Shield as a 'Gift to Russia,'" Punditfact, March 23, 2014, accessed March 12, 2018, at http://www.politifact.com/punditfact/statements/2014/mar/23/mitt-romney/romney-obama-stopped-missile-defense-shield-gift-r/.

4. Martin Dangerfield, "Visegrad Group Cooperation and Russia," *Journal of Common Market Studies* 50, no. 6 (2012): 958–74.

5. Samuel Charap, "The Ghost of Hybrid War," *Survival* 57, no. 6 (2015): 52, states, "Western analysis gives the impression that Russia is already conducting hybrid war against the West. This is a dangerous misuse of the word 'war.'"

6. Steve Lee Myers, *The New Tsar: The Rise and Reign of Vladimir Putin* (New York: Vintage, 2015), 51.

7. Timothy Snyder, *The Road to Unfreedom: Russia, Europe, America* (New York: Tim Duggan Books, 2018).

8. Bobo Lo, *Russia and the New World Disorder* (London: Royal Institute of International Affairs and Washington, DC: Brookings Institution Press, 2015), 101.

9. David Satter, *The Less You Know, The Better You Sleep: Russia's Road to Terror and Dictatorship under Yeltsin and Putin* (New Haven, CT: Yale University Press, 2016), 163. See also Karen Dawisha, *Putin's Kleptocracy: Who Owns Russia?* (New York: Simon and Schuster, 2014); Garry Kasparov, *Winter Is Coming* (New York: Public Affairs, 2015); Janusz Bugajski, *Dismantling the West: Russia's Atlantic Agenda* (Washington, DC: Potomac Books, 2009); Marcel H. Van Herpen, *Putin's Wars: The Rise of Russia's New Imperialism*, 2nd ed. (Lanham, MD: Rowman and Littlefield, 2015).

10. Putin's responsibility for souring relations with the West is attested to by a number of excellent studies, including Kramer, *Back to Containment*; Lilia Shevtsova, *Putin's Russia*, rev. ed. (Washington, DC: Carnegie Endowment, 2010); Walter Laqueur, *Putinism: Russia and Its Future with the West*

(New York: Macmillan, 2015); Katherine Stoner and Michael McFaul, "Who Lost Russia (This Time)? Vladimir Putin," *Washington Quarterly* 38, no. 2 (2015): 167–87.

11. John J. Mearsheimer, "Why the Ukraine Crisis Is the West's Fault: The Liberal Delusions That Provoked Putin," *Foreign Affairs*, September–October 2014: 1–12; Joshua R. Itzkowitz Shifrinson, "Deal or No Deal? The End of the Cold War and the U.S. Offer to Limit NATO Expansion," *International Security* 40, no. 4 (Spring 2016): 7–44; Samuel Charap and Timothy Colton, *Everybody Loses: The Ukraine Crisis and the Ruinous Contest for Post-Soviet Eurasia* (New York: Routledge, 2017); Michael E. O'Hanlon, *Beyond NATO: A New Security Architecture for Eastern Europe* (Washington, DC: Brookings Institution Press, July 28, 2017); James Dobbins and Andrei Zagorski, "Lessons Learned from Russia-West Interactions on European Security," in Samuel Charap, Alyssa Demus, and Jeremy Shapiro, eds., *Getting Out from "In Between": Perspectives on the Regional Order in Post-Soviet Europe and Eurasia* (Santa Monica, CA: RAND Corporation, 2018).

12. Oleksander Chalyi, "Approaches to Resolving the Conflict over the States In Between," in Charap, Demus, and Shapiro, *Getting Out*, writes, "All parties, including Ukraine, Russia, and the West, should acknowledge responsibility for the security crisis in and around Ukraine. The West and Russia should take responsibility for not reaching a consensus on a mutually acceptable security arrangement for Ukraine" (p. 36).

13. Andrei P. Tsygankov, *Russia and the West from Alexander to Putin: Honor in International Relations* (New York: Cambridge University Press, 2012).

14. Dmitri Trenin, *Should We Fear Russia?* (Cambridge: Polity Press, 2016); Dmitri Trenin, *Post-Imperium: A Eurasian Story* (Washington, DC: Carnegie Endowment for International Peace, 2011); Celeste Wallander, "Russian Transimperialism and Its Implications," *Washington Quarterly* 30, no. 2 (Spring 2007): 107–22; Van Herpen, *Putin's Wars*; Lo, *Russia and the New World Disorder*.

15. Charles A. Kupchan, "NATO's Final Frontier: Why Russia Should Join the Atlantic Alliance," *Foreign Affairs* 89, no. 3 (May–June 2010): 100–112.

16. See also O'Hanlon, *Beyond NATO*, 20; he points to "a confluence of events in 2007 and 2008 that probably marked the decisive turning point in relations between Vladimir Putin and the West."
17. Transcript, "Putin's Prepared Remarks at the 43rd Munich Conference on Security Policy," *Washington Post*, February 12, 2007, accessed March 12, 2018, at http://www.washingtonpost.com/wp-dyn/content/article/2007/02/12/AR2007021200555.html.
18. Dobbins and Zagorski, "Lessons Learned," 9.
19. Stent, *The Limits of Partnership*, ch. 7.
20. Dmitry Medvedev, "Why I Had to Recognize Georgia's Breakaway Regions," *Financial Times*, August 26, 2008, accessed October 2, 2018, at https://www.ft.com/content/9c7ad792-7395-11dd-8a66-0000779fd18c.
21. Meghann Myers, "Back to Europe: The Army Is Sending More Troops, Tanks and Helicopters to Deter Russia," *Army Times*, March 19, 2017, accessed October 19, 2018, at https://www.armytimes.com/news/your-army/2017/03/19/back-to-europe-the-army-is-sending-more-troops-tanks-and-helicopters-to-deter-russia/.
22. "Nobel Peace Prize Awarded to European Union," BBC, October 12, 2012, accessed July 28, 2017, at http://www.bbc.com/news/world-europe-19921072.
23. Dawisha, *Putin's Kleptocracy*; Vladimir Gel'man, *Authoritarian Russia: Analyzing Post-Soviet Regime Changes* (Pittsburgh: University of Pittsburgh Press, 2015).
24. Milada Anna Vachudova, "Democratization in Postcommunist Europe: Illiberal Regimes and the Leverage of International Actors," University of Pittsburgh Center for European Studies Working Paper No. 138 (2006), accessed July 18, 2017, at http://aei.pitt.edu/9023/1/Vachudova.pdf.
25. Trenin, *Should We Fear Russia?*, 49. For a full analysis, see Gel'man, *Authoritarian Russia*; M. Stephen Fish, *Democracy Derailed in Russia: The Failure of Open Politics* (New York: Cambridge University Press, 2005).
26. Steven Levitsky and Lucan A. Way, "The Rise of Competitive Authoritarianism," *Journal of Democracy* 13, no. 2 (April 2002): 51–65.

27. "Putin's Asymmetric Assault on Democracy in Russia and Europe: Implications for U.S. National Security," Minority Staff Report Prepared for the Use of the Committee on Foreign Relations of the United States Senate, 115th Congress, Second Session, January 10, 2018.

28. Marc Bennetts, "Russian TV Launches Series following Putin's Weekly Activities," *Guardian*, September 3, 2018, accessed October 19, 2018, at https://www.theguardian.com/world/2018/sep/03/russian-tv-launches-series-devoted-vladimir-putins-weekly-activities.

29. Dawisha, *Putin's Kleptocracy*; Bálint Magyar, *Post-Communist Mafia State: The Case of Hungary* (Budapest: Central European University Press, 2016).

30. Satter, *The Less You Know*.

31. Dobbins and Zagorski, "Lessons Learned," 9.

32. Thomas Ambrosio, *Authoritarian Backlash: Russian Resistance to Democratization in the Former Soviet Union* (New York: Routledge, 2016).

33. Mark Leonard and Nicu Popescu, "A Power Audit of EU-Russia Relations," European Council on Foreign Relations Policy Brief, 2007, 53.

34. Margot Light, "Russia and the EU: Strategic Partners or Strategic Rivals?," *Journal of Common Market Studies* 46 (2008): 7–27, http://proxy.library.upenn.edu:2278/doi/10.1111/j.1468-5965.2008.00808.x/epdf.

35. Light, "Russia and the EU."

36. Katja Richters, *The Post-Soviet Russian Orthodox Church: Politics, Culture and Greater Russia* (London: Routledge, 2013).

37. Mitchell A. Orenstein, "Putin's Western Allies: Why Europe's Far Right Is on the Kremlin's Side," *Foreign Affairs*, Snapshot, March 25, 2014.

38. Mitchell A. Orenstein, Péter Krekó, and Attila Juhász, "The Hungarian Putin? Viktor Orbán and the Kremlin's Playbook," *Foreign Affairs*, Snapshot, February 8, 2015.

39. Andrei P. Tsygankov, "The Irony of Western Ideas in a Multicultural World: Russians' Intellectual Engagement with the 'End of History' and 'Clash of Civilizations,'" *International Studies Review* 5, no. 1 (March 2003): 53–76.

40. Bugajski, *Dismantling the West.*
41. A number of authors have pointed out that Russia has no official military strategy of "hybrid war," but what Western analysts call hybrid war is sometimes referred to within Russia's defense ministry as "strategic deterrence," described as "a coordinated system of military and non-military (political, diplomatic, legal, economic, ideological, scientific-technical and others) measures taken consecutively or simultaneously . . . with the goal of deterring military action entailing damage of a strategic character." See Kristin Ven Bruusgaard, "Russian Strategic Deterrence," *Survival* 58, no. 4 (2016): 7–26; Maria Snegovaya, *Putin's Information in Ukraine: Soviet Origins of Russia's Hybrid Warfare* (Washington, DC: Institute for the Study of War, 2015), uses the term "reflexive control" to denote Russia's hybrid warfare. A well-researched French report claims that Russia uses the term, "new generation warfare": Jean-Baptiste Jeangene Vilmer et al., "Information Manipulation: A Challenge for Our Democracies," Report by the Policy Planning Staff (CAPS, Ministry for Europe and Foreign Affairs) and the Institute for Strategic Research (IRSEM, Ministry for the Armed Forces), Republic of France, 2018, 55.
42. For a more comprehensive description, see "Putin's Asymmetric Assault."
43. Bugajski, *Dismantling the West*, 17–18.
44. Satter, *The Less You Know.*
45. Andrew Rettman, "Belgian Intelligence Chief Talks to EUobserver: Transcript," *EUobserver*, September 17, 2012, accessed July 18, 2017, at https://euobserver.com/secret-ue/117554.
46. The "false" Dmitry refers to several real pretenders to the Russian throne, during Russia's "time of troubles" from 1598 to 1613, who claimed to be the youngest son of Ivan the Terrible.
47. Richard Field, "Jobbik MEP 'KGBéla' Kovács and Wife Outed as Russian Spies," *Budapest Beacon*, September 24, 2014, accessed July 18, 2017, at http://budapestbeacon.com/news-in-brief/jobbik-mep-kgbela-kovacs-and-wife-outted-as-russian-spies/13537; Mitchell A. Orenstein and Péter Krekó, "A Russian Spy in Brussels? The Case of 'KGBéla'—and What It Means for Europe," *Foreign Affairs*, May 29, 2014, accessed July 19, 2017,

https://www.foreignaffairs.com/articles/hungary/2014-05-29/russian-spy-brussels; "Parliament Lifts Hungarian MEP's Immunity over Russia Spy Probe," *Euractive*, October 15, 2015, accessed July 19, 2017, http://www.euractiv.com/section/europe-s-east/news/parliament-lifts-hungarian-mep-s-immunity-over-russia-spy-probe/; Hungary Matters, "European Parliament Lifts Immunity of Jobbik MEP Béla Kovács," *Politics.hu*, June 2, 2017, accessed July 19, 2017, at http://www.politics.hu/20170602/european-parliament-lifts-immunity-of-jobbik-mep-bela-kovacs/; Dezsõ András, "A Beautiful Match Made in Moscow," Index.hu, September 28, 2014, accessed July 31, 2017, at http://index.hu/belfold/2014/09/28/a_glorious_match_made_in_russia/.

48. Anton Shekhovtsov, *Russia and the Western Far Right: Tango Noir* (Abingdon, UK: Routledge, 2017).

49. Max Seddon and Michael Stothard, "Putin Awaits Returns on Le Pen Investment," *Financial Times*, May 4, 2017, accessed July 19, 2017, at https://www.ft.com/content/010eec62-30b5-11e7-9555-23ef563ecf9a?mhq5j=e1.

50. Anton Shekhovtsov, "Foreign Politicians' Visit to Crimea Is Russia's Latest Disinformation Failure," *Moscow Times*, March 29, 2017, accessed July 19, 2017, at https://themoscowtimes.com/articles/foreign-politicians-visit-to-crimea-is-russias-latest-disinformation-failure-57569.

51. Alina Polyakova et al., "The Kremlin's Trojan Horses: Russian Influence in France, Germany, and the United Kingdom," Atlantic Council, November 2016, accessed October 27, 2017, at http://www.atlanticcouncil.org/images/publications/The_Kremlins_Trojan_Horses_web_0228_third_edition.pdf.

52. Agnia Grigas, "Legacies, Coercion, and Soft Power: Russian Influence in the Baltic States," Chatham House Briefing Paper, August 2012, 10.

53. Snyder, *The Road to Unfreedom.*

54. Office of the Director of National Intelligence, "Assessing Russian Activities and Intentions in Recent US Elections," January 6, 2017, 4, accessed August 21, 2018, at https://www.dni.gov/files/documents/ICA_2017_01.pdf; Steven Erlanger, "Russia's RT Network: Is It More BBC or K.G.B.?," *New York Times*, March

8, 2017, accessed October 7, 2017, at https://www.nytimes.com/ 2017/03/08/world/europe/russias-rt-network-is-it-more-bbc-or-kgb.html; Rosie Gray, "How the Truth Is Made at Russia Today," *Buzzfeed*, March 13, 2014, accessed October 7, 2017, at https:// www.buzzfeed.com/rosiegray/how-the-truth-is-made-at-russia-today?utm_term=.euwEAJkqK#.or57gqrzb.

55. Office of the Director of National Intelligence, "Assessing Russian Activities," 4; Erlanger, "Russia's RT Network"; Adrain Chen, "The Agency," *New York Times*, June 2, 2015, accessed July 19, 2017, at https://www.nytimes.com/2015/06/07/magazine/the-agency.html; Lawrence Alexander, "Social Network Analysis Reveals Full Scale of Kremlin's Twitter Bot Campaign," *Global Voices*, April 2, 2015, accessed October 7, 2017, at https://globalvoices.org/2015/04/02/ analyzing-kremlin-twitter-bots/.

56. "Putin's Asymmetric Assault," 39. See also Peter Pomerantsev, "The Kremlin's Information War," *Journal of Democracy* 26, no. 4 (2015), accessed October 14, 2017, at https://proxy.library.upenn. edu:2576/article/595921.

57. Denise Clifton, "How Trump and His Allies Have Run with Russian Propaganda," *Mother Jones*, June 5, 2017, accessed October 7, 2017, at http://www.motherjones.com/politics/2017/06/russian-active-measures-trump-propaganda-conspiracy-theories/.

58. Robert Orttung, Elizabeth Nelson, and Anthony Livshen, "How Russia Today Is Using YouTube," *Washington Post*, March 23, 2015, accessed July 19, 2017, at https://www.washingtonpost. com/news/monkey-cage/wp/2015/03/23/how-russia-today-is-using-youtube/; Elias Groll, "Kremlin's 'Sputnik' Newswire Is the Buzzfeed of Propaganda," *Foreign Policy*, November 10, 2014, accessed October 7, 2017, at https://foreignpolicy.com/2014/11/10/ kremlins-sputnik-newswire-is-the-buzzfeed-of-propaganda/.

59. "Nigel Farage's Relationship with Russian Media Comes under Scrutiny," *Guardian*, March 31, 2014, accessed October 28, 2017, at https://www.theguardian.com/politics/2014/mar/31/ nigel-farage-relationship-russian-media-scrutiny.

60. "Green Party Candidates to Face Off in Debate Hosted by RT (Watch Live)," RT, May 9, 2016, accessed October 7, 2017, at https:// www.rt.com/usa/342395-green-party-rt-debate/; "America to

Choose Either 'Proto-fascist' or 'Corruption Queen'—Jill Stein to RT," RT, November 2, 2017, accessed October 7, 2017, at https://www.rt.com/usa/365045-jill-stein-elections-candidates/; "The Other Guys: Meet Third-Party US Candidates for President," RT, November 7, 2016, accessed October 7, 2017, at https://www.rt.com/usa/365681-us-elections-other-candidates/; "Debunking the Media's Smear Campaign against Green Presidential Candidate Jill Stein," RT, August 25, 2016, accessed October 7, 2017, at https://www.rt.com/usa/355444-debunking-jill-stein-smears/.

61. Peter Walker, "Russia 'Spreading Fake News about Refugees to Sow Discord in Europe' Says Ex-Spy," *Independent*, March 22, 2017, accessed October 7, 2017, at http://www.independent.co.uk/news/world/europe/russia-europe-threat-refugee-crisis-europe-aggravate-propaganda-kremlin-farenc-katrei-hungarian-spy-a7642711.html.

62. Stefan Meister, "The 'Lisa Case': Germany as a Target of Russian Disinformation," *NATO Review*, 2016, accessed October 28, 2017, at https://www.nato.int/docu/review/2016/Also-in-2016/lisa-case-germany-target-russian-disinformation/EN/index.htm.

63. Andy Greenberg, "How an Entire Nation Became Russia's Test Lab for Cyberwar," *Wired*, June 20, 2017, accessed October 28, 2017, at https://www.wired.com/story/russian-hackers-attack-ukraine/.

64. Andrew Wilson, *Ukraine's Orange Revolution* (New Haven, CT: Yale University Press, 2005).

65. Mark Galeotti, "Controlling Chaos: How Russia Manages Its Political War in Europe," European Council on Foreign Affairs, September 2017, 7, accessed October 28, 2017, at http://www.ecfr.eu/page/-/ECFR228_-_CONTROLLING_CHAOS1.pdf.

66. Stephanie Kirchgaessner, Dan Collyns, and Luke Harding, "Revealed: Russia's Secret Plan to Help Julian Assange Escape from UK," *Guardian*, September 21, 2018, accessed October 19, 2018, at https://www.theguardian.com/world/2018/sep/21/julian-assange-russia-ecuador-embassy-london-secret-escape-plan.

67. Jason Le Miere, "Russia Election Hacking: Countries Where the Kremlin Has Allegedly Sought to Sway Votes," *Newsweek*, May

9, 2017, accessed October 7, 2017, at http://www.newsweek. com/russia-election-hacking-france-us-606314; Mark Clayton, "Ukraine Election Narrowly Avoided 'Wanton Destruction' from Hackers," *Christian Science Monitor*, June 17, 2014, accessed October 7, 2017, at https://www.csmonitor.com/World/ Passcode/2014/0617/Ukraine-election-narrowly-avoided-wanton-destruction-from-hackers-video.

68. Andy Greenberg, "'Crash Override': The Malware That Took Down a Power Grid," *Wired*, June 12, 2017, accessed October 28, 2017, at https://www.wired.com/story/crash-override-malware/.

69. Andy Greenberg. "Hackers Gain Direct Access to US Power Grid Controls," Wired, September 6, 2017, accessed October 28, 2017, at https://www.wired.com/story/hackers-gain-switch-flipping-access-to-us-power-systems/.

70. Dezsõ András and Szabolcs Panyi, "Russian Diplomats Exercised with Hungarian Cop Killer's Far-Right Gang," *Index*, October 28, 2016, accessed July 19, 2017, at http://index.hu/belfold/2016/10/ 28/russian_diplomats_exercised_with_hungarian_cop_killer_s_ far-right_gang/.

71. Petra Vejvodová, Jakub Janda, and Veronika Víchová, "The Russian Connections of Far-Right and Paramilitary Organizations in the Czech Republic," *Political Capital*, April 2017, accessed July 20, 2017, at http://www.politicalcapital.hu/pc-admin/source/documents/PC_NED_country_study_CZ_20170428.pdf; Péter Krekó et al., "Marching toward Eurasia: The Kremlin Connections of the Slovak Far-Right," *Political Capital*, January 2015, accessed July 20, 2017, at https://www.researchgate.net/publication/287218227_ Marching_towards_Eurasia_The_Kremlin_connections_of_the_ Slovak_far-right; "The Russian Connection: The Spread of Pro-Russian Policies on the European Far Right," Political Capital Institute, March 14, 2014, accessed October 7, 2017, at http:// www.riskandforecast.com/useruploads/files/pc_flash_report_ russian_connection.pdf.

72. Josh Lederman, Courtney Kube, Abigail Williams, and Ken Dilanian, "U.S. officials suspect Russia in mystery 'attacks' on diplomats in Cuba, China," *Guardian,* September 11, 2018, accessed

October 19, 2018, at https://www.nbcnews.com/news/latin-america/u-s-officials-suspect-russia-mystery-attacks-diplomats-cuba-china-n908141.

73. Agnia Grigas, *The New Geopolitics of Natural Gas* (Cambridge, MA: Harvard University Press, 2017); Stephen F. Szabo, *Germany, Russia, and the Rise of Geo-Economics* (London: Bloomsbury, 2015).

74. Dimitar Bechev, *Rival Power: Russia in Southeast Europe* (New Haven, CT: Yale University Press, 2017).

75. Mitchell A. Orenstein and R. Daniel Keleman, "Trojan Horses in EU Foreign Policy," *Journal of Common Market Studies* 55, no. 1 (2016): 87–102, accessed August 7, 2017, at http://proxy.library.upenn.edu:2278/doi/10.1111/jcms.12441/full.

76. Bechev, *Rival Power*.

77. BBC, "Greece's Tsipras Condemns Sanctions against Russia," BBC News, May 28, 2016, accessed May 4, 2018, at http://www.bbc.com/news/world-europe-36403129.

78. Orenstein and Keleman, "Trojan Horses."

79. Vejvodová, Janda, and Víchová, "Russian Connections."

80. Galeotti, "Controlling Chaos," 7.

Chapter 3

1. European Union Committee, "The EU and Russia: Before and beyond the Crisis in Ukraine," House of Lords, February 20, 2015, accessed August 21, 2018, at https://publications.parliament.uk/pa/ld201415/ldselect/ldeucom/115/115.pdf.

2. Stephen White, Margot Light, and Ian McAllister, "Russia and the West: Is There a Values Gap?" *International Politics* 42, no. 3 (2005): 314–33, at https://proxy.library.upenn.edu:2320/content/pdf/10.1057%2Fpalgrave.ip.8800114.pdf.

3. Kramer, *Back to Containment*.

4. Putin, "Putin's Prepared Remarks"; Kramer, *Back to Containment*, describes the weak Bush administration response to Putin's attack on US dominance of the international system.

5. Szabo, *Germany, Russia*.

6. Francis Fukuyama, *The End of History and the Last Man* (New York: Free Press, 1992).

7. James Sherr, "A War of Narratives and Arms," in Keir Giles et al., *The Russian Challenge* (London: Royal Institute of International Affairs, 2105), 23–32.
8. Josh Rogin, "Germany Helped Prep Russia for War, U.S. Sources Say," *Daily Beast*, April 22, 2014, accessed May 4, 2018, at https://www.thedailybeast.com/germany-helped-prep-russia-for-war-us-sources-say.
9. Gel'man, *Authoritarian Russia*.
10. "A Scripted War," *Economist*, August 14, 2008, accessed May 8, 2018, at https://www.economist.com/node/11920992.
11. Margriet Drent, Rob Hendriks, and Dick Zandee, "New Threats, New EU, and NATO Responses," Clingendael Netherlands Institute of International Relations, accessed May 4, 2018, at https://www.clingendael.org/sites/default/files/pdfs/New%20Threats_New%20EU_Nato%20Responses_Clingendael_July2015.pdf, 9.
12. Hilary Appel and Mitchell A. Orenstein, *From Triumph to Crisis: Neoliberal Economic Reform in Postcommunist Countries* (New York: Cambridge University Press, 2018), ch. 5.
13. Polyakova et al., "The Kremlin's Trojan Horses."
14. Szabo, *Germany, Russia*, 77.
15. Bugajski, *Dismantling the West*; Edward Lucas, *The New Cold War: Putin's Russia and the Threat to the West* (New York: Palgrave Macmillan, 2008).
16. Kramer, *Back to Containment*.
17. Tuomas Forsberg, "From *Ostpolitik* to 'Frostpolitik'? Merkel, Putin, and German Foreign Policy towards Russia," *International Affairs* 92, no. 1 (2016): 21–42; Szabo, *Germany, Russia*.
18. Vladimir Gel'man, "Cracks in the Wall: Challenges to Electoral Authoritarianism in Russia," Problems of Post-Communism 60, no. 2 (2013): 3–10.
19. Ralf Neukirch and Matthias Schepp, "German-Russian Relations Enter a New Ice Age," *Spiegel Online*, May 30, 2012, accessed May 6, 2018, at http://www.spiegel.de/international/germany/german-and-russian-relations-are-at-an-impasse-a-835862.html.
20. Glenn Kessler, "Flashback: Obama's Debate Zinger on Romney's '1980s' Foreign Policy (Video)," *Washington Post*, March 20, 2014,

accessed May 6, 2018, at https://www.washingtonpost.com/news/
fact-checker/wp/2014/03/20/flashback-obamas-debate-zinger-
on-romneys-1980s-foreign-policy/?utm_term=.4d72ae40a58e.

21. Ali Watkins, "Obama Team Was Warned in 2014 about Russian
Interference," *Politico*, August 14, 2017, accessed May 6, 2018,
at https://www.politico.com/story/2017/08/14/obama-russia-
election-interference-241547.

22. Jan Strupczewski and Paul Taylor, "Russia Is a Strategic Problem for the
EU: Tusk," *Reuters*, December 18, 2014, at http://www.reuters.com/
article/us-ukraine-crisis-russia-eu-idUSKBN0JW2S620141218.

23. David Cadier, "Eastern Partnership vs Eurasian Union? The EU-
Russia Competition in the Shared Neighbourhood and the Ukraine
Crisis," *Global Policy* 5, no. 1 (2014), accessed May 7, 2018, at
https://onlinelibrary.wiley.com/doi/full/10.1111/1758-5899.12152.

24. "Agreement on the Settlement of Crisis in Ukraine—Full Text,"
Guardian, February 21, 2014, accessed October 8, 2017, at
https://www.theguardian.com/world/2014/feb/21/agreement-
on-the-settlement-of-crisis-in-ukraine-full-text.

25. Rajan Menon and Eugene Rumer, *Conflict in Ukraine: The
Unwinding of the Post-Cold War Order* (Cambridge, MA: MIT
Press, 2015), 80.

26. Harriet Alexander and Yekaterina Kravtsova, "Vladimir Putin
Held Secret Meeting to Agree Crimea Annexation Weeks before Referendum," *Telegraph*, March 20, 2014, accessed May 8,
2018, at https://www.telegraph.co.uk/news/worldnews/vladimir-
putin/10712866/Vladimir-Putin-held-secret-meeting-to-agree-
Crimea-annexation-weeks-before-referendum.html.

27. Matthieu Crozet and Julian Hinz, "Collateral Damage: The Impact
of the Russia Sanctions on Sanctioning Countries Exports," CEPII
Working Paper No. 2016-16 (June), Paris: CEPII.

28. Russian International Affairs Council (RIAC), "The Ukrainian
Challenge for Russia," Russian International Affairs Council
Working Paper 24/2015, Moscow, accessed October 28, 2017,
at https://www.slideshare.net/RussianCouncil/wp-ukraine
russia24eng.

29. Taras Kuzio, "Ukraine between a Constrained EU and Assertive
Russia," *Journal of Common Market Studies* 55, no. 1 (2016): 1–18.

30. Country Fact Sheet: Russian Federation, UNCTAD World Investment Report 2017, United Nations Conference on Trade and Development, 2017, accessed May 9, 2018, at http://unctad.org/sections/dite_dir/docs/wir2017/wir17_fs_ru_en.pdf.
31. Russian International Affairs Council, "Ukrainian Challenge for Russia."
32. Stephen Blank, "Georgia: The War Russia Lost," Military Review, November–December 2008, 40.
33. Orenstein and Kelemen, "Trojan Horses."
34. Luke Harding, *A Very Expensive Poison: The Assassination of Alexander Litvinenko and Putin's War with the West* (New York: Knopf Doubleday, 2017).
35. Forsberg, "From *Ostpolitik* to Frostpolitik," 26. This is an excellent and detailed article on changes to German foreign policy on Russia.
36. Ian Traynor and Patrick Wintour, "Ukraine Crisis: Vladimir Putin Has Lost the Plot, Says German Chancellor," *Guardian*, March 3, 2014, accessed August 21, 2018, at https://www.theguardian.com/world/2014/mar/03/ukraine-vladimir-putin-angela-merkel-russian.
37. "Rattachement de la Crimée à la Russie: La colère de Hollande, Merkel et Obama," *L'Express*, March 18, 2014, accessed August 21, 2018, at https://www.lexpress.fr/actualite/monde/europe/rattachement-de-la-crimee-a-la-russie-la-colere-de-hollande-merkel-et-obama_1501058.html.
38. Andrew Rettman, "Italy Dangles Veto Threat on EU's Russia Sanctions," *EU Observer*, October 25, 2018, accessed October 25, 2018, at https://euobserver.com/foreign/143207.
39. Somini Sengupta and Andrew E. Kramer, "Dutch Inquiry Links Russia to 298 Deaths in Explosion of Jetliner over Ukraine," *New York Times*, September 28, 2016, accessed October 8, 2017, https://www.nytimes.com/2016/09/29/world/asia/malaysia-air-flight-mh17-russia-ukraine-missile.html?mcubz=3&_r=0; "Top AIDS Researcher Killed in Malaysia Airlines Crash," *Time,* July 17, 2014, accessed October 8, 2017, at http://time.com/3003840/malaysia-airlines-ukraine-crash-top-aids-researchers-killed-aids2014-mh17/.

40. Jessica Elgot, "Dutch Foreign Minister Frans Timmermans Gives Perfect Response to Horror of MH17," *Huffington Post*, July 23, 2014, accessed October 8, 2017, at http://www.huffington post.co.uk/2014/07/22/speech-un-mh17_n_5609363. html.

41. Rebecca M. Nelson, *US Sanctions and Russia's Economy*, CRS Report Prepared for Members of Congress 7-5700 (Washington, DC: Congressional Research Service, February 17, 2017), 4, with updated data from World Bank.

42. Michael Birnbaum, "Russia Bans Food Imports from U.S., E.U.," *Washington Post*, August 7, 2014, accessed August 21, 2018, at https://www.washingtonpost.com/world/russia-bans-food-imports-from-us-eu/2014/08/07/a29f5bea-1e14-11e4-82f9-2cd6fa8da5c4_story.html?utm_term=.11bdec97d971.

43. Jason Bush, "Russia's Import-Substitution Drive Will Take Years—and May Be Misguided," Reuters, October 1, 2015, accessed August 21, 2018, at https://www.reuters.com/article/us-russia-economy-import-substitution/russias-import-substitution-drive-will-take-years-and-may-be-misguided-idUSKCN0RV4W920151001.

44. Vladimir Alexandrovich Davydenko, Gulnara Fatykhovna Romashkina, and Ruzilya Maratovna Nasyrova, "Models of Russian Consumer Behaviour: Retail under Crisis Pressure," *Ekonomska Misao i Praksa* [Economic Thought and Practice] (Croatia) 2017, no. 2: 697–714.

45. Average Inflation Russia (CPI) by Year, Inflation.EU, accessed January 8, 2018, at http://www.inflation.eu/inflation-rates/russia/historic-inflation/cpi-inflation-russia.aspx.

46. Russia Food Inflation, Trading Economics, accessed January 9, 2018, at https://tradingeconomics.com/russia/food-inflation.

47. Nelson, *US Sanctions and Russia's Economy*.

48. International Monetary Fund, Russian Federation: Staff Report for the 2015 Article IV Consultation, August 2015, 5.

49. Nikolaus Blome, Kai Diekmann, and Daniel Biskup, "Interview with Putin," *Bild* (Germany), November 1, 2016.

50. "Russia Faces '100 Years of Solitude' (or More), Putin Aide Says," Radio Free Europe / Radio Liberty, April 10, 2018, accessed

August 21, 2018, at https://www.rferl.org/a/putin-adviser-surkov-says-russia-abandoning-hopes-integrating-with-west-loneliness-isolation-/29155700.html.

51. Emma Ashford, "Not-So-Smart Sanctions: The Failure of Western Restrictions against Russia," *Foreign Affairs* 114, 2016: 114–23.

52. Daisy Sindelar, "Out with a Whimper: Novorossia, 2014–2015," Radio Free Europe / Radio Liberty, May 21, 2015, accessed May 8, 2018, at https://www.rferl.org/a/death-of-novorossia/27029267.html.

53. Danila Bochkarev, "Gazprom Plays Ball: The Depoliticization of the European Gas Market," *EnergyPost*, January 25, 2017, accessed August 3, 2017, at http://ec.europa.eu/eurostat/statistics-explained/index.php/File:Main_origin_of_primary_energy_imports,_EU-28,_2005-2015_(%25_of_extra_EU-28_imports)_YB17.png.

54. Szabo, *Germany, Russia*, 71.

55. Grigas, *New Geopolitics*.

56. "Main Origin of Primary Energy Imports, EU-28, 2005–2015 (5% of Extra EU-28 Imports) YB17," *Eurostat,* July 12, 2017, accessed October 8, 2017, at http://ec.europa.eu/eurostat/statistics-explained/index.php/File:Main_origin_of_primary_energy_imports,_EU-28,_2005-2015_(%25_of_extra_EU-28_imports)_YB17.png.

57. Euractiv with Reuters, "EU Wants Same Price for Russian Gas for All Its Members: Oettinger," *Euractiv*, May 2, 2014, accessed August 3, 2017, at https://www.euractiv.com/section/energy/news/eu-wants-same-price-for-russian-gas-for-all-its-members-oettinger/.

58. Florent Silve and Pierre Noël, "Cost Curves for Gas Supply Security: The Case of Bulgaria," Electricity Policy Research Group Working Paper 1031, September 2010, accessed October 8, 2017, at https://www.repository.cam.ac.uk/bitstream/handle/1810/257219/cwpe1056.pdf?sequence=1&isAllowed=y. "Bulgaria and Romania Launch Gas Pipeline," Reuters, November 11, 2016, accessed August 3, 2017, at http://www.reuters.com/article/bulgaria-gas-romania-idUSL8N1DB2YX.

59. Bochkarev, "Gazprom Plays Ball."

60. Jacob Cohen, "Let's Drink to All the Russian Gas: How Energy Dependence Affects European Union Energy Strategy towards

Russing," Senior Honors Thesis, University of Pennsylvania, April 2018.

61. "Communication from the Commission to the European Parliament, the Council, the European Economic and Social Committee and the Committee of the Regions on an EU Strategy for Liquefied Natural Gas and Gas Storage," European Commission, p. 6, February 16, 2016, accessed October 8, 2017, at https://ec.europa.eu/energy/sites/ener/files/documents/1_EN_ACT_part1_v10-1.pdf.

62. "Question and Answers on the Third Legislative Package for an Internal EU Gas and Electricity Market," European Commission, March 2, 2011, accessed October 13, 2017, at http://europa.eu/rapid/press-release_MEMO-11-125_en.htm?locale=en/.
Dagmara Stoerring and Susanne Horl, "Fact Sheets on the European Union: Internal Energy Market," European Parliament, June 2017, accessed October 13, 2017, at http://www.europarl.europa.eu/atyourservice/en/displayFtu.html?ftuId=FTU_5.7.2.html.

63. Yuliya Lovochkina, Member of Parliament of Ukraine, interview by Mitchell A. Orenstein, June 13, 2017.

64. Sergei Komlev, "Third Energy Package and Its Impact on Gazprom Activities in Europe," EBC Working Committee "Energy," *Gazprom*, Essen, March 18, 2011, accessed October 13, 2017, at gazpromexport.ru/files/komlev_speech_essen_18_03_1124.pdf.

65. Jakob Hedenskog and Robert L. Larsson, *Russian Leverage on the CIS and the Baltic States* (Stockholm: Swedish Defence Research Agency, 2007).

66. Komlev, "Third Energy Package."

67. "TIMELINE-EU's Anti-monopoly Case against Russia's Gazprom," Reuters, October 25, 2016, at https://af.reuters.com/article/idAFL8N1CV6WG.

68. Stanley Reed and Milan Schreuer, "E.U. Settles with Russia's Gazprom over Antitrust Charges," *New York Times*, May 24, 2018.

69. Benjamin Fox, "EU Launches Anti-trust Case against Gazprom," *EUobserver*, October 4, 2013, accessed October 13, 2017, at https://euobserver.com/political/121659; Simone Tagliapietra, "The EU Antitrust Case: No Big Deal for Gazprom," *Bruegel*,

March 15, 2017, accessed October 13, 2017, at http://bruegel. org/2017/03/the-eu-antitrust-case-no-big-deal-for-gazprom/; David Sheppard and Henry Fox, "US and Russia Step Up Fight to Supply Europe's Gas," *Financial Times*, August 3, 2017, accessed October 13, 2017, at https://www.ft.com/content/352f4cac-6c7a-11e7-b9c7-15af748b60d0; Alexei Lossan, "Gazprom Recognizes EU Restrictions for the First Time," *Russia beyond the Headlines*, March 29, 2016, accessed October 13, 2017, at https://www.rbth. com/business/2016/03/29/gazprom-recognizes-eu-restrictions-for-the-first-time_579955; Georgi Gotev, "Nord Stream 2 Official: We See a Lot of Smokescreens Thrown Around," *Euractiv*, March 23, 2017, accessed October 13, 2017, at https://www. euractiv.com/section/energy/interview/nord-stream-2-official-we-see-a-lot-of-smokescreens-thrown-around/.

70. Lo, *Russia and the New World Disorder*, 86; Szabo, *Germany, Russia*.

71. Stefan Nicola, Carol Matlack, and Birgit Jennen, "Germany Builds an Election Firewall to Fight Russian Hackers," *Bloomberg*, June 14, 2017, accessed October 13, 2017, at https://www.bloomberg. com/news/articles/2017-06-14/germany-builds-an-election-firewall-to-fight-russian-hackers.

72. European Parliament, "EU Strategic Communication to Counteract Anti-EU Propaganda by Third Parties," P8_TA(2016)0441, accessed August 21, 2018, at http://www.europarl.europa.eu/sides/getDoc. do?pubRef=-//EP//NONSGML+TA+P8-TA-2016-0441+0+DOC+PDF+V0//EN.

73. "Facebook to Start Disclosing Identity of Political Advertisers," *Radio Free Europe / Radio Liberty*, April 7, 2018, at https:// www.rferl.org/a/facebook-start-disclosing-identity-political-advertiser-network-russian-election-meddling-/29151116.html.

74. Vilmer et al., "Information Manipulation," 105–53.

75. Galeotti, "Controlling Chaos," 7.

76. Charap and Colton, *Everybody Loses*.

77. Drent, Hendriks, and Zandee, "New Threats," 25.

78. NATO Public Diplomacy Division, "Defence Expenditure of NATO Countries (2010–2017), Press Release PR/CP(2017)111, accessed May 12, 2018, at https://www.nato.int/nato_static_fl2014/assets/pdf/pdf_2017_06/20170629_170629-pr2017-111-en.pdf, 4.

79. "Donald Trump Tells NATO Allies to Pay Up at Brussels Talks," BBC News, May 25, 2017.

80. The Data Team, "Military Spending by NATO Members," Economist, February 16, 2017, accessed October 30, 2017, at https://www.economist.com/blogs/graphicdetail/2017/02/daily-chart-11. See also Kaija Schilde, "European Military Capabilities: Enablers and Constraints on EU Power?," Journal of Common Market Studies 55, no. 1 (2017): 37–53.

81. Magnus Nordenman, "Lessons from Sweden's Sub Hunt," USNI News, October 28, 2014, accessed May 21, 2018, at https://news.usni.org/2014/10/28/lessons-swedens-sub-hunt.

82. Steve Brusk and Ralph Ellis, "Russian Planes Intercepted Near U.S., Canadian Airspace," CNN, November 13, 2014, accessed May 21, 2018, at https://www.cnn.com/2014/09/19/us/russian-plane-incidents/index.html.

83. Reuters Staff, "Russia Threatens to Aim Nuclear Missiles at Denmark Ships If It Joins NATO Shield," March 22, 2015, accessed May 21, 2018, at https://www.reuters.com/article/us-denmark-russia/russia-threatens-to-aim-nuclear-missiles-at-denmark-ships-if-it-joins-nato-shield-idUSKBN0MI0ML20150322.

84. Zachary Fryer-Biggs, "British Fighter Jets Intercept Russian Bombers Once Again Taunting U.K.: Report," Newsweek, January 15, 2018, accessed May 21, 2018, at http://www.newsweek.com/russian-bombers-taunt-uk-again-fly-781741.

85. Schilde, "European Military Capabilities."

86. Daniel Kochis, "Support for Montenegro's Accession to NATO Would Send a Message of Strength," Heritage Foundation Issue Brief 4647, January 12, 2017, accessed May 21, 2018, at https://www.heritage.org/sites/default/files/2017-01/IB4647_0.pdf.

87. Esther Ademmer, Russia's Impact on EU Policy Transfer to the Post-Soviet Space: The Contested Neighborhood (London: Routledge, 2017); Julia Langbein, Transnationalization and Regulatory Change in the EU's Eastern Neighbourhood: Ukraine between Brussels and Moscow (London: Routledge, 2017); László Bruszt and Julia Langbein, "Varieties of Dis-embedded Liberalism: EU Integration Strategies in the Eastern Peripheries of Europe," Journal of European Public Policy 2017 24, no. 2 (2017): 297–315; Tanja A. Börzel and Frank Schimmelfennig, "Coming Together or

Drifting Apart? The EU's Political Integration Capacity in Eastern Europe," *Journal of European Public Policy* 24, no. 2 (2017): 278–96; Antoaneta Dimitrova and Elitsa Kortenska, "What Do Citizens Want? And Why Does It Matter? Discourses among Citizens as Opportunities and Constraints for EU Enlargement," *Journal of European Public Policy* 24, no. 2 (2017): 259–77.

88. Michael Emerson and Denis Cenusa, eds., *Deepening EU-Moldovan Relations: What, Why, and How?* (London: Rowman & Littlefield International; Brussels: Centre for European Policy Studies, 2016).

89. Anahit Shirinyan, "What Armenia's New Agreement with the EU Means," *EU Observer*, November 24, 2017; Esther Ademmer and Yaroslav Lissovolik, "Thoughts on Inclusive Economic Integration," in Charap, Demus, and Shapiro, *Getting Out*.

Chapter 4

1. Andrei Makhovsky, "Belarus Won't Choose between the EU and Russia: Lukashenko," Reuters, March 23, 2016, accessed July 27, 2017, at http://www.reuters.com/article/us-belarus-eu-poland-idUSKCN0WP1HI; Elena Korosteleva, "The EU and Belarus: Seizing the Opportunity?," Swedish Institute for Policy Studies Working Paper, November 2016, accessed July 27, 2017, at https://kar.kent.ac.uk/59637/1/Belarus%20policy%20brief%20final%20oct%202016.pdf.

2. Korosteleva, "The EU and Belarus."

3. Omer Bartov and Eric D. Weitz, eds., *Shatterzone of Empires: Coexistence and Violence in the German, Habsburg, Russian, and Ottoman Borderlands* (Bloomington: Indiana University Press, 2013).

4. Taras Kuzio, "Viktor Pinchuk Wants Ukraine to Capitulate to Russia," *Euromaidan Press*, January 4, 2017, accessed May 14, 2018, at http://euromaidanpress.com/2017/01/04/victor-pinchuk-wants-ukraine-to-capitulate-to-russia-crimea-donbas/.

5. "Abkhazia Profile—Overview," BBC, August 27, 2015, accessed August 16, 2017, at http://www.bbc.com/news/world-europe-18175394.

6. AFP News Agency, "New Armenian Prime Minister Assures Putin of 'Strategic Alliance,'" *Radio Free Europe / Radio Liberty*, May 14, 2018, accessed May 14, 2018, at https://www.rferl.org/a/pashinian-putin-meeting-sochi/29226096.html.

7. "Armenia, Azerbaijan Closer to War over Nagorno-Karabakh Than at Any Time since 1994," Reuters, June 1, 2017, accessed May 14, 2018, at https://www.reuters.com/article/armenia-azerbaijan-conflict-idUSL8N1IY402.

8. "Kremlin Pushes for Russian Airbase in Belarus after Presidential Elections," *Belarus in Focus*, April 22, 2016, accessed May 14, 2018, at https://belarusinfocus.info/society-and-politics/kremlin-pushes-russian-airbase-belarus-after-presidential-elections.

9. David R. Cameron and Mitchell A. Orenstein, "Post-Soviet Authoritarianism: The Influence of Russia in Its 'Near Abroad,'" *Post-Soviet Affairs* 28, no. 1 (2017): 1–44; Ian Bond, "Contested Space: Eastern Europe between Russia and the EU," *Centre for European Reform*, March 2017, accessed July 25, 2017, at http://www.cer.eu/sites/default/files/pb_eastern_part_IB_9march17.pdf.

10. T.J. Chisinau, "Why Has Russia Banned Moldovan Wine?," *Economist*, November 25, 2013, accessed July 25, 2017, at https://www.economist.com/blogs/economist-explains/2013/11/economist-explains-18; "Russia Lifts Ban on Imports of Moldovan Wines," *Real Russia Today*, May 15, 2017, accessed October 14, 2017, at http://realrussiatoday.com/2017/05/15/russia-lifts-ban-on-imports-of-moldovan-wines/.

11. "Russia Is Destroying Its Food," *Stratfor*, August 11, 2015, accessed October 14, 2017, at https://worldview.stratfor.com/article/russia-destroying-its-food.

12. Denis Cenusa et al., "Russia's Punitive Trade Policy Measures towards Ukraine, Moldova, and Georgia," *Centre for European Policy Studies*, September 2014, 7, accessed July 25, 2017, at http://infoeuropa.md/files/masurile-de-politica-comerciala-punitiva-a-rusiei-fata-de-ucraina-moldova-si-georgia.pdf.

13. Cenusa et al., "Russia's Punitive Trade Policy."

14. "Bringing Plurality and Balance to the Russian Language Media Space," *European Endowment for Democracy*, June 25, 2015,

accessed October 14, 2017, at https://www.democracyendowment.
eu/news/bringing-plurality-1/; Pomerantsev, "The Kremlin's
Information War."

15. Peter Pomerantsev, *Nothing Is True and Everything Is Possible: The
Surreal Heart of the New Russia* (New York: PublicAffairs, 2014).

16. "Ukraine Bans Russian Media Outlets, Websites," *Committee to
Protect Journalists*, May 17, 2017, accessed July 26, 2017, at https://
cpj.org/2017/05/ukraine-bans-russian-media-outlets-websites.
php.

17. Robert C. Blitt, "Russia's 'Orthodox' Foreign Policy: The Growing
Influence of the Russian Orthodox Church in Shaping Russia's
Policies Abroad," *Penn Law: Legal Scholarship Repository*,
November 28, 2011, accessed July 26, 2017, at http://scholarship.
law.upenn.edu/cgi/viewcontent.cgi?article=1058&context=jil;
Stanislav Zlenko, "Trust to Social Institutions," *Kiev International
Institute of Sociology*, February 1, 2017, accessed October 14,
2017, at http://kiis.com.ua/?lang=eng&cat=reports&id=678&pa
ge=1; "IMAS: Mass-Media, Second Most Trusted Institution in
Moldova," *Media AZI*, November 19, 2013, accessed October 14,
2017, at http://media-azi.md/en/stiri/imas-mass-media-second-
most-trusted-institution-moldova; Bureau of Democracy, Human
Rights, and Labor, "Belarus: International Religious Freedom
Report 2005," *U.S. Department of State*, 2005, accessed October
14, 2017, at https://www.state.gov/j/drl/rls/irf/2005/51542.htm;
Central Intelligence Agency, "The World Factbook: Religions,"
accessed October 14, 2017, at https://www.cia.gov/library/publi-
cations/the-world-factbook/fields/2122.html.

18. Igor Munteanu, interview with Mitchell A. Orenstein, Chisinau,
June 2017.

19. James J. Coyle, 2016, "Ukrainians Desert Russian Orthodox
Church En Masse," *Newsweek*, June 25, 2016, accessed July 26,
2017, at http://www.newsweek.com/ukrainian-desert-russian-
orthodox-church-en-masse-474357.

20. Roman Olearchyk and Max Seddon, "Ukraine's Orthodox church
emerges from Russia's shadow," *Financial Times*, September 29,
2018, accessed October 19, 2018, at https://www.ft.com/content/
1bdfb854-c26e-11e8-95b1-d36dfef1b89a.

21. Appel and Orenstein, From Triumph to Crisis.

22. Emerson and Cenusa, *Deepening EU-Moldovan Relations.*
23. European Union External Action, "Eastern Partnership," October 10, 2016, accessed May 14, 2018, at https://eeas.europa.eu/head-quarters/headquarters-homepage/419/eastern-partnership_en.
24. Béla Galgóczí, "Why Central and Eastern Europe Needs a Pay Rise," European Trade Union Institute Working Paper 2017.01.
25. Ecaterina Locoma, PhD diss., Department of Political Science, Rutgers University, 2018.
26. Information and Communication Department of the Secretariat of the CMU, "Ukraine and Moldova Have Intensified a Dialogue on Topical Issues of Political and Economic Cooperation— Outcomes of Negotiations of Heads of Government," October 6, 2017, accessed May 14, 2018, at http://old.kmu.gov.ua/kmu/control/en/publish/article?art_id=250331167&cat_id=244314975.
27. Henry Foy, "Moldova Voters Face Stark Choice between East and West," Financial Times, November 27, 2014, accessed May 14, 2018, at https://www.ft.com/content/4a4f7dea-7647-11e4-a777-00144feabdc0.
28. Gergana Noutcheva, "Whose Legitimacy? The EU and Russia in Contest for the Eastern Neighbourhood," Democratization 25, no. 2 (2018), accessed August 21, 2018, at https://www.tandfonline.com/doi/full/10.1080/13510347.2017.1363186.
29. Yuliya Lovochkina, Member of Parliament of Ukraine, interview by Mitchell A. Orenstein, June 13, 2017.
30. Noutcheva, "Whose Legitimacy?"
31. President of Russia, "Orthodox-Slavic Values: The Foundation of Ukraine's Civilisational Choice Conference," July 27, 2013, accessed August 21, 2018, at http://en.kremlin.ru/events/president/news/18961.
32. "Russia Faces '100 Years of Solitude' (or More), Putin Aide Says," Radio Free Europe / Radio Liberty, April 10, 2018, accessed August 21, 2018, at https://www.rferl.org/a/putin-adviser-surkov-says-russia-abandoning-hopes-integrating-with-west-loneliness-isolation-/29155700.html.
33. Rating Group Ukraine, "Public Opinion Survey Residents of Ukraine, May 28–June 14, 2016," Center for Insights in Survey Research, International Republican Institute, 2016, 37,

accessed October 14, 2017, at http://www.iri.org/sites/default/files/wysiwyg/2016-07-08_ukraine_poll_shows_skepticism_glimmer_of_hope.pdf.

34. "Opposition Bloc Reports 50,000 People Hurt by Repression in Ukraine," *Interfax-Ukraine*, November 18, 2016, accessed October 14, 2017, at http://en.interfax.com.ua/news/general/384855.html.

35. Tom Balmforth, "As Ukraine Says 'Farewell Unwashed Russia,' Putin Says Take Care in 'Gay' Europe," Radio Free Europe / Radio Liberty, June 15, 2017, accessed May 15, 2018, at https://www.rferl.org/a/putin-unwashed-russia-poroshenko-ukraine-gay/28557438.html.

36. Mariusz Maszkiewicz, "State Ideology in Belarus—Main Problems and Concepts," unpublished manuscript, University of Cardinal Stephan Wyszynski, Warsaw, 2012; Natalia Leshchenko, "The National Ideology and the Basis of the Lukashenka Regime in Belarus," *Europe-Asia Studies* 60, no. 8 (2008): 1419–33.

37. Maxim Edwards, "Moldova's New President: His Bark Is Worse Than His Bite," *World Policy*, November 28, 2016.

38. Denis Cenusa, "Geopolitical Games Expected Ahead of Moldova's 2018, Elections," Foreign Policy Research Institute, Moldova Monthly, October 10, 2017, accessed May 15, 2018, at https://www.fpri.org/article/2017/10/geopolitical-games-expected-ahead-moldovas-2018-elections/.

39. Cenusa, "Geopolitical Games Expected."

40. Kit Gillet, "Moldova's Banking Sector Edges towards Stability," Banker, April 3, 2018, accessed May 15, 2018, at http://www.thebanker.com/World/Central-Eastern-Europe/Moldova/Moldova-s-banking-sector-edges-towards-stability; Ivana Kottasova, "How to Steal $1 Billion in Three Days," CNN Money, May 7, 2015, accessed May 15, 2018, at http://money.cnn.com/2015/05/07/news/economy/moldova-stolen-billion/index.html.

41. "Former Moldovan PM Jailed for Nine Years," Radio Free Europe / Radio Liberty, June 27, 2016, accessed May 15, 2018, at https://www.rferl.org/a/moldova-former-prime-minister-filat-jailed-9-years/27823377.html.

42. David Cadier and Samuel Charap, "The Polarisation of Regional Politics: The Impact of the EU-Russia Confrontation on Countries in the Common Neighborhood," in Łukasz Kulesa,

Ivan Timofeev, and Joseph Dobbs, eds., *Damage Assessment: EU-Russia Relations in Crisis*, European Leadership Network and Russian International Affairs Council, June 15, 2017, accessed October 14, 2017, at http://www.europeanleadershipnetwork. org/damage-assessment-eu-russia-relations-in-crisis_4846. html.

43. Lucan A. Way, "Weak States and Pluralism: The Case of Moldova," *East European Politics and Societies* 17, no. 3 (2003).

44. Cadier and Charap, "Polarisation of Regional Politics."

45. Andrew Osborne, "Inside the Fantasy Home of the £3.5bn Politician," *Telegraph*, November 27, 2011, accessed August 21, 2018, at https://www.telegraph.co.uk/culture/art/art-features/ 8917730/Inside-the-fantasy-home-of-the-3.5bn-politician.html.

46. European Commission, "Georgia—Trade," accessed October 20, 2017, at http://ec.europa.eu/trade/policy/countries-and-regions/ countries/georgia/. The EU-Georgia Association Agreement was signed June 27, 2014.

47. Regis Gente, "Bidzina Ivanishvili, a Man Who Plays according to Russian Rules?," *Caucasus Survey* 1, no. 1 (2013): 117–26, at http://www.tandfonline.com/doi/pdf/10.1080/23761199.2013. 11417276; The Economist Intelligence Unit, "Georgia Economy: Enter the Oligarch," *Economist*, September 17, 2004, accessed July 27, 2017, at https://proxy.library.upenn.edu:7450/docview/ 466737823?pq-origsite=summon; Christopher Caldwell, "Back in the USSR? Georgia Elects an Oligarch," *Weekly Standard*, October 22, 2012, accessed July 27, 2017, at http://proxy.library.upenn. edu:2261/ps/i.do?p=AONE&u=upenn_main&id=GALE|A3054 70287&v=2.1&it=r&sid=summon&authCount=1; Hans Gutbrod and Nana Papiashvili, "Georgian Attitudes to Russia: Surprisingly Positive," *Russian Analytical Digest* 68, no. 9 (2009): 8–12, at http://home.gwu.edu/~cwelt/Russian_Analytical_Digest_68.pdf.

48. Korosteleva, "The EU and Belarus."

49. Stanislav Markus and Volha Charnysh, "The Flexible Few: Oligarchs and Wealth Defense in Developing Democracies," *Comparative Political Studies* 50, no. 12 (2017): 1632–65, at http:// journals.sagepub.com/doi/abs/10.1177/0010414016688000.

50. Maria Levcenko, "Vlad Plahotniuc: Moldova's Man in the Shadows," *openDemocracy*, February 25, 2016, accessed October

20, 2017, at https://www.opendemocracy.net/od-russia/maria-levcenco/vlad-plahotniuc-moldova-s-man-in-shadows; "Prime," *Викинедия*, September 28, 2017, accessed October 20, 2017, at https://ru.wikipedia.org/wiki/Prime; "Canal 2," *Point*, accessed October 20, 2017, at https://point.md/ru/tv/2plus; "Разное," *Canal 3*, accessed October 20, 2017, at http://www.canal3.md/ru/raznoe. html; publikaTV broadcasts (Kremlin-owned) Russia 24, among others: "Publika TV," *Викинедия*, September 28, 2017, accessed October 20, 2017, at https://ru.wikipedia.org/wiki/Publika_TV.

51. Mariana Rață, "Money, Businesses, and Interests of Igor Dodon and "Crucial" Alliances of PD-PSRM," *Centrul de Investigații Jurnalistice*, October 16, 2016, accessed August 21, 2018, at https://anticoruptie.md/en/elections-2016/money-businesses-and-interests-of-igor-dodon-and-crucial-alliances-of-pd-psrm.

52. "Moldova Declares Russian Deputy PM Rogozin Persona Non Grata," Reuters, August 2, 2017, accessed September 2, 2017, at http://www.reuters.com/article/us-moldova-rogozin/moldova-declares-russian-deputy-pm-rogozin-persona-non-grata-idUSKBN1AI1MZ; "Moldova Expels Five Russian Diplomats," *Aljazeera*, May 29, 2017, accessed September 2, 2017, at http://www.aljazeera.com/news/2017/05/moldova-expels-russian-diplomats-170529175133505.html; Touma, "Moldovan President Ridiculed"; Eugen Tomiuk, "Despite Russian Allegations, Moldova's Dodon Finds No Fault with Training Base," Radio Free Europe / Radio Liberty, August 14, 2017, accessed August 21, 2018, at https://www.rferl.org/a/moldova-dodon-refutes-russia-rt-allegations-military-base/28676040.html.

53. Arzu Geybullayeva, "Azerbaijan: Striking a Balance between Russia and the West," *Sofia Platform*, June 2015, accessed September 2, 2017, at http://sofiaplatform.org/wp-content/uploads/2015/06/Azerbaijan_Striking_a_Balance_between_Russia_and_the_West.pdf; European Union External Action, "EU-Azerbaijan Relations," accessed October 20, 2017, at https://eeas.europa.eu/headquarters/headquarters-homepage_en/4013/EU-Azerbaijan%20relations; Stratfor, "Azerbaijan Seeks a Balance between Russia and the West," *Stratfor*, June 18, 2014, accessed September 2, 2017, at https://www.stratfor.com/geopolitical-diary/azerbaijan-seeks-balance-between-russia-and-west.

54. Economist Intelligence Unit, "Armenia Joins Eurasian Union," *Economist*, October 14, 2014, accessed September 2, 2017, at http://country.eiu.com/article.aspx?articleid=592382843& Country=Armenia&topic=Politics&subtopic=Forecast&su bsubtopic=International+relations; Hrant Kostanyan, "EU-Armenian Relations: Seizing the Second Chance," *Centre for European Policy Studies*, October 31, 2016, accessed September 2, 2017, at https://www.ceps.eu/publications/ eu-armenian-relations-seizing-second-chance.

55. Bartov and Weitz, *Shatterzone of Empires*.

Chapter 5

1. Ruth Fraňková, "Zeman: Russian Television Lies on 1968 Invasion of Czechoslovakia," Radio Praha, June 3, 2015, accessed October 19, 2018, at http://www.radio.cz/en/section/news/zeman-russian-television-lies-on-1968-invasion-of-czechoslovakia.

2. Jakub Janda, "How Czech President Miloš Zeman Became Putin's Man," *Observer*, January 26, 2018, accessed October 19, 2018 at http://observer.com/2018/01/how-czech-president-milos-zeman-became-vladimir-putins-man/.

3. ČTK, "MfD: Russian Lukoil Pays Huge Debt of Zeman's Key Aide Nejedlý," *Prague Daily Monitor*, November 7, 2016, accessed September 9, 2017, at http://praguemonitor.com/2016/ 11/07/mfd-russian-lukoil-pays-huge-debt-zemans-key-aide-nejedl%C3%BD.

4. Neil MacFarquhar, "How Russians Pay to Play in Other Countries," *New York Times*, December 30, 2016, accessed October 20, 2017, at https://www.nytimes.com/2016/12/30/world/europe/czech-republic-russia-Miloš-zeman.html.

5. Orenstein and Keleman, "Trojan Horses."

6. Balázs Orbán, "Guest Post: Hungary Tries to Balance between Russia and EU," *Financial Times*, February 16, 2015, accessed August 1, 2017, at http://blogs.ft.com/beyond-brics/2015/02/16/ guest-post-hungary-tries-to-balance-between-russia-and-eu/;

Rick Lyman, "Putin Swaggers into Hungary as Europe Worries about U.S.," *New York Times*, February 2, 2017, accessed August 1, 2017, at https://www.nytimes.com/2017/02/02/world/europe/vladimir-putin-hungary.html.

7. Hedenskog and Larsson, *Russian Leverage*.
8. Bechev, *Rival Power*.
9. Vija Pakalkaite, "Lithuania's Strategic Use of EU Energy Policy Tools: A Transformation of Gas Dynamics," *Oxford Institute for Energy Studies*, September 2016, 13, accessed September 8, 2017, at https://www.oxfordenergy.org/wpcms/wp-content/uploads/2016/09/Lithuanias-Strategic-Use-of-EU-Energy-Policy-Tools-A-transformation-of-Gas-Market-Dynamics-NG-111.pdf.
10. Tsvetana Paraskova, "After Poland, Lithuania Becomes U.S. LNG Buyer," *Pipeline&GasJournal*, June 27, 2017, accessed August 2, 2017, at https://pgjonline.com/2017/06/27/after-poland-lithuania-becomes-u-s-lng-buyer/.
11. Independent Balkan News Agency, "Bulgaria-Romania Gas Interconnector Pipeline Finished," *Sofia Globe*, November 11, 2016, accessed May 15, 2018, at https://sofiaglobe.com/2016/11/11/bulgaria-romania-gas-interconnector-pipeline-finished/. See also Bechev, *Rival Power*.
12. Vladimir Milov, "Can South Stream Be Revived?," *Bulgaria Analytica*, July 8, 2016, accessed August 1, 2017, at http://bulgariaanalytica.org/en/2016/07/08/може-ли-южен-поток-да-се-възроди/.
13. Bechev, *Rival Power*, 215.
14. Milov, "Can South Stream Be Revived?"; Jim Yardley and Jo Becker, "How Putin Forged a Pipeline Deal That Derailed," *New York Times*, December 30, 2014, accessed August 1, 2017, at https://www.nytimes.com/2014/12/31/world/europe/how-putin-forged-a-pipeline-deal-that-derailed-.html.
15. Georgi Gotev, "Russian MP: We Will Buy Bulgaria, We Already Bought Half of the Coast," Euractiv, September 20, 2016, accessed November 1, 2017, at https://www.euractiv.com/section/central-europe/news/russian-mp-we-will-buy-bulgaria-we-already-bought-half-of-the-coast/.

16. "Russian Ambassador Says Hungary Could Become Regional Gas Distribution Hub," *Daily News Hungary*, March 23, 2015, accessed May 15, 2018, at https://dailynewshungary.com/russian-ambassador-says-hungary-could-become-regional-gas-distribution-hub/.

17. Andrew Byrne and Neil Buckley, "EU Approves Hungary's Russian-Financed Nuclear Station," *Financial Times*, March 6, 2017, accessed August 1, 2017, at https://www.ft.com/content/0478d38a-028a-11e7-ace0-1ce02ef0def9.

18. Euractiv.com with Reuters, "Putin and Orbán Contemplate Stronger Energy Ties," *Euractiv*, February 18, 2015, accessed October 20, 2017, at http://www.euractiv.com/section/central-europe/news/putin-and-orban-contemplate-stronger-energy-ties/.

19. "Annual Report of the Security Information Service for 2014," *Security Information Service*, accessed October 20, 2017, at https://www.bis.cz/vyrocni-zpravaEN6c8d.html?ArticleID=1096.

20. Bechev, *Rival Power*; Yardley and Becker, "How Putin Forged a Pipeline Deal."

21. Cohen, "Russian Gas."

22. Agnia Grigas, "Compatriot Games: Russian-Speaking Minorities in the Baltic States," *World Politics Review*, October 21, 2014, accessed August 2, 2017, at http://www.worldpoliticsreview.com/articles/14240/compatriot-games-russian-speaking-minorities-in-the-baltic-states.

23. Snyder, *The Road to Unfreedom*.

24. Łukasz Wenerski and Michal Kacewicz, "Russian Soft Power in Poland: The Kremlin and Pro-Russian Organizations," in Lóránt Győri, ed., *Political Capital*, April 2017, accessed October 20, 2017, at http://www.politicalcapital.hu/pc-admin/source/documents/PC_NED_country_study_PL_20170428.pdf.

25. Wenerski and Kacewicz, "Russian Soft Power."

26. András and Panyi, "Russian Diplomats Exercised"; Andrew Higgins, "Intent on Unsettling E.U., Russia Taps Foot Soldiers from the Fringe," *New York Times*, December 24, 2016, accessed August 2, 2017, at https://www.nytimes.com/2016/12/24/world/europe/intent-on-unsettling-eu-russia-taps-foot-soldiers-from-the-fringe.html.

27. Grigorij Mesežnikov and Radovan Bránik, "Hatred, Violence and Comprehensive Military Training: The Violent Radicalisation and Kremlin Connections of Slovak Paramilitary, Extremist and Neo-Nazi Groups," in Győri, *Political Capital*.

28. Péter Krekó, Lóránt Győri, and Edit Zgut, "From Russia with Hate: The Activity of Pro-Russian Extremist Groups in Central-Eastern Europe," in Győri, *Political Capital*.

29. Radovan Geist, "Russia Targets Slovakia as the Weakest Link in V4," *Euractiv*, March 16, 2017, accessed October 20, 2017, at https://www.euractiv.com/section/central-europe/news/russian-targets-slovakia-as-the-weakest-link-in-v4/; "Demand for Right-Wing Extremism Index (DEREX)," *Political Capital*, November 11, 2016, accessed October 20, 2017, at http://www.politicalcapital.hu/hireink.php?article_read=1&article_id=315.

30. GLOBSEC, "Vulnerability Index: Subversive Russian Influence in Central Europe," *GLOBSEC Policy Institute*, 2017, accessed August 2, 2017, at http://www.cepolicy.org/sites/cepolicy.org/files/attachments/vulnerability_index.pdf.

31. E. L., "Orbán and the Wind from the East," *Economist*, November 14, 2011, accessed August 2, 2017, at https://www.economist.com/blogs/easternapproaches/2011/11/hungarys-politics.

32. Magyar, *Post-Communist Mafia State*.

33. Szabolcs Panyi, "Hungarian Secret Agent Reveals in Detail How Serious the Russian Threat Is," *Index*, March 21, 2017, accessed October 20, 2017, at http://index.hu/belfold/2017/03/21/hungarian_secret_agent_reveals_how_serious_the_russian_threat_is/.

34. Anne Applebaum, "Russia's New Kind of Friends," *Washington Post*, October 16, 2015, accessed October 20, 2017, at https://www.washingtonpost.com/opinions/neither-agents-of-influence-nor-useful-idiots/2015/10/16/73fdc478-7423-11e5-8248-98e0f5a2e830_story.html.

35. "Annual Report of the Security Information Service for 2015," *Security Information Service*, accessed October 20, 2017, at https://www.bis.cz/vyrocni-zpravaEN890a.html?ArticleID=1104.

36. Alena Kudzko, "Information War Monitor for Central Europe: June 2017 Part 1," *GLOBSEC*, July 26, 2017, accessed

October 20, 2017, at http://www.cepolicy.org/publications/ information-war-monitor-central-europe-june-2017-part-1.

37. GLOBSEC, "Vulnerability Index."
38. Thomas Frear, Łukasz Kulesa, and Ian Kearns, "Dangerous Brinkmanship: Close Military Encounters between Russia and the West in 2014," *European Leadership Network*, November 2014, accessed October 20, 2017, at http://www. europeanleadershipnetwork.org/medialibrary/2014/11/09/ 6375e3da/Dangerous%20Brinkmanship.pdf; Thomas Frear, "List of Close Military Encounters between Russia and the West, March 2014—March 2015," *European Leadership Network*, March 12, 2015, accessed October 20, 2017, at http://www. europeanleadershipnetwork.org/medialibrary/2015/03/11/ 4264a5a6/ELN%20Russia%20-%20West%20Full%20List%20 of%20Incidents.pdf.
39. Matthew Dey, "Russia 'Simulates' Nuclear Attack on Poland," *Telegraph*, November 1, 2009, accessed September 9, 2017, at http://www.telegraph.co.uk/news/worldnews/europe/poland/ 6480227/Russia-simulates-nuclear-attack-on-Poland.html.
40. Samuel Osborne, "Russian Naval Activity in Europe 'Exceeds Cold War Levels' Says Nato Admiral," *Independent*, April 10, 2017, accessed August 3, 2017, at http://www.independent. co.uk/news/world/europe/russia-navy-europe-cold-war-levels- nato-admiral-michelle-howard-warships-submarines-aircraft- a7675771.html.

Chapter 6

1. Thomas Risse and Nelli Babayan, "Democracy Promotion and the Challenges of Illiberal Regional Powers: Introduction to the Special Issue," Democratization 22, no. 3, special issue on "Democracy Promotion and the Challenges of Illiberal Regional Powers" (2015): 381–99.
2. Larry Wolff, *Inventing Eastern Europe: The Map of Civilization on the Mind of the Enlightenment* (Stanford, CA: Stanford University Press, 1994), 4.

3. "Сепаратисты Техаса рассказали о своих 'российск их' контактах в Facebook," *РБК,* September 15, 2017, accessed October 21, 2017, at http://www.rbc.ru/rbcfreenews/ 59bb26fe9a7947d77e25d2c5; "СМИ рассказали о попытках 'фабрики троллей' устроить митинг в США," *РБК,* September 12, 2017, accessed October 21, 2017, at http://www.rbc.ru/politics/12/09/2017/59b7b88a9a79475a418953dd.

4. Jon Swaine and Luke Harding, "Russia Funded Facebook and Twitter Investments through Kushner Investor," *Guardian,* November 5, 2017, accessed October 19, 2018, at https:// www.theguardian.com/news/2017/nov/05/russia-funded-facebook-twitter-investments-kushner-investor

5. Snyder, *The Road to Unfreedom,* 124.

6. Natalya Kanevskaya, "How the Kremlin Wields Its Soft Power In France," Radio Free Europe / Radio Liberty, June 24, 2014, accessed October 21, 2017, https://www.rferl.org/a/russia-soft-power-france/25433946.html.

7. Kanevskaya, "How the Kremlin Wields."

8. Yair Rosenberg, "Friends Don't Let Friends Vote for Jill Stein," *Tablet,* August 10, 2016, accessed August 21, 2018, at https://www.tabletmag.com/scroll/210549/friends-dont-let-friends-vote-for-jill-stein.

9. Andrew Feinberg, "My Life at a Russian Propaganda Network," *Politico,* August 21, 2017, accessed October 21, 2017, at http:// www.politico.com/magazine/story/2017/08/21/russian-propaganda-sputnik-reporter-215511.

10. Jim Rutenberg, "RT, Sputnik, and Russia's New Theory of War," *New York Times,* September 13, 2017, accessed October 21, 2017, at https://www.nytimes.com/2017/09/13/magazine/rt-sputnik-and-russias-new-theory-of-war.html?nl=todaysheadlines&emc= edit_th_20170916; Office of the Director of National Intelligence, "Assessing Russian Activities," 4; Katie Zavadski, "Putin's Propaganda TV Lies about Its Popularity," *Daily Beast,* September 17, 2015, accessed October 21, 2017, at http://www.thedailybeast. com/putins-propaganda-tv-lies-about-its-popularity.

11. Clint Watts and Andrew Weisburd, "How Russia Wins an Election," *Politico,* December 13, 2016, accessed October 21,

2017, at http://www.politico.com/magazine/story/2016/12/how-russia-wins-an-election-214524.

12. Ben Knight, "Teenage Girl Admits Making Up Migrant Rape Claim That Outraged Germany," *Guardian*, January 31, 2016, accessed August 3, 2017, at https://www.theguardian.com/world/2016/jan/31/teenage-girl-made-up-migrant-claim-that-caused-uproar-in-germany.

13. Chen, "The Agency."

14. Bridge R., "911 Reasons Why 9/11 Was (Probably) an Inside Job," RT, June 28, 2010, accessed June 10, 2014, at http://rt.com/usa/911-attack-job/; Ilya Yablokov, "Conspiracy Theories as a Russian Public Diplomacy Tool: The Case of *Russia Today* (*RT*)," *Politics* 35, nos. 3–4 (2015), accessed October 21, 2017, at http://proxy.library.upenn.edu:2487/doi/pdf/10.1111/1467-9256.12097.

15. Oliver Bullough, "Inside Russia Today: Counterweight to the Mainstream Media, or Putin's Mouthpiece?," *New Statesman*, May 10, 2013, accessed October 21, 2017, at http://www.newstatesman.com/world-affairs/world-affairs/2013/05/inside-russia-today-counterweight-mainstream-media-or-putins-mou.

16. Margaret Vice, "Publics Worldwide Unfavorable toward Putin, Russia," Pew Research Center, August 16, 2017, accessed October 21, 2017, at http://www.pewglobal.org/2017/08/16/publics-worldwide-unfavorable-toward-putin-russia/.

17. Wilson, *Ukraine's Orange Revolution*.

18. Michael Riley and Jordan Robertson, "Russian Cyber Hacks on U.S. Electoral System Far Wider Than Previously Known," *Bloomberg*, June 13, 2017, accessed October 21, 2017, at https://www.bloomberg.com/news/articles/2017-06-13/russian-breach-of-39-states-threatens-future-u-s-elections.

19. Damien Sharkov, "France's Front National Accepts €9M Loan from Russian Bank," *Newsweek*, November 25, 2014, accessed August 3, 2017, at http://www.newsweek.com/frances-front-national-accepts-eu9m-loan-russian-bank-286999.

20. Marine Turchi and Mathias Destal, "Le Pen–Putin Friendship Goes Back a Long Way," *EUobserver*, April 22, 2017, accessed August 3, 2017, at https://euobserver.com/elections/137629.

21. Emilio Ferrera, "Disinformation and Social Bot Operations in the Run Up to the 2017 French Presidential Election," *University*

of Southern California, Information Sciences Institute, 2017, accessed August 3, 2017, at https://arxiv.org/ftp/arxiv/papers/1707/1707.00086.pdf.

22. "The Julian Assange Show," RT, at https://www.rt.com/tags/the-julian-assange-show/.

23. Reuters, "Emmanuel Macron's Campaign Team Bans Russian News Outlets from Events," *Guardian*, April 27, 2017, accessed October 21, 2017, at https://www.theguardian.com/world/2017/apr/27/russia-emmanuel-macron-banned-news-outlets-discrimination.

24. Stefan Wagstyl, "German Politics: Russia's Next Target?," *Financial Times*, January 29, 2017, accessed August 3, 2017, at https://www.ft.com/content/31a5758c-e3d8-11e6-9645-c9357a75844a; Patrick Beuth et al., "Cyberattack on the Bundestag: Merkel and the Fancy Bear," *Zeit Online*, May 12, 2017, accessed October 21, 2017, at http://www.zeit.de/digital/2017-05/cyberattack-bundestag-angela-merkel-fancy-bear-hacker-russia/seite-4.

25. Gregory Krieg and Joshua Berlinger, "Hillary Clinton: Donald Trump Would Be Putin's 'Puppet,'" CNN, October 20, 2016, accessed August 3, 2017, at http://www.cnn.com/2016/10/19/politics/clinton-puppet-vladimir-putin-trump/index.html.

26. Ashley Parker and David E. Sanger, "Donald Trump Calls on Russia to Find Hillary Clinton's Missing Emails," *New York Times*, July 27, 2016, accessed August 3, 2017, at https://www.nytimes.com/2016/07/28/us/politics/donald-trump-russia-clinton-emails.html.

27. Maggie Haberman and Jonathan Martin, "Paul Manafort Quits Donald Trump's Campaign after a Tumultuous Run," *New York Times*, August 19, 2016, accessed August 3, 2017, at https://www.nytimes.com/2016/08/20/us/politics/paul-manafort-resigns-donald-trump.html; Andrew E. Kramer, Mike McIntire, and Barry Meier, "Secret Ledger in Ukraine Lists Cash for Donald Trump's Campaign Chief," *New York Times*, August 14, 2016, accessed August 3, 2017, at https://www.nytimes.com/2016/08/15/us/politics/paul-manafort-ukraine-donald-trump.html.

28. Rajeev Syal, "Brexit: Foreign States May Have Interfered in Vote, Report Says," *Guardian*, April 12, 2017, accessed August 3, 2017, at https://www.theguardian.com/politics/2017/apr/12/foreign-states-may-have-interfered-in-brexit-vote-report-says;

Neil Barnett, "United Kingdom: Vulnerable but Resistant," in *The Kremlin's Trojan Horses,* Atlantic Council, November 2016, accessed August 3, 2017, at http://www.atlanticcouncil.org/images/publications/The_Kremlins_Trojan_Horses_web_0228_third_edition.pdf.

29. Patrick Foster, "Kremlin-Backed Broadcaster RT Offers Nigel Farage His Own Show," *Telegraph*, September 7, 2016, accessed October 21, 2017, at http://www.telegraph.co.uk/news/2016/09/07/kremlin-backed-broadcaster-rt-offers-nigel-farage-his-own-show/.

30. Carole Cadwalladr, "Arron Banks: 'Brexit Was a War. We Won. There's No Turning Back Now," *Guardian*, April 2, 2017, accessed October 21, 2017, at https://www.theguardian.com/politics/2017/apr/02/arron-banks-interview-brexit-ukip-far-right-trump-putin-russia; Jim Waterson, "Major UKIP Donor Says 'KGB Man' Took Him to Russian Embassy," *Buzzfeed*, November 1, 2016, accessed October 21, 2017, at https://www.buzzfeed.com/jimwaterson/major-ukip-donor-says-kgb-man-took-him-to-russian-embassy?utm_term=.pcPAPWaEg#.llMj85kZl; Luke Harding, "Offshore Secrets of Brexit Backer Arron Banks Revealed in Panama Papers," *Guardian*, October 16, 2016, accessed October 21, 2017, at https://www.theguardian.com/world/2016/oct/15/panama-papers-reveal-offshore-secrets-arron-banks-brexit-backer.

31. Polyakova et al., "The Kremlin's Trojan Horses."

32. Stephanie Kirchgaessner, "Former Farage Aide Gives US Information in Plea Deal, Court Files Show," *Guardian*, June 7, 2017, accessed October 27, 2017, at https://www.theguardian.com/politics/2017/jun/07/former-nigel-farage-aide-us-information-plea-deal-court-files-george-cottrell.

33. Snyder, *The Road to Unfreedom*, 126.

34. Benjamin Novak, "Jobbik MEP Accused of Spying for Russia," *Budapest Beacon*, May 17, 2014, accessed October 27, 2017, at https://budapestbeacon.com/jobbik-mep-accused-of-spying-for-russia/.

35. Reuters Staff, "Bulgaria's Borisov Names New Coalition Government," *Reuters*, March 26, 2017, accessed October 27,

2017, at https://www.reuters.com/article/us-bulgaria-government/
bulgarias-borisov-names-new-coalition-government-
idUSKBN17Z0XO; Clive Leviev-Sawyer, "Bulgaria's GERB, United
Patriots Announce Agreement on Governance Programme for
Coalition Government," *Sofia Globe*, April 13, 2017, accessed
October 27, 2017, at http://sofiaglobe.com/2017/04/13/bulgarias-
gerb-united-patriots-announce-agreement-on-governance-
programme-for-coalition-government-2/.

36. Snyder, *The Road to Unfreedom*, 128.
37. Shekhovtsov, *Russia and the Western Far Right*.
38. Andrew Rettman, "Fight Club: Russian Spies Seek EU Recruits,"
    EUobserver, May 26, 2017, accessed October 27, 2017, at https://
    euobserver.com/foreign/137990.
39. Mark Galeotti, "Crimintern: How the Kremlin Uses Russia's
    Criminal Networks in Europe," *European Council on Foreign
    Relations*, April 18, 2017, accessed October 27, 2017, at http://
    www.ecfr.eu/publications/summary/crimintern_how_the_
    kremlin_uses_russias_criminal_networks_in_europe.
40. Snyder, *The Road to Unfreedom*, 290.
41. Conor Friedersdorf, "Is Russia Behind a Secession Effort in
    California?," *Atlantic*, March 1, 2017, accessed October 27, 2017,
    at https://www.theatlantic.com/politics/archive/2017/03/is-
    russia-behind-a-secession-effort-in-california/517890/.
42. Katy Murphy, "'Calexit' Campaign Dropped as Leader Bolts for
    Russia," *Mercury News*, April 17, 2017, accessed October 27, 2017,
    at http://www.mercurynews.com/2017/04/17/calexit-leaders-
    drop-ballot-measure-to-break-from-the-u-s/.
43. Murphy, "'Calexit' Campaign."
44. Graham Keeley, "Russia Meddled in Catalonia Independence
    Referendum, Says German Intelligence Boss," The Times (London),
    May 16, 2018, accessed May 16, 2018, at https://www.thetimes.
    co.uk/article/russia-meddled-in-catalonia-vote-p6g5nttpm.
45. Wagstyl, "German Politics."
46. Polyakova et al., "The Kremlin's Trojan Horses."
47. Maria Snegovaya, "Russian Propaganda in Germany: More
    Effective Than You Think," *American Interest*, October 17, 2017,
    accessed May 22, 2018, at https://www.the-american-interest.
    com/2017/10/17/russian-propaganda-germany-effective-think/.

48. Stephanie Kirchgasessner, "Italy's Five Star Movement Part of Growing Club of Putin Sympathisers in the West," *Guardian*, January 5, 2017, accessed May 16, 2017 at https://www.theguardian.com/world/2017/jan/05/five-star-movement-beppe-grillo-putin-supporters-west.

49. Frear, Kulesa, and Kearns, "Dangerous Brinkmanship"; Frear, "List of Close Military Encounters."

50. Laura Smith-Spark, "Why Is Russia Sending Bombers Close to U.S. Airspace?" *CNN*, July 27, 2015, accessed October 27, 2017, at http://www.cnn.com/2015/07/27/world/us-russia-bombers-intentions/index.html; "Russia Simulated an Attack on Denmark," *The Local*, October 31, 2014, accessed October 27, 2017, at https://www.thelocal.dk/20141031/russia-simulated-a-military-attack-on-denmark.

51. Elisabeth Braw, "How to Deal with Russian Information Warfare? Ask Sweden's Subhunters," *Defense One*, April 3, 2018, accessed May 16, 2018, at https://www.defenseone.com/ideas/2018/04/how-deal-russian-information-warfare-ask-sweden/147154/.

52. Reuters Staff, "Russia Threatens to Aim"; Ian Johnston, "Russia Threatens to Use 'Nuclear Force' over Crimea and the Baltic States," *Independent*, April 1, 2015, accessed October 27, 2017, at http://www.independent.co.uk/news/world/europe/russia-threatens-to-use-nuclear-force-over-crimea-and-the-baltic-states-10150565.html.

53. Damien Sharkov, "NATO: Russian Aircraft Intercepted 100 Times above Baltic in 2016," *Newsweek*, January 4, 2017, accessed October 27, 2017, at http://www.newsweek.com/nato-intercepted-110-russian-aircraft-around-baltic-2016-538444.

54. Risse and Babayan, "Democracy Promotion"; Tanja A. Borzel, "The Noble West and the Dirty Rest? Western Democracy Promoters and Illiberal Regional Powers," *Democratization* 22, no. 3 (2015): 519–35.

55. James Crisp, "Macron Warns of European 'Civil War' over Growing East-West Divide," *Telegraph*, April 17, 2018, accessed May 22, 2018, at https://www.telegraph.co.uk/news/2018/04/17/macron-warns-european-civil-war-growing-east-west-divide/.

56. Fred Hiatt, "McMaster Warned against Officials Who 'Glamorize and Apologize' for Dictators. Hmm.," *Washington Post*, April 8, 2018.

57. Shada Islam, "Sober Times for Liberal Democracies," Friends of Europe, October 5, 2016, accessed May 16, 2018, at https://www.friendsofeurope.org/publication/sober-times-liberal-democracies; Robert D. Kaplan, "Was Democracy Just a Moment?," *Atlantic*, December 1997.

58. Adam Davidson, "Trump's Business of Corruption," *New Yorker*, August 21, 2017, accessed November 2, 2017, at https://www.newyorker.com/magazine/2017/08/21/trumps-business-of-corruption.

59. Craig Unger, "Trump's Russian Laundromat," *New Republic*, July 13, 2017.

Chapter 7

1. Snyder, *The Road to Unfreedom*, 94.

2. Robert Legvold, *Return to the Cold War* (Cambridge, UK: Polity Press, 2016).

3. Michael McFaul, *From Cold War to Hot Peace* (New York: Houghton Mifflin Harcourt, 2018).

4. Mearsheimer, "Ukraine Crisis."; Shifrinson, "Deal or No Deal?"; Charap and Colton, *Everybody Loses*.

5. Mary Sarotte, *The Struggle to Create Post–Cold War Europe* (Princeton, NJ: Princeton University Press, 2009).

6. Trenin, *Should We Fear Russia*?; Trenin, *Post-imperium*; Wallander, "Russian Transimperialism"; Lo, *Russia and the New World Disorder*.

7. Gerald Toal, *Near Abroad: Putin, the West, and the Contest over Ukraine and the Caucasus* (Oxford: Oxford University Press, 2017).

8. Many facets of the Putin era were already on display at Moscow State University in the fall of 2000: rising anti-Western sentiment, pervasive corruption, and efforts to dominate democracy through propaganda. Courses and students had already shifted from pro-Western to anti-Western in the course of a year. Students often commented to me that they used to support Western democracy and values, but now saw that the West had subverted Russia during the 1990s, and they had adopted a more nationalistic outlook. They told me about massive and organized corruption at the university. While some outstanding students were admitted to the university after succeeding on rigorous placement tests, others

paid bribes for admission, for grades, to pass exams, and to get jobs and job recommendations after. Students knew exactly who the scholarship students were. Ten years later, I learned that the dean of the faculty that I worked with, Alexey Surin, was removed from his position in 2010 after his twenty-six-year-old daughter, also on the faculty, was accused of accepting a 35,000-euro admission bribe ("MGU Lecturer Quits in Bribe Case," *Moscow Times*, May 13, 2010, accessed August 21, 2018, at http://old.themoscowtimes. com/sitemap/free/2010/5/article/mgu-lecturer-quits-in-bribe-case/405856.html/). Dean Surin was also responsible for reversing the decline of the 1990s, turning the faculty into a high-quality academic institution, and building an impressive new facility for the faculty of public administration. At the time, one of the faculty's biggest problems was that it had invested heavily in teaching Western approaches to public administration, but was facing competition from a new school of "political technology" that taught the dark arts of winning and manipulating democratic elections, associated with Gleb Pavlovsky, a Kremlin-connected political scientist and media guru of the Putin administration.

9. Associated Press, "Putin: Soviet Collapse a 'Genuine Tragedy,'" NBC, April 25, 2005, accessed August 4, 2017, at http://www. nbcnews.com/id/7632057/ns/world_news/t/putin-soviet-collapse-genuine-tragedy/; Putin also said, "Whoever does not miss the Soviet Union has no heart. Whoever wants it back has no brain," YouTube, at https://www.youtube.com/ watch?v=TSI7WJW8wqE and perhaps elsewhere; Lo, *Russia and the New World Disorder*, suggests that Russia seeks a "post-modern" empire in which "physical features of empire have disappeared, but where the imperial spirit is still present and even resurgent" (101).

10. "Russian Federation," The World Bank | Data, 2017, accessed October 27, 2017, at http://data.worldbank.org/country/russian-federation; Russia's GDP in 1989 was 506.5 billion USD. In 1999, at the lowest point of recession, it had fallen to 195.9 billion USD.

11. "Russian Federation," The World Bank | Data, 2017, accessed October 27, 2017, at http://data.worldbank.org/country/russian-federation; in 1989, Russia's total life expectancy (for men and women) at birth was 69.2 years. In 1994, it had fallen to 64.5 years.

12. Kuzio, "Ukraine between a Constrained EU"; *"An Open Letter to the Obama Administration from Central and Eastern Europe,"* July 16, 2009, Radio Free Europe / Radio Liberty, accessed May 3, 2018, at https://www.rferl.org/a/An_Open_Letter_To_The_Obama_Administration_From_Central_And_Eastern_Europe/1778449.html.

13. Mitchell A. Orenstein, "Vladimir Putin: An Aspirant Metternich?," Foreign Policy Research Institute e-Notes, January 2015, accessed May 16, 2018, at https://www.fpri.org/docs/orenstein_on_putin_1.pdf.

14. Richard Weitz, "The Rise and Fall of Medvedev's European Security Treaty," German Marshall Fund of the United States, May 29, 2012.

15. Sergei Karaganov, "Goals for Russia," Russia in Global Affairs, August 28, 2006, accessed May 4, 2018, at http://eng.globalaffairs.ru/pubcol/n_7095.

16. Samuel Huntington, *The Clash of Civilizations and the Remaking of World Order* (New York: Simon and Schuster, 1996).

17. Timothy Snyder, *On Tyranny: Twenty Lessons from the Twentieth Century* (New York: Tim Duggan Books, 2017).

18. Jaroslav Hašek, *The Good Soldier Svejk and His Fortunes in the World War* (New York: Penguin Classics, 2005).

19. Richard Pérez-Peña, "Britain Signals Harder Look at Wealthy Russians and Russian Wealth," *New York Times*, March 29, 2018, accessed August 21, 2018, at https://www.nytimes.com/2018/03/29/world/europe/uk-britain-russia-russian-wealth-putin.html

20. Zeeshan Aleem, "The UK Could Seriously Punish Russia for the Spy Attack. Here's Why It Probably Won't," *Vox*, March 16, 2018, accessed August 21, 2018, at https://www.vox.com/world/2018/3/16/17123918/russia-nerve-agent-attack-uk-sanctions-spy-skripal.

21. UK Parliament, "Moscow's Gold: Russian Corruption in the UK," May 21, 2018, accessed August 21, 2018, at https://publications.parliament.uk/pa/cm201719/cmselect/cmfaff/932/93206.htm#_idTextAnchor022.

22. Reuters, "Emmanuel Macron's Campaign Team."

23. Reid Standish, "Russia's Neighbors Respond to Putin's 'Hybrid War,'" *Foreign Policy*, October 12, 2017, accessed August 21,

2018, at http://foreignpolicy.com/2017/10/12/russias-neighbors-respond-to-putins-hybrid-warlatvia-estonia-lithuania-finland/.

24. Sarah Perez, "Facebook's New Authorization Process for Political Ads Goes Live in the US," *Tech Crunch*, April 23, 2018, accessed August 21, 2018, at https://techcrunch.com/2018/04/23/facebooks-new-authorization-process-for-political-ads-goes-live-in-the-u-s/.

25. "Australia Passes Foreign Meddling Laws amid China Tensions," *Business Times*, June 29, 2018, accessed August 21, 2018, at https://www.businesstimes.com.sg/government-economy/australia-passes-foreign-meddling-laws-amid-china-tensions.

26. European Union Committee, "The EU and Russia," 96; see also O'Hanlon, *Beyond NATO*, 2.

27. Kramer, *Back to Containment*.

28. Reinhard J. Krumm, "Small Steps: How to Start Improving Security in Europe," in Charap, Demus, and Shapiro, *Getting Out*, 17–24.

29. Ivan Krastev and Gleb Pavlovsky, "The Arrival of Post-Putin Russia," European Council on Foreign Relations Policy Brief, March 1, 2018, accessed May 17, 2018, at http://www.ecfr.eu/publications/summary/the_arrival_of_post_putin_russia.

30. Trenin, *Should We Fear Russia?*

31. Philip Oltermann, Rosie Scammell, and Gordon Darroch, "Brexit Causes Resurgence in Pro-EU Leanings across Continent," *Guardian*, July 8, 2016, accessed August 7, 2017, at https://www.theguardian.com/world/2016/jul/08/brexit-causes-resurgence-in-pro-eu-leanings-across-continent.

32. Orenstein and Keleman, "Trojan Horses."

33. Alessandra Stanley, "Moscow Journal: The Americans Who Saved Yeltsin (or Did They?)," *New York Times*, July 9, 1996, accessed August 7, 2017, at http://www.nytimes.com/1996/07/09/world/moscow-journal-the-americans-who-saved-yeltsin-or-did-they.html; Jennifer Wilson, "Spinning Hillary: A History of America and Russia's Mutual Meddling," *Guardian*, August 3, 2016, accessed August 7, 2017, at https://www.theguardian.com/world/2016/aug/03/spinning-hillary-a-history-of-america-and-russias-mutual-meddling.

34. Mark Blyth, *Austerity: The History of a Dangerous Idea* (Oxford: Oxford University Press, 2013).
35. European Union Committee, "The EU and Russia."
36. Ulrich Speck, "How the EU Sleepwalked into a Conflict with Russia," *Carnegie Europe*, July 10, 2014, accessed October 27, 2017, at http://carnegieeurope.eu/2014/07/10/how-eu-sleepwalked-into-conflict-with-russia-pub-56121.

INDEX

Page numbers followed by *f* indicate figures